Character,
Scene,
and Story

Books by Will Dunne

The Dramatic Writer's Companion: Tools to Develop Characters, Cause Scenes, and Build Stories

Character, Scene, and Story: New Tools from the Dramatic Writer's Companion

The Architecture of Story: A Technical Guide for the Dramatic Writer

NEW TOOLS
FROM THE DRAMATIC
WRITER'S COMPANION

Character, Scene, and Story

WILL DUNNE

THE UNIVERSITY OF CHICAGO PRESS

CHICAGO AND LONDON

The University of Chicago Press, Chicago 60637
The University of Chicago Press, Ltd., London
© 2017 by Will Dunne
Published 2017
Printed in the United States of America

26 25 24 23 22 21 20 19 18 17   1 2 3 4 5

ISBN-13: 978-0-226-39347-6 (cloth)
ISBN-13: 978-0-226-39350-6 (paper)
ISBN-13: 978-0-226-39364-3 (e-book)
DOI: 10.7208/chicago/9780226393643.001.0001

Library of Congress Cataloging-in-Publication Data
Names: Dunne, Will, author. | Supplement to (work): Dunne, Will. Dramatic writer's companion.
Title: Character, scene, and story : new tools from The dramatic writer's companion / Will Dunne.
Description: Chicago ; London : The University of Chicago Press, 2017.
Identifiers: LCCN 2017008987 | ISBN 9780226393476 (cloth : alk. paper) | ISBN 9780226393506 (pbk. : alk. paper) | ISBN 9780226393643 (e-book)
Subjects: LCSH: Drama—Technique—Handbooks, manuals, etc. | Drama—Technique—Problems, exercises, etc. | Playwriting—Handbooks, manuals, etc. | Playwriting—Problems, exercises, etc. | Authorship—Handbooks, manuals, etc. | Authorship—Problems, exercises, etc. | Motion picture authorship—Handbooks, manuals, etc. | Motion picture authorship—Problems, exercises, etc.
Classification: LCC PN1661 .D859 2017 | DDC 808.2—dc23 LC record available at https://lccn.loc.gov/2017008987

♾ This paper meets the requirements of ANSI/NISO Z39.48-1992 (Permanence of Paper).

For RUSS TUTTEROW,

the godfather of

Chicago playwriting

CONTENTS

About This Guide xiii
Exercises at a Glance xix

DEVELOPING YOUR CHARACTER 1
STAGE 1. FLESHING OUT THE BONES

A) Character Interview 3

Use an interview process to uncover information about your character in a dramatic way—from the character's perspective and in the character's voice.

B) Beyond Belief 7

Explore your character's credo: what key beliefs it includes, how these beliefs arose, and what impact they might have on the dramatic journey.

C) The Emotional Character 12

Characters tend to be emotional beings. Learn more about your characters by exploring their dominant emotions and how they might translate into dramatic elements.

D) Meet the Parents 17

Whether or not your character's mother and father are in the story, they have probably played a critical role in shaping his or her physical, psychological, and social makeup. Use this exercise to learn more about your character's parents and how they might influence story events.

STAGE 2. GETTING TO KNOW THE CHARACTER BETTER

A) Sensing the Character 21

Sense memory is a technique in which actors recall a specific physical detail from a past experience in order to relive the experience emotionally. Writers can use a similar technique to trigger emotional truths about their characters.

B) The Imperfect Character 23

If to err is to be human, you can ground your character in humanity by identifying his or her weaknesses, flaws, and limitations and exploring how these imperfections might contribute to story events.

C) Objects of Interest 27

What do objects and other physical elements reveal about your character? Explore the physical realm of your story to gain new insights about the character at two key points: the beginning and the end of the dramatic journey.

D) The Invisible Character 30

Though the audience never meets them, offstage characters can have a profound effect on story events. This exercise helps you identify the most important offstage characters in your story and why they matter.

E) Side by Side 36

Flesh out two characters at a specific time in the story and record your responses side by side so that you can easily compare them in telling categories, such as "most important relationship," "dominant emotion," and "burning desire."

STAGE 3. UNDERSTANDING WHO THE CHARACTER REALLY IS

A) Character Fact Sheet 41

Develop a fact sheet that highlights critical truths about your character that could affect how your story unfolds.

B) Two Views of One Character 47

Find out more about a character by asking two other characters from your story to describe him or her. In the end, your findings may reveal important information about all three characters and their relationships.

C) Nothing but the Truth 52

What would your character write in a journal, secret letter, or other private document that he or she would never tell others? Use instinctive writing to explore a character's innermost thoughts and desires.

D) What Is the Character Doing Now? 57

What characters do is often more important than what they say, especially when their actions contradict their words. Use this exercise to explore the doings of a character—before, during, and after the story.

CAUSING A SCENE 63

STAGE 1. MAKING THINGS HAPPEN

A) The Real World 65

Discover new ideas for dramatic action by exploring a scene's physical life: the setting and what's in it.

B) **What's New? What's Still True?** 71

  *A dramatic story depicts changes that occur as characters pursue their
  goals and deal with obstacles. But sometimes what doesn't change is
  also important. Use this exercise to explore how new circumstances and
  unwavering truths can both affect how a scene unfolds.*

C) **The Past Barges In** 76

  *The backstory is everything that happened in the world of the characters
  before the story begins. The only parts of this backstory that matter,
  however, are those that influence the characters here and now. Use this
  exercise to explore how the past can force its way into the present to ignite
  dramatic action.*

D) **Levels of Desire** 82

  *In drama, desire operates on three levels: story (what the character wants
  overall), scene (what the character wants at a particular time and place),
  and beat (what the character wants from moment to moment). Explore
  these different levels of desire and their impact on the dramatic action of a
  scene.*

E) **Mother Conflict** 88

  *How might your character be his or her own worst enemy? Who else might
  pose an obstacle to the character's success? How might the setting or
  current situation add to the problem? Explore different types of conflicts that
  your character might face when pursuing a scenic objective.*

F) **Why Did the Character Cross the Road?** 94

  *Objective is what the character wants. Motivation is why the character
  wants it. Define a character's objective for a scene, and explore two levels
  of motivation to achieve it: the apparent reasons for the character's actions
  and the hidden reasons, whether conscious or subconscious.*

G) **The Strategics of the Scene** 100

  *Learn more about characters by exploring how they try to get what they
  want: what strategies and tactics they choose, how well they execute these
  actions, how they manage the unexpected, and how they act under rising
  pressure.*

H) **The Scenes within the Scene** 106

  *Some scenes divide into smaller units of action called "French scenes,"
  which are each demarcated by the entrance or exit of a character. Flesh out
  character motivations for arriving in a scene after it starts or leaving before
  it ends, and explore the results of such comings and goings.*

STAGE 2. REFINING THE ACTION

A) The Color of Drama 112

Color is a basic component of the physical realm that grounds your characters in the truths of the world they inhabit. Work intuitively to tap the power of color and find new ideas and insights for a scene.

B) The Emotional Onion 117

Emotions tend to exist not in isolation but in layers. Explore the conscious and subconscious feelings that might influence the thoughts and actions of your characters as they interact here and now to cause a dramatic event.

C) Why This? Why Now? 123

We enter the lives of dramatic characters when they have compelling reasons to act without delay. Develop a scene by focusing on two of its fundamental elements: importance and urgency.

D) Relationship Storyboard 128

Map out a scene through the filter of a character relationship and how it both affects and reflects the dramatic action.

E) Classified Information 133

What is your character hiding? Find new ideas for a scene by exploring the secrets that may influence the character's behavior at this time in the story.

STAGE 3. REFINING THE DIALOGUE

A) Phrase Book 138

Learn more about your characters by exploring how they talk, what words they choose, and how their language reflects the world they inhabit.

B) Better Left Unsaid 143

Approach the development of a scene by focusing on the subtext—what is not said—and how this flow of unuttered thoughts and feelings can influence character behavior.

C) Anatomy of Speech 147

Once you have a draft of a scene, you can refine the dialogue by reviewing it from a technical perspective. This editing exercise helps you identify lines that are essential to the scene and lines that need to be clarified, condensed, or cut.

BUILDING YOUR STORY 153

STAGE 1. TRIGGERING THE CHAIN OF EVENTS

A) Facts of Life 155

Whether the world of a story is realistic or nonrealistic, it has certain operating rules that determine how things usually work here, what is possible under certain circumstances, and what is never possible under any circumstances. Use this exercise to flesh out the facts of life for the story you want to tell.

B) In the Beginning 160

When should you first bring the audience into the lives of your characters? This exercise helps you explore ideas for one of the most critical times in any dramatic story: the opening scene and its opening moment, or point of attack.

C) Character on a Mission 167

A dramatic story is a quest driven by a character's need to accomplish something that is extremely important but also extremely difficult. Answer more than thirty questions to explore your main character's quest and how it begins.

STAGE 2. DEVELOPING THE THROUGHLINE

A) Decision Points 171

Characters often have to make difficult decisions as they pursue their goals. Explore two important decision points in your character's dramatic journey, how they affect the story, and what each reveals about the decision maker.

B) Living Images 176

Visual images on stage or on screen are different from those in a book or on canvas. They include elements, such as action and sound, that make them dynamic. Translate a big moment from your story into a living image that can heighten its emotional impact.

C) What Just Happened? 180

A dramatic story is made up of events that each change the lives of the characters in either a good or a bad way. Identify different types of events in your script, and explore in more depth the one you understand least.

D) The Dramatic Continuum 184

The past, present, and future of your characters' lives are intrinsically linked and constantly changing as the dramatic journey unfolds. Flesh out the throughline of your story by focusing on how scenes in sequence connect.

6) **An End in Sight** 189

> *Once you know how the story ends, you may have a better idea of what needs to happen during the dramatic journey. This exercise helps you evaluate a final scene and what it demands of the characters and events leading up to it.*

STAGE 3. SEEING THE BIG PICTURE

A) **Two Characters in Search of a Story** 194

> *Get a clearer big-picture view of your story by studying the dramatic journeys of the two most important characters and how these individual arcs of action compare, contrast, and affect each other.*

B) **Found in Translation** 199

> *While drama is primarily an emotional experience, it is often rich in ideas as well. Identify the most important topics your story addresses, and then use character traits, dramatic action, dialogue, visual imagery, and other elements to translate these concepts into character and story specifics.*

C) **List It** 204

> *Tap the power of free association to develop a series of lists that can help you identify and evaluate the key elements of your story.*

D) **Different Sides of the Story** 208

> *Flesh out the main event of your story by examining it objectively from your perspective as the writer and then by looking at it again subjectively through the eyes of three different characters.*

E) **Coming Soon to a Theater near You!** 212

> *While theatrical posters are designed to sell tickets, they also display what's important and interesting about a play or film. Gain new insights into your subject matter, theme, and plot by looking at these elements through the eyes of a marketer and exploring ideas for a hypothetical marketing poster.*

FIXING THAT PROBLEM SCENE 217

> *Some scenes are harder to write than others and may be indicative of problems elsewhere in the script. This section helps you analyze a troublesome scene, identify exercises from this guide to address the issues raised, and find the solutions that best fit your story.*

Glossary 231
Acknowledgments 237

ABOUT THIS GUIDE

From beginners to professionals, working alone or in groups, thousands of writers have used *The Dramatic Writer's Companion* to develop characters, cause scenes, and build stories. This guide complements that resource by using a similar structure and approach to offer new storytelling tools for dramatic writers. For best results, please review this introduction, which explains more about this guide and how to use it.

■ A NEW RESOURCE FOR SCRIPT DEVELOPMENT

Character, Scene, and Story: New Tools from the Dramatic Writer's Companion is a creative and analytical reference guide composed of self-contained exercises that can be used in any order, as needed, to write or revise a dramatic script. Each exercise has been workshop tested and designed as a series of action steps to help you flesh out your own material—not someone else's. The exercises thus become part of your writing process rather than something you do in addition to it.

THE AUDIENCE FOR THIS GUIDE

While written from a playwright's perspective, this guide addresses both playwrights and screenwriters, since they share many of the same challenges. For example, both must figure out how to translate character and story information into observable terms so that the audience can witness the story rather than have it explained to them. Parts of this guide also may be useful to fiction writers, many of whom have used *The Dramatic Writer's Companion* to explore ideas for their stories.

HOW THE TWO GUIDES COMPARE

Some of the tools in this guide focus on topics not covered in *The Dramatic Writer's Companion*. Others explore the same topics but do so from a different angle or in more depth. Many call for intuitive responses. They help you dig deeper into your script by fleshing out images, exploring characters from an emotional perspective, tapping the power of color and sense memory to trigger ideas, and trying other visceral techniques. The guide concludes with a troubleshooting section to help you tackle problem scenes.

It is not necessary to have the original guide in order to use this one. Each stands alone as a writing companion. If you do have the original, you can use it in combination with this guide to flesh out your characters, scenes, and stories. Each chapter in this guide refers to related tools in *The Dramatic Writer's Companion* so you have the option to explore certain topics further.

Together, the two guides offer more than one hundred script-development tools that can be adapted to your writing process.

TOOLS FOR THE STORY YOU WANT TO TELL

This guide builds on the idea that there is no sure formula for a successful play or screenplay. Each comes into the world with a set of characters, plot points, and operating rules that must be defined and developed by the writer with the understanding that what works for one story does not necessarily work for another. It is for such reasons that American playwright and director Moss Hart once said that you never really learn how to write a play. You learn only how to write *this* play.

As you figure out what is right for your story, however, you can benefit from understanding storytelling principles that have been common in dramatic scripts through the ages—for example, that characters don't speak or act unless they want something, that conflict is almost always present in some form as a story unfolds, and that high stakes typically hang in the balance. The exercises in this guide demonstrate such principles while giving you leeway to adapt them to your individual needs.

For more about tools and techniques that successful dramatists have used and questions to facilitate analysis of your own scripts, try *The Architecture of Story: A Technical Guide for the Dramatic Writer* by Will Dunne (Chicago: University of Chicago Press, 2016).

CHARACTER: THE FOUNDATION OF DRAMATIC STORYTELLING

Character is the root of scene and story. To develop a dramatic script is to examine its characters: who they are, what they want, why they want it, and how they deal with obstacles. In the end, the character and the story are the same thing. Every exercise in this guide can thus be approached as a character exploration, even when the focus is on scene or story development.

Plot is essential to dramatic writing, but a script dictated by plot points can lead to false characters and melodrama. By letting the plot evolve primarily from the characters rather than vice versa, you can develop dramatic stories that shed light on human truths rather than sacrifice them for dramatic effect.

This collection of dramatic writing exercises builds on a simple but powerful idea: The character is not something added to the scene or to the story. Rather, the character is the scene. The character is the story.

■ HOW TO USE THIS GUIDE

Like *The Dramatic Writer's Companion*, this guide invites you to review its contents, select the specific information you currently need, and use it to produce results. Most exercises can be completed in about thirty minutes.

NONLINEAR DESIGN TO FIT YOUR WRITING NEEDS
The tools on the following pages are each self-contained, so you can use them in any order at any time and repeat them at different times with different results. This approach reflects the idea that there is no single way to develop story and lets you adapt the guide to your writing process and level of experience.

SIMPLE STRUCTURE TO FACILITATE GUIDE USE
Exercises are divided into three main sections focusing on character, scene, and story. Each section is further divided into three stages to suggest when an exercise might be most appropriate during script development.

At the end of this guide, you will find a troubleshooting section to help you tackle difficult scenes. It includes twelve sets of questions for problem solving and suggests exercises in this guide to address related topics further. This section is followed by a glossary of key terms used throughout the guide.

EXAMPLES TO ILLUSTRATE TOOLS AND TECHNIQUES
The guide is sprinkled with hundreds of examples from dramatic stories, many of which have been developed as both plays and films. Some examples are quick references. Others include more detailed script analysis. The dramatic works used most often or in most depth include *Anna in the Tropics* by Nilo Cruz; *Bent* by Martin Sherman; *Circle Mirror Transformation* by Annie Baker; *Becky Shaw* by Gina Gionfriddo; *Birdman or (The Unexpected Virtue of Ignorance)* by Alejándro Gonzalez Iñárritu, Nicolas Giacobone, Alexander Dinelaris Jr., and Armando Bo; *The Clean House* by Sarah Ruhl; *The Cripple of Inishmaan* by Martin McDonagh; *The Curious Incident of the Dog in the Night-Time*, adapted for the stage by Simon Stephens from a novel by Mark Haddon; *Defiance* by John Patrick Shanley; *Doubt* by John Patrick Shanley; *Fences* by August Wilson; *Glengarry Glen Ross* by David Mamet; *The Goat* by Edward Albee; *Hamlet* by William Shakespeare; *In the Next Room (or the vibrator play)* by Sarah Ruhl; *Joe Turner's Come and Gone* by August Wilson; *The Lieutenant of Inishmore* by Martin McDonagh; *Love and Drowning* by Will Dunne; *A Marriage Proposal* by Anton Chekhov; *Of Mice and Men* by John Steinbeck; *The Piano Lesson* by August Wilson; *The Roper* by Will Dunne; *Ruined* by Lynn Nottage; *Seminar* by Theresa Rebeck; *The Sixth Sense* by M. Night Shyamalan; *A Streetcar Named Desire* by Tennessee Williams; *Topdog/Underdog* by Suzan-Lori Parks; and *Water by the Spoonful* by Quiara Alegría Hudes.

GETTING STARTED

You can use this guide in whatever way works best for you. The following suggestions are similar to those for *The Dramatic Writer's Companion*. If you are not familiar with the original guide, be sure to review these steps:

1. **Select a section.** Think about where you are now in the development of your script. Then go to the table of contents and choose the section that feels appropriate.

    - Use "Developing Your Character" to flesh out the population of your story. Exercises range from a character interview to in-depth character analysis.
    - Use "Causing a Scene" to plan, write, or revise any scene. Exercises range from an exploration of the physical setting to more advanced tools for refining dramatic action and dialogue.
    - Use "Building Your Story" to develop a throughline and clarify what you are really writing about. Exercises range from defining the rules for the world of your story to developing a hypothetical marketing poster.

2. *(Optional) Select a level.* If you prefer a more structured approach to exercise selection, choose the level that matches where you are now in script development.

    - *Stage 1* starter tools can help lay the groundwork for new material during the early stages of script development, when you have the most to figure out.
    - *Stage 2* exploratory tools can help you learn more about a character, scene, or story that you've already begun.
    - *Stage 3* focusing tools can help you simplify, prioritize, and clarify your work during later story development, when you have the most to track and manage.

    You may do these stages in chronological order. Or you may choose instead to intuitively create your own system of use. For example, you might try a stage 1 exercise during later script development. The leap backward can shake up material that has grown stale. Or try a stage 3 exercise during early script development. The leap forward can help you plan the work that lies ahead.

3. **Select an exercise.** Scan the exercise summaries in this category at this level. Trust your instinct and pick the most appealing one. If you encounter any unfamiliar terms, check the glossary at the end of the guide.

    As you do exercises, you may occasionally not know how to answer a question. In some cases this may signal that you need to devote more attention to a certain aspect of character, scene, or story development. In other cases your lack of response may simply mean that this topic is not relevant to your particular script. Remember that the purpose of this guide is to support you and that you are the final authority on what matters in the world of your story.

4. *(Optional) Explore the topic further.* By reviewing the table of contents or the streamlined "Exercises at a Glance," you may find other tools in this guide related to the topic at hand. If you have *The Dramatic Writer's Companion* available, you can continue exploring the topic or a related one in that guide as well. To keep you aware of what the other guide offers, each chapter in this guide concludes with suggestions of additional exercises to consider.

> For best results, approach each exercise as if there are no wrong answers. Look for what's new rather than rehash what you already know. If a question has you stumped but feels important, trust your instinct and take a creative leap into what's possible in the world of your story. You may find your best material where you least expect it.

INTEGRATING THIS GUIDE INTO YOUR WRITING PROCESS

You can continue to use this guide as an ongoing writing companion to warm up, explore ideas, and develop scripts. Use the troubleshooting section at the end for any scenes that are difficult to write and the glossary for any terms that are unfamiliar.

As you become familiar with the guide, you can shortcut exercise selection by using "Exercises at a Glance," which begins on the next page.

EXERCISES AT A GLANCE

DEVELOPING YOUR CHARACTER

Stage 1. Fleshing Out the Bones

Exercise Title	*Exercise Subject*	
Character Interview	Traits and experiences	3
Beyond Belief	Credo	7
The Emotional Character	Emotional life	12
Meet the Parents	Backstory	17

Stage 2. Getting to Know the Character Better

Exercise Title	*Exercise Subject*	
Sensing the Character	Sense memory	21
The Imperfect Character	Weaknesses and flaws	23
Objects of Interest	Physical life	27
The Invisible Character	Offstage population	30
Side by Side	How characters compare	36

Stage 3. Understanding Who the Character Really Is

Exercise Title	*Exercise Subject*	
Character Fact Sheet	Defining truths	41
Two Views of One Character	What others think	47
Nothing but the Truth	Innermost thoughts and desires	52
What Is the Character Doing Now?	Telling moments of behavior	57

CAUSING A SCENE

Stage 1. Making Things Happen

Exercise Title	*Exercise Subject*	
The Real World	Setting	65
What's New? What's Still True?	Given circumstances	71
The Past Barges In	Backstory	76
Levels of Desire	Objectives	82
Mother Conflict	Sources of conflict	88
Why Did the Character Cross the Road?	Motivation	94
The Strategics of the Scene	Strategies and tactics	100
The Scenes within the Scene	French scenes	106

Stage 2. Refining the Action

Exercise Title	*Exercise Subject*	
The Color of Drama	Physical life	112
The Emotional Onion	Emotions in layers	117
Why This? Why Now?	Importance and urgency	123
Relationship Storyboard	Relationship and action	128
Classified Information	Hidden truths	133

Stage 3. Refining the Dialogue

Exercise Title	*Exercise Subject*	
Phrase Book	Key terms and idioms	138
Better Left Unsaid	Subtext	143
Anatomy of Speech	Technical analysis of dialogue	147

BUILDING YOUR STORY

Stage 1. Triggering the Chain of Events

Exercise Title	*Exercise Subject*	
Facts of Life	How this story works	155
In the Beginning	Opening scene	160
Character on a Mission	Inciting event and quest	167

Stage 2. Developing the Throughline

Exercise Title	*Exercise Subject*	
Decision Points	Critical character choices	171
Living Images	Image and action	176
What Just Happened?	Nature of a dramatic event	180
The Dramatic Continuum	How scenes connect	184
An End in Sight	Foreshadowing	189

Stage 3. Seeing the Big Picture

Exercise Title	*Exercise Subject*	
Two Characters in Search of a Story	Character arcs	194
Found in Translation	Dramatization of ideas	199
List It	Key story elements	204
Different Sides of the Story	Main event	208
Coming Soon to a Theater near You!	Subject, theme, and plot	212

Developing Your Character

Character is the heart and soul of story. This section can help you flesh out your characters as you prepare to write, make ongoing discoveries about them as your story unfolds, and focus on what matters most. Use these exercises anytime. You can always benefit from knowing more about your characters, especially if you begin to lose interest in them, get stuck in a scene, or feel unsure about the direction in which your story should proceed.

A) CHARACTER INTERVIEW

THE QUICK VERSION
Use the interview process to learn more about a character

BEST TIME FOR THIS
Anytime you need to know a character better

FLESHING OUT CHARACTERS: AN ONGOING PROCESS
Dramatic characters are each a combination of physical, psychological, and social traits shaped by the lifetime of experiences that have brought them to the threshold of a story. Some of these traits are common: we see ourselves and others we know mirrored in them. This enables us to understand and often sympathize with the character as conflict ensues. Other traits may be uncommon: we see what sets the character apart from the crowd. If we approve of such distinctions, we may root for the character to succeed. If we disapprove, we may wait for the character to get his or her just deserts. Either way, we are drawn into the story because we care about what will happen next.

To develop the kinds of characters who can grab our attention and keep us engaged, dramatic writers need to know whom they are writing about and how these characters will cause a dramatic journey to take place. This journey will be the most memorable period of their lives. They will have to do things they have never done before and find resources they didn't know they had. They will make discoveries that affect them and those around them in profound ways.

Fleshing out characters who can accomplish such feats is not a simple or one-time task. It is a multidimensional process that can be both enjoyable and challenging and that requires the writer's attention throughout script development, including revisions. When it comes to any character in a dramatic story, there is always more to be discovered.

ABOUT THE EXERCISE
You can learn a lot about your characters by interviewing them. This exercise offers forty revealing, emotionally charged questions to help you do this. Answer each question not as the writer but as the character. Since you will be responding from the character's perspective and in the character's voice, this process will be similar to writing dialogue.

The answers to some questions will depend on when in the story your character responds. If you are exploring a new character or starting a new script, try focusing on the character at the beginning of the dramatic journey. This can help you learn more about who is entering the world of your story. If you are well into script development, you may benefit more from focusing on the character at a later point in the story— the middle or end. This can help you learn more about how the dramatic journey is affecting him or her. To begin the exercise,

- *identify a character* to interview, preferably a principal character, and
- *choose a timeframe* for the interview: beginning, middle, or end of story.

As you conduct the interview, remember that the character may be truthful and insightful at some times and mistaken, misinformed, or deluded at other times. As a result, the answers will reveal what the character believes but not necessarily what is true and accurate in the world of the story. Keep in mind, too, that your character's responses may be influenced by the timeframe you have chosen for the interview.

For best results, try to find your character's response to every question. If he or she has no response, you need to determine whether the subject at hand is irrelevant to the story or a sign that you need to dig deeper into the character's identity and life.

■ TO THE CHARACTER

1. In one word, how would you describe yourself as a child?
2. When you were growing up, who loved you most?
3. Whether good or bad, what is your most vivid childhood memory?
4. In two or three sentences, how would you describe yourself today?
5. Who among your friends and family would describe you in the most positive light, and what would this person say?
6. Who among your friends and family would describe you in the most negative light, and what would that person say?
7. Have you ever had a serious illness or injury? If so, what happened, and how has this affected you?
8. Think about where you live now and whom, if anyone, you live with. How would you describe your home life today?
9. If there were a fire in your home, what three things would you save first?
10. How do you feel about your current job or the type of work you do?
11. What is your current financial status, and how does this affect you?
12. What would you do if you suddenly inherited a fortune?
13. What is the biggest lie you ever told? To whom did you tell it, and why?
14. What makes you angry?
15. When are you the happiest?
16. What is your greatest fear, and what has it stopped you from doing?

17. What turns you on sexually?
18. How would you describe your current love life?
19. When is the last time you cried, and why?
20. On an everyday basis, which do you tend to live in most: the past, present, or future? Why?
21. What trait do you admire most in others?
22. Who is your closest ally?
23. What about your closest ally do you most dislike?
24. Who is your worst adversary?
25. What about your worst adversary do you most admire?
26. Living or dead, what famous person would you most like to meet, and why?
27. How would you sum up your spiritual beliefs?
28. What would you never do under any circumstances?
29. What illegal or immoral act would you consider if the price were right?
30. For whom or for what would you be willing to give your life?
31. Who, if anyone, would be willing to give his or her life for you?
32. What is the scariest experience you've ever had, and how has that affected you?
33. When you think back about your life and the things you have done and not done, what are you most proud of?
34. What are you most ashamed of?
35. What is the greatest loss you have experienced, and how has this affected you?
36. What are your three greatest secrets?
37. If you could have a second chance in life, what would you do differently?
38. What is the most important lesson you've learned in life?
39. If you could ask God one question, what would it be?
40. How would you title your autobiography?

■ CHARACTER SUMMARY

Using what you've discovered during the exercise, sum up who your character is by writing two simple descriptions:

- *Literal description* that identifies the character factually. From the play *Doubt: A Parable* by John Patrick Shanley, for example, Sister Aloysius might be described literally as the principal of a Catholic elementary school in the Bronx.
- *Figurative description* that uses a poetic comparison, such as a metaphor or simile, to sum up the essence of the character. For example, Sister Aloysius might be described figuratively as a guard in a tower overseeing a prison yard.

WRAP-UP

You can use a variety of techniques to flesh out your characters, such as developing a biography that focuses on major events of the past, writing a typical day in their lives around the time the story begins, and imagining them in other situations not related to the story so you can see how they behave without the encumbrance of a dramatic plot. Character interview is an especially valuable tool when it is emotionally based. By interacting with characters directly, you can not only learn more about their lives but also gain a working sense of each one's unique perspective and dramatic voice.

Related tools in *The Dramatic Writer's Companion*. From "Basic Character Builder" to "In So Many Words," any exercise in the "Developing Your Character" section can help you learn more about your characters. Be sure to try "Defining Trait," "The Secret Lives of Characters," and "Character as Paradox."

BEYOND BELIEF

THE QUICK VERSION
Flesh out a character's personal credo

BEST TIME FOR THIS
Anytime you need to know a character better

CREDO: WHAT A CHARACTER BELIEVES TO BE TRUE
A dramatic character's belief system, or credo, evolves from his or her life experiences, both positive and negative, and consists of the various conclusions the character has reached as a result of what has happened. The credo reflects what the character believes to be true—even if it's not. It is often a character's credo that explains why he or she behaves a certain way under certain circumstances.

Since this credo is so closely tied to the character's individual identity and life, it is unique. Even in the case of twins, such as Myrna and Myra in *The Mineola Twins* by Paula Vogel, no two credos are alike. More often than not, a character's credo is also dynamic. It changes as the character enters the new, uncharted territory of the story and begins to acquire new experiences.

ABOUT THE EXERCISE
Use this exercise to explore the credo of one of your characters: what types of beliefs this credo includes, how these beliefs arose, and, most importantly, how they might affect the character's emotions and behavior during the story.

Examples are from August Wilson's play *The Piano Lesson*, which received, among other honors, the 1990 Pulitzer Prize for Drama. Set in Pittsburgh in 1934 just after the Great Depression, the story centers on a fight between brother and sister about what to do with the family piano. The brother, Boy Willie, wants to sell it and use the money to buy land where their ancestors once worked as slaves. The sister, Berniece, wants to keep the piano, which she views as a sacred family heirloom. Exercise examples focus on Berniece.

To begin, choose a character from your story whom you would like to know better. As you explore this character's credo, keep looking for a new belief in each round. Do not repeat a response you've already given.

■ TOPICS

Through character traits, dialogue, actions, images, events, and other dramatic elements, *The Piano Lesson* addresses certain topics about which Berniece has certain opinions and beliefs. In random order, such topics include historical legacy, family, ghosts, murder, racism, slavery, making a mark in the world, vengeance, reparation, self-worth, memory, and music. Think about the character you chose to explore. In a word or phrase each, identify at least a dozen topics that your story addresses and that are important to your character at some point in the dramatic journey.

■ SHARED BELIEF

You and your character most likely have some important beliefs in common. These similarities can help you understand the character.

1. *Topic.* Review your list of topics and choose one to explore. Trust your first instinct and mark your choice—for example, historical legacy.
2. *Belief.* Your character may have a number of different opinions and beliefs about the topic you chose. In regard to historical legacy, Berniece believes that it is important to remember the past and to protect and honor the memory of one's ancestors. Think about the topic you marked. Identify a strong character belief about this topic with which you agree. This is an example of how you and your character are alike.
3. *Trigger.* Berniece's belief about historical legacy was taught to her by her mother, who is now dead and who bequeathed the family piano to Berniece and her brother. The piano bears the faces of their ancestors carved in wood. Think about the character belief you are exploring. Recount an experience from any time in the character's life, past or present, that led to this belief or reinforced it.
4. *Emotion.* Strong beliefs tend to arouse strong emotions. Berniece's belief about historical legacy inspires reverence. What is your character's emotional connection to the belief you are exploring?
5. *Action.* Strong beliefs can also lead to decisive action. Because of her view of historical legacy, Berniece will fiercely resist her brother's plan to sell the family piano. Her resistance fuels the central conflict of the story. Think about the belief you are exploring and what it might motivate your character to do. Identify an important action your character could initiate at any time during the story as a result of this belief.

■ UNIQUE BELIEF

Your character most likely has certain important beliefs that you do not share. These differences help make your character unique and may sometimes require you to do research to understand the character's perspective.

1. *Topic.* Review your list of topics and choose another to explore. Trust your first instinct and mark your choice—for example, ghosts.

2. *Belief.* As before, your character may have a number of opinions and beliefs, right or wrong, about the second topic you chose. Berniece believes actively in the presence of ghosts. In fact, she believes that there is one living upstairs in her house. She also believes that the spirits of her ancestors reside in the family piano. Think about the second topic you chose to explore. Name a strong belief about this topic that your character holds but that you do not share. This is an example of how you and your character are different.

3. *Trigger.* Berniece believes that her house is haunted because she has seen a ghost at the top of her stairs. (She thinks it is the vengeful spirit of a man whom her brother murdered.) She believes that ancestral spirits reside in the family piano because this is what her mother taught her. Think about the second belief you're exploring and how your character came to this conclusion. Recount an experience from any time in the character's life, past or present, that led to this belief or reinforced it.

4. *Emotion.* Berniece's belief in ghosts makes her feel fearful. What is your character's emotional response to the belief you are exploring?

5. *Action.* Because she believes her house is haunted, Berniece asks a preacher to bless the house and exorcise the ghost. Because she believes that ancestral spirits reside in the family piano, she refuses to cooperate with her brother's plan to sell it. This belief also keeps her from playing the piano, for fear that it will wake the dead. Think about the belief you are exploring and what it might motivate your character to do. Identify an important action that your character could initiate at any time during the story as a result of this belief.

■ MISTAKEN BELIEF

Not all of your character's beliefs are accurate. These mistaken views and delusions can often lead to trouble.

1. *Topic.* Review your list of topics and choose another to explore. Trust your first instinct and mark your choice.

2. *Belief.* Identify an important character belief about this topic that is inaccurate within the world of your story. This is a belief that reflects wrong thinking. It might be the result of delusion, ignorance, error in judgment, a lie that someone told, or some other deception or

misinformation. Without repeating a previous response, state one of the character's mistaken beliefs.

3. *Trigger.* Think about how your character came to this conclusion. Describe one experience from any time in the character's life, past or present, that led to this mistaken belief or reinforced it.
4. *Emotion.* How does this belief make your character feel?
5. *Action.* What might this mistaken belief motivate your character to do at some time during the story?

■ HIDDEN BELIEF

For one reason or another, your character may keep some beliefs hidden from most others in the world of the story.

1. *Topic.* Review your list of topics and choose another to explore.
2. *Belief.* Identify a belief about this topic that your character tends to keep secret. From the character's perspective, this hidden belief may be too unusual, too unpopular, too shameful, or too painful to share publicly. Without repeating a previous response, state your character's hidden belief and explain why he or she keeps it secret.
3. *Trigger.* Think about how your character came to this conclusion. Recount an experience from any time in the character's life, past or present, that led to this hidden belief or reinforced it.
4. *Emotion.* How does this belief make your character feel?
5. *Action.* What might this hidden belief motivate your character to do at some time during the story?

■ BELIEF THAT WILL CHANGE

Some of your character's beliefs may change as a result of what happens during the dramatic journey.

1. *Topic.* Review your list of topics and choose another to explore.
2. *Belief.* Identify a belief that your character has early in the story but not later. State the belief that the character brings into the story.
3. *Trigger.* Recount an experience from the character's life that led to this early belief or reinforced it.
4. *Emotion.* How does this belief make your character feel?
5. *Action.* What might this belief motivate your character to do? This will most likely be an action that your character initiates early in the story.

■ NEW BELIEF

Your character is likely to develop many new beliefs as a result of story events.

1. *Belief.* Think about the belief you explored in the last round and how it might change during the story. State the new belief.
2. *Trigger.* Think about how your character comes to this new conclusion during the story. Identify the experience that results in this new belief.
3. *Emotion.* How does this new belief make your character feel?
4. *Action.* What might this belief motivate your character to do? This will most likely be an action that your character initiates late in the story or after the story ends.

◼ MOST IMPORTANT BELIEF

Right or wrong, what is your character's most important belief? This might be a belief that you've identified during the exercise or a new one. It might be about the character himself or herself, or about someone else or something else in the specific world of the story. Or it might be a universal belief about humanity, nature, or life in general. It is "most important" because it will have the greatest impact on how the story unfolds. Identify this critical belief and how it affects the dramatic journey.

WRAP-UP

Belief systems evolve from what the characters have experienced in life, what they have been taught by others, and how they have responded to all of this over time. Knowing each character's credo is an important step toward understanding his or her desires and motivations during the dramatic journey. The credo of the main character is often a link to the story's main subject and theme.

> **Related tools in *The Dramatic Writer's Companion*. To continue exploring a character's credo, go to the "Developing Your Character" section and try "What the Character Believes."**

THE EMOTIONAL CHARACTER

THE QUICK VERSION
Use different emotions to discover new truths about your characters

BEST TIME FOR THIS
Anytime you need to know a character better

THE EMOTIONAL LIVES OF CHARACTERS
Drama is primarily an emotional experience. As a result, dramatic characters tend to be emotional beings who experience a wide range of feelings as story events unfold. To know a character's emotional identity and emotional point of view is to understand the character where it counts most—at a gut level.

ABOUT THE EXERCISE
Use this exercise to uncover new truths about the characters in your story. Examples are based on an interpretation of *Topdog/Underdog* by Suzan-Lori Parks. Recipient of the 2002 Pulitzer Prize for Drama, the play explores the competitive relationship of two African American brothers—one a thief, the other a reformed card hustler—who live together in a seedy furnished room.

During the exercise, you will be asked to think about different emotions and name the character from your story whom you most associate with each one. You may choose some characters repeatedly during this process and other characters not at all. In each round you will explore one of your emotional associations in more depth.

To prepare, list the characters from your story so you can see them all at a glance. For best results, include at least six characters. If you have fewer than that in your story, find the rest from the offstage world. For example, Booth and Lincoln are the only onstage characters in *Topdog/Underdog*. Offstage characters include their Moms and Pops, who abandoned them years ago; Booth's ex-girlfriend Grace, whom he is trying to win back; and Lincoln's ex-wife, Cookie, who will have nothing more to do with him.

■ **FIRST EMOTIONAL FOCUS**

Learn more about your characters through their dominant emotions.
   1. *Three associations.* Identify the character from your story whom you most associate with

- *love*—for example, Booth, who wants to win back his ex-girlfriend Grace
- *sorrow*—for example, Lincoln, who has lost almost everyone important in his life
- *hate*—for example, Cookie, who kicked Lincoln out for being unfaithful

2. *Primary association.* Choose one of your three emotional associations to explore in more depth—for example, Lincoln and sorrow.

3. *Credo.* Emotion and intellect are closely linked. Feelings affect how the character thinks. Thinking affects how the character feels. For example, Lincoln's sorrow has led him to conclude that loved ones are not to be trusted: they inevitably betray and abandon you. Translate your primary emotional association into a belief, right or wrong, that could affect the character's behavior at an important time in the story.

4. *Desire.* Know what the character wants and you're on the way to understanding who the character is. As a result of the sorrow in his life, Lincoln wants to protect his relationship with his brother, his only remaining family member and friend. Translate your primary emotional association into an important desire or need that the character might experience at some time during the story.

5. *Physical life.* Characters exist in a certain physical reality made up of settings, material elements, and objects that reflect who they are and how they live. Lincoln's sorrow might be embodied by his old, beat-up guitar. Since he has trouble revealing his true feelings, Lincoln uses this guitar to play the songs that he makes up about loneliness. Translate your primary emotional association into an object or physical element and explain how it is important to the story.

6. *Image.* We go to the theater to *see* plays, not to *hear* them. Visual imagery is thus a key tool of dramatic storytelling. Lincoln's sorrow might be depicted by his lying awake in an old recliner late at night and staring up at the ceiling with a blanket over him (in this one-room dwelling, this chair is where he must spend the night). His brother, Booth, is sound asleep in the single bed across the room. There is a folding screen between them for privacy. Translate your primary emotional association into a visual image that is not in your script now.

7. *Hidden truth.* We tend to get most engaged in a dramatic story not when it is explained to us but rather when it is implied: when we have to lean forward in our seat, piece together bits and pieces of information, and make inferences about what we have observed. In a great story there are many hidden truths to be discovered. If Lincoln's sorrow were to mask a hidden truth, it would be that of all the people in his life whom he has lost, the one he misses most is his

father, who abandoned him when he was a teenager. Translate your primary emotional association into a hidden truth that underlies your character's words and actions.

■ **SECOND EMOTIONAL FOCUS**

Try a new set of emotions to reveal new truths about your characters.

1. *Three associations.* Identify the character whom you most associate with
   - *anger*—for example, Booth, who is mad at the world and almost everyone in it
   - *jealousy*—for example, Booth, who wishes he were his older brother
   - *joy*—for example, Booth's ex-girlfriend Grace, who is living her dream by going to beauty school
2. *Primary association.* Choose one of your three emotional associations to explore in more depth—for example, Booth and anger.
3. *Credo.* Booth's anger has led him to conclude that life is unfair and that it is okay, therefore, to do whatever is necessary—lie, cheat, steal, or even kill—in order to get what he wants. Translate your primary emotional association into a belief, right or wrong, that could affect your character's behavior at an important time in the story.
4. *Desire.* As a result of his anger, Booth wants to conquer the world around him and everyone in it, particularly his older brother, in whose shadow he has lived since childhood. Translate your primary emotional association into an important desire or need that the character might experience at some time during the story.
5. *Physical life.* Booth's anger might be embodied by the gun he keeps in his pants even when he's home alone. Translate your primary emotional association into physical life—a setting, object, or physical element—and explain how it is important to the story.
6. *Image.* Booth's anger might be depicted by the image of him grabbing Lincoln from behind and thrusting a gun into the left side of his neck. Booth is trying to stop his brother from cutting open the stocking that he won in their game of three-card monte. The stocking is a sacred object to Booth because it was the last thing his mother gave him before she disappeared. It contains his inheritance from her: $500 cash. Translate your primary emotional association into a visual image that is not in your script now.
7. *Hidden truth.* If there were a hidden truth behind Booth's anger, it would be that he has never actually looked inside the stocking that his departing mother gave him twenty years ago. His anger is masking a deeper fear that the stocking may contain no money at all and that his mother lied to him. Translate your primary emotional association into a hidden truth that underlies your character's words and actions.

■ THIRD EMOTIONAL FOCUS

Continue to use emotional life as a tool for character development.

1. *Three associations.* Identify the character whom you most associate with
   - *fear*—for example, Lincoln, who gave up card hustling after his partner was murdered
   - *guilt*—for example, Pops, who deserted his sons two years after their mother left
   - *hope*—for example, Booth, who always has big plans for the future
2. **Primary association.** Choose one of your three emotional associations to explore in more depth—for example, Booth and hope.
3. *Credo.* Booth's hope has led him to believe that it is possible to win back his beautiful ex-girlfriend Grace and live happily ever after. Translate your primary emotional association into a belief, right or wrong, that could affect your character's behavior at an important time in the story.
4. *Desire.* Booth's hopes and dreams lead him to want to become the world's best three-card monte dealer and make so much money that Grace will come crawling back to him. Translate your primary emotional association into an important desire or need that the character might experience at some time during the story.
5. *Physical life.* Booth's hope might be embodied by the three-card monte setup in his room: two stacked milk crates with a cardboard playing board on top and three cards, two black and one red. Translate your primary emotional association into physical life—a setting, object, or physical element—and explain how it is important to the story.
6. *Image.* Booth's hope might be depicted by his sitting alone at the three-card monte setup and pretending to be a dealer who is hustling an imaginary sucker from the street. It is clear from the look on Booth's face that in his imagining of this con game, he is winning. Translate your primary emotional association into a visual image that is not in your script now.
7. *Hidden truth.* Behind Booth's hope lies the hidden truth that he has no skill whatsoever at throwing the cards. For his plan to work, he will need the help of his brother, a master dealer who swore off the cards after his partner was murdered. Translate your primary emotional association into a hidden truth that underlies your character's words and actions.

WRAP-UP

Whether healthy or unhealthy, unbridled or repressed, emotional life is a vital element of a dramatic character's identity. Knowing this emotional life can often help you make key decisions at the scenic level. For example, the feelings of the characters may influence how they enter the scene, what they want here and now, and how they go about trying to get it. If you have trouble developing a scene, try changing the emotional life of at least one character and see what happens.

Related tools in *The Dramatic Writer's Companion*. To explore a character's emotional life in more depth, go to the "Developing Your Character" section and try "Getting Emotional." Or go to the "Causing a Scene" section and try "The Emotional Storyboard."

MEET THE PARENTS

THE QUICK VERSION
Learn more about a character by fleshing out his or her parents

BEST TIME FOR THIS
Anytime you need to know a character better

IT ALL BEGINS WITH MOM AND POP
Behind every dramatic character are a mother and father who have influenced his or her development in some way, even if only biologically. In some cases parents are so important that they become onstage or onscreen characters, such as Violet and Beverly Weston in *August: Osage Country* by Tracy Letts or Mag Folan in *The Beauty Queen of Leenane* by Martin McDonagh. In other cases the parents do not appear in the story but are nevertheless important to it. In *Topdog/Underdog* by Suzan-Lori Parks, Moms and Pops abandoned their teenage sons twenty years ago but remain a focal point of the conflict between the brothers today. Their final deadly clash is over a money stocking left to one of them by their mother before she disappeared.

In many cases parents do not play a direct role in the dramatic journeys of the characters, such as the real estate salesmen in *Glengarry Glen Ross* by David Mamet, who are too worried about losing their jobs to dwell on their moms and dads. Yet it is reasonable to assume that the self-images, value systems, and behaviors of these ruthless salesmen can be traced back to parental influences.

As you develop your script, then, it can be useful to know what role parents have played in a character's life and how much they influence the character's behavior during the dramatic journey, even if the character is not aware of that influence.

ABOUT THE EXERCISE
Use this exercise to flesh out a character's mother and father and then explore in more depth the influence of the dominant parent. If your character did not know his or her biological parents, substitute whoever fulfilled these roles. Unless otherwise directed, answer the questions from the global perspective of the writer, who knows more about the world of the story than any single character does.

■ YOUR CHARACTER'S MOTHER

Answer the following twenty questions with your character's mother in mind.

Getting to know this parent
1. What is this parent's name?
2. When the story begins, what is this parent's age? Ethnic background? Educational level? Social class?
3. Has this parent had any health issues that have affected his or her life in a significant way, and if so, what?
4. What is or was this parent's primary line of work?
5. How successful has this parent been at work, and why?
6. What is this parent's relationship to wealth and money?
7. How much importance does this parent attach to social status, and why?
8. How would you describe this parent's politics?
9. What are this parent's views of spirituality, religion, or the supernatural?
10. Whether at home, at work, or in the community, what has been this parent's greatest strength? This may be a physical, psychological, or social trait.
11. What has been this parent's greatest weakness?
12. What is a place, past or present, that your character might associate with this parent, and why?
13. What is an object or physical element that your character might associate with this parent, and why?
14. What is the strongest emotion that your character might associate with this parent, and why?
15. In a line or two, what is the most important thing that this parent thought or believed but never said? In other words, what has been his or her main subtext in life?
16. Where does this parent reside when the story begins?
17. Looking backwards from the start of the story, when is the last time your character saw this parent? It may have been a few moments ago or decades ago. Identify how long it's been.
18. Where did the last meeting with this parent occur, and—whether positive or negative, routine or unusual—what was the most important thing that happened?
19. Around the time the story begins, how would your character describe this parent? Answer from the character's perspective and in the character's voice, as if you were writing dialogue. Write as much as you can for at least three minutes.

20. Whether accurate or not, how would your character describe this parent in only one or two words?

■ YOUR CHARACTER'S FATHER

Now go back and answer the same twenty questions under "Getting to know this parent" with your character's father in mind.

■ IMPACT OF WHO MATTERS MOST

For the purposes of the exercise, the parent who has had the greatest influence on your character's development is Parent 1. This influence may have been positive or negative, direct or indirect, obvious or subtle. Identify your character's Parent 1. Then answer the following questions, and try not to repeat a response you've already given.

1. How would you describe the general relationship between your character and Parent 1?
2. What is the most significant physical trait or condition that your character has inherited from Parent 1?
3. How has Parent 1 affected the character's self-image and general outlook on life?
4. How has Parent 1 affected the character's approach to other people, organizations, and life in society?
5. What three things does your character value most as a result of Parent 1? These values might reflect the character's desire to emulate this parent or to rebel against him or her. Look for values that could be relevant to the story.
6. Your character may have many wants and needs as the dramatic journey unfolds. These translate into strategies and tactics, scenic objectives, and an overall story goal. Whether the character is aware of it or not, what is an important desire or need that can be traced back to Parent 1?
7. Different types of conflict may make it difficult for your character to get what he or she wants. These obstacles may arise from within the character, from other characters with opposing needs, or from the various situations that the character encounters. What significant problem of your character can be traced back to Parent 1?
8. Think about your character's strengths and assets. Without repeating a previous response, give an example of how Parent 1 has been a good influence.
9. Think about your character's faults and weaknesses. Without repeating a previous response, give an example of how Parent 1 has been a bad influence.

10. Right or wrong, what is the greatest lesson that your character has learned from Parent 1? State this lesson in the character's voice and from the character's perspective, as if you were writing dialogue.

WRAP-UP

Even if your character's parents are never mentioned in the story, their influence is likely to affect the character—and thus your story—in profound ways. If you get stuck during scriptwriting, try learning more about your character's family background and how it has affected his or her physical, psychological, and social development.

Related tools in *The Dramatic Writer's Companion*. To learn more about your character's early years, go to the "Developing Your Character" section and try "Into the Past."

SENSING THE CHARACTER

THE QUICK VERSION
Use sense memories to uncover new truths about your character

BEST TIME FOR THIS
After you have a working sense of the character

EXPERIENCING THE STORY
Characters live in a physical ream full of sights, sounds, smells, tastes, and sensations. The audience experiences this realm literally through sight and sound and vicariously through their other senses. Whether real or imagined, such input can provide powerful clues to who the characters are and what the story is about. It is often the physical realm that draws the audience most deeply into the dramatic journey by stirring personal memories, conscious and subconscious, of prior sense experiences.

ABOUT THE EXERCISE
To capture the mood of a scene, some actors use a technique called sense memory in which they relive a past emotion by recalling a physical detail from the experience that triggered it. Sometimes even a small detail, such as the sight of a certain necklace or the smell of a certain room, can trigger powerful memories. This exercise can help you adapt this technique to the development of a character in your story.

The process is a visceral one that asks you to explore a character's life by responding instinctively to a series of physical triggers. For each prompt,
- *identify a memory* for your character from any time in the story or backstory, and
- *describe an emotion* that your character associates with this memory.

Suppose that the stimulus was "an unopened box" and the character was Ella. The prompt might conjure up the memory of a hat box in Ella's attic full of old love letters that her husband, Hank, wrote to her twenty years ago when they were dating in college. She used to revisit this box regularly to reread those letters but hasn't opened it now in many years. The sight of the box arouses in Ella a feeling of sadness, since the love that once inspired those letters has faded away.

As you move from one prompt to the next, you may find sense memories from your own life mixing in with those from the life of your character. That is ultimately what the exercise is about: getting more personal, understanding your character emotionally through shared experiences, and rooting your findings in a specific physical reality.

To begin, choose a character to explore.

■ THE POWER OF SENSE MEMORY

Use the following physical triggers to find memories and emotions that reveal important information about your character.

Unopened box	Stifling heat
Christmas tree	Dark room on a sunny day
Smell of something burning	Cigar smoke
Unexpected knock at the door	Freshly dug grave
Pair of old boots	Birthday cake
Foggy, foggy road	Scent of roses
Sip of champagne	Thunderstorm
Bloodstains	Church bells ringing
Aroma of cookies baking	Shattering glass
Barking dog	An empty room

WRAP-UP

Sense memory can be a key tool to develop characters. By using physical details to trigger emotions and ideas, you may discover new ways in which your characters' lives mirror your own. No matter how well you know your characters, there is always more to learn.

Related tools in *The Dramatic Writer's Companion*. To continue using sensory input to trigger story ideas, go to the "Causing a Scene" section and try "In the Realm of the Senses" or "The Voice of the Setting."

THE IMPERFECT CHARACTER

THE QUICK VERSION
Explore a character's flaws and vulnerabilities

BEST TIME FOR THIS
Anytime you want to know the character better

DWELLING ON THE NEGATIVE
When we think of great characters who have moved us, it is often their flaws and vulnerabilities that we remember most. Consider what comes to mind when you think of Richard III, Lady Macbeth, Othello, Norma Desmond in *Sunset Boulevard*, Ratso Rizzo in *Midnight Cowboy*, Mama Nadi in *Ruined*, Violet Weston in *August: Osage County*, Jules Winnfield in *Pulp Fiction*, Randle McMurphy in *One Flew over the Cuckoo's Nest*, Mrs. Robinson in *The Graduate*, Vito Corleone in *The Godfather*, or Scarlett O'Hara in *Gone with the Wind*. To know characters is to know what makes them imperfect and to understand how their flaws and misdeeds affect their dramatic journeys scene by scene.

ABOUT THE EXERCISE
This exercise can help you explore the traits, qualities, and deeds that make a dramatic character less than saintly. It's based on the idea that perfect characters tend to be boring and that it is through character liabilities and limitations that we come to know them as human, get invested in their dramatic journey, and root for them to succeed or fail. For the purposes of the exercise, "the past" refers to the time before the story. "The present" refers to the time of the story.

To begin, choose a character to explore. Then respond to each exercise question as the writer who decides what's true and not true in the world of the story. Unless directed otherwise, feel free to repeat a response if it feels appropriate to do so. The repetition may signal that something important has been uncovered.

■ CHARACTER IMPERFECTIONS

Explore what makes your character vulnerable.
1. *Shortcomings.* Most dramatic characters are a combination of positive and negative traits. Identify three of your character's personal shortcomings when the story begins. These are physical, psychological, or social traits that put the character at a disadvantage at certain times

during the story. For example, he's ugly. She isn't very bright. He's deep in debt.

2. *Vice or bad habit.* Without repeating a previous response, identify a significant vice or bad habit of your character when the story begins. For example, she's greedy. He's a chronic liar. She has a gambling addiction.

3. *Worst fear.* Fear is a healthy emotion when it contributes to one's safety, well-being, or survival. Fear becomes unhealthy when it occurs inappropriately and prevents one from living a successful life. Identify your character's worst fear when the story begins and how it affects him or her.

4. *Greatest guilt.* Guilt is an emotion that reflects values. It is triggered by the belief that one has violated one's moral code or personal standards of conduct. Guilt becomes unhealthy when it is based on inaccurate beliefs or when it is disproportionate to the violation. Identify a time, past or present, when your character felt guilty. Identify the cause of this guilt and how it affects the character.

5. *Biggest delusion.* Characters are not always accurate in their perceptions of themselves, others, and the world around them. As a result of intellectual error, ignorance, or the willful deception of others, characters may have misconceptions and delusions that affect their behavior. Identify one of your character's greatest delusions when the story begins and how this affects him or her.

6. *Worst secret.* A good place to find imperfection is the realm of the character's life that he or she would prefer to keep hidden. Identify one of the character's biggest secrets when the story begins. Explore the reasons the character hides this.

7. *Wildest emotion.* Most characters experience a gamut of emotions as a dramatic journey unfolds. Some of these feelings—such as anger, fear, jealousy, and lust—may be harder to control than others. When your story begins, what is your character's wildest, or most unbridled, emotion, and how does this affect him or her?

8. *Biggest contradiction.* Great characters are multidimensional beings who sometimes embody contradictions. Identify a contradiction that your character manifests during the dramatic journey. For example, she's a health fanatic, but she smokes cigarettes and drinks too much. He loves his wife and family but frequents prostitutes. She controls everyone around her but can't control herself.

9. *Bad influence.* Some character imperfections are a result of a bad influence, such as a family member, friend, teacher, classmate, boss, or coworker, or even a famous person whom the character has never met. Identify someone from your character's life, past or present, who is a bad influence, and describe the harmful impact.

10. *Lack of control.* Power is the ability to control oneself, others, groups,

situations, or environments. It typically fluctuates depending on who's here now and what's happening. Think about others who can turn your character into proverbial putty for any reason—for example, because they seem so awesome, beautiful, or threatening. Identify an important power grabber in your character's life, past or present. Explain how and why this individual makes your character feel helpless.

11. **Worst decision.** Characters are decision makers who cause stories to happen. Their decisions often center on issues of vital importance and can have consequences that affect others as well. Think about your character's biggest decisions, past or present, with a focus on difficult choices that ultimately prove to be bad due to intellectual or moral error. Identify your character's worst decision and describe its consequences.

12. **Bad deed.** What characters do is often more important than what they say. Their actions not only move the story forward but also reveal important information about them. Without repeating a previous response, identify one of your character's worst deeds, past or present, and its consequences.

13. **Careless mistake.** Sometimes characters get into trouble because they fail to think before they act. Identify one of your character's careless mistakes, past or present, and its consequences. Look for the kind of mistake that leads to regret.

14. **Most self-destructive act.** Dramatic characters are sometimes their own worst enemies. They do things that are self-destructive. In some cases they know that their actions will harm them. In other cases they are unaware of the consequences. Identify one of your character's most self-destructive acts, past or present, and its results.

15. **Most malicious act.** Sometimes it is someone else's destruction that the character has in mind. Are there any times, past or present, when your character set out to cause someone else's downfall? If so, identify the character's most malicious act. Tell what happened to whom, why your character did this, and what occurred as a result.

16. **Biggest lie.** Characters may knowingly stray from the truth when something else appears more important. Their falsehoods can range from little fibs to devastating lies with far-reaching effects. Identify your character's biggest lie, past or present, why it was told, and what happened as a result of it.

17. **Sin of omission.** Sometimes problems arise because of what characters *don't* do. Through forgetfulness, fear, laziness, or intention, they fail to take important action, and as a result, they or others must suffer the consequences. For your character, identify an important failure to act, past or present, and its results.

18. **Victimization.** Dramatic characters tend to be active. They cause events as they pursue their goals. Inevitably, others in their lives

have different agendas and create physical, psychological, or social obstacles. Identify a notable time in the past when your character was a victim of someone else's agenda. Explain who the culprit was, what happened, and how it has affected your character.

19. *Tough luck.* Some problems are due to accident or unfortunate coincidence. Identify an example of tough luck from your character's life, past or present, and describe its consequences.

20. *Greatest flaw.* In classical tragedy, the hero's downfall is often the result of a "tragic flaw," an intellectual or moral lapse that leads to self-destruction. In classical comedy, such flaws are overcome so that the story can have a happy ending. Whether you are writing tragedy or comedy, or something in between, think about the character weaknesses, vulnerabilities, and limitations that you've discovered through this exercise. What is your character's greatest flaw? What is its most significant impact?

WRAP-UP

If to err is to be human, this exercise reflects an effort to ground your character in humanity by exploring his or her flaws and limitations. As you develop your script, stay aware of such imperfections, what they reveal about the character, and how they influence the dramatic journey. Characters tend to become more interesting when we see what makes them vulnerable.

Related tools in *The Dramatic Writer's Companion.* To explore your character's imperfections further, go to the "Developing Your Character" section and try "Seven Deadly Sins" or "The Character You Like Least."

OBJECTS OF INTEREST

THE QUICK VERSION
Use physical life to learn more about a character's dramatic journey

BEST TIME FOR THIS
After you are well into the story

CHARACTER IS A MANY-SPLENDORED THING
Objects in a dramatic story matter. They embody truths about the characters and their world, enable certain events to occur as the dramatic journey unfolds, and contribute to visual images that show, not tell, the story. Great moments in drama often involve an object or physical element of pivotal importance, such as a white painting in *Art* by Yasmina Reza, a 35mm film projector in *The Flick* by Annie Baker, or a pricey engagement ring in *Between Riverside and Crazy* by Stephen Adly Guirgis.

ABOUT THE EXERCISE
Use this exercise to develop a character by focusing on important objects from his or her life at two points in the dramatic journey: the beginning and the end. You can find these objects anywhere in the world of the story. They may be large or small, old or new, familiar or unfamiliar, and the character's perception of their importance may be accurate or inaccurate. For the purposes of the exercise, an "object" is a tangible thing, such as a cell phone, or a single set of tangible things, such as a pair of shoes. This is a visceral exercise that asks you to respond intuitively. Stay open to new possibilities and see what you can discover, rather than rehashing what you already know.

To begin, choose a character whom you would like to know better.

■ AS THE JOURNEY BEGINS

As you respond to the following two sets of exercise prompts, "Physical life" and "The thing that matters most," focus on your character at the beginning of the dramatic journey. Since the story has not happened yet, you will be exploring the world that has evolved from the backstory.

Physical life
Look for new discoveries as you explore your character's physical realm.
1. *Good thing.* Find an important object that your character perceives as a "good thing" at this time in the story. The value of this desirable object

may be obvious or hidden. Briefly identify this thing—for example, an unpublished memoir, the key to a safe deposit box, or a blackthorn walking stick.

2. *Bad thing.* Identify an important object that your character perceives as a "bad thing" at this time in the story. The problem that this undesirable object represents may be obvious or hidden.

3. *Another thing.* Identify a third object that is important to your character at this time in the story. Your character may perceive this object as either good or bad. It may be in your character's possession now or elsewhere, and its significance may be obvious or hidden.

The thing that matters most

Of the three physical items you named, choose one to examine in more depth.

1. *Subjective description.* From your character's perspective, right or wrong, and in your character's voice, as if you were writing dialogue, describe this object. Include what it looks like and why it's important. Remember where you are now in the dramatic journey.

2. *Objective description.* How would an impartial outside observer view this same object? In a few sentences, describe what this thing looks like and explain why it actually is or isn't important in the unique world of your story.

3. *Origin.* Whether purchased, created, received from someone else, stolen, found, or acquired by chance or accident, how did this object first come into the character's life?

4. *Memory.* What is a personal memory that this object could trigger for your character at this time in the story? Write the memory in your character's voice.

5. *Emotion.* What is the strongest emotion that this object might stir in your character now, and why?

6. *Desire.* What is the most important desire or need that this object might trigger or represent for your character at this time in the story?

7. *Action.* At any time in your character's life, past or present, what might this object motivate your character to do?

8. *Belief.* Imagine that this object reflects an important belief that your character has about life, people, or the world in general. Right or wrong, this is a universal insight—for example, that crime doesn't pay or that crime does pay if you do it right. From your character's perspective and in your character's voice, what universal idea might this object inspire or represent?

9. *Values.* The importance that a character attaches to an object can reveal a lot about his or her values. For example, a personal photo album might suggest that the owner values family. A pair of battered old shoes might suggest that the owner values comfort over image.

What values are suggested by your character's perception of the object you are exploring?

10. *Surprising fact.* Imagine that there is something surprising about this object that you didn't realize until now. This surprising fact may have something to do with the object's makeup, use, value, significance, or history. What is the surprising fact?

11. *Image.* Objects can reveal important truths about characters and move the story forward by providing tools for imagery. Think about the images that passed through your mind as you thought about this object in your character's life. What is the most powerful image that comes to mind now? Think of it as a portrait of your character at this time in the story, and let the object take focus as you describe the image.

■ AS THE JOURNEY ENDS

Shift your focus to the character's life near the end of the dramatic journey. Most of the story has happened now. Life has changed in some ways and not changed in others. There may be new objects of importance in your character's life. Some objects from the beginning of the story may no longer exist or matter. Or they may have acquired new meaning.

Use the same two sets of questions, "Physical life" and "The thing that matters most," to explore your character at the end of the dramatic journey. Look for what's new. If you wish to repeat an object from the beginning of the journey, find new information and feelings about it.

WRAP-UP

Working with objects, you have found two important images for your character—one from the beginning of the dramatic journey and one from the end. Think about how these images compare and contrast. What story do they suggest when you imagine them side by side?

Related tools in *The Dramatic Writer's Companion.* To explore the impact of physical life on dramatic action, go to the "Causing a Scene" section and try "Where In the World Are We?"

THE INVISIBLE CHARACTER

THE QUICK VERSION
Explore offstage characters who influence story events

BEST TIME FOR THIS
After you are well into the story

IMPORTANT CHARACTERS WHOM WE NEVER MEET
Dramatic stories often include characters who influence story events but never appear before the audience. In some cases these characters remain elsewhere because they are not important enough for the audience to meet. In other cases they remain out of sight because their absence is more powerful dramatically than their presence.

The importance of offstage characters is measured by how much they affect story events. Such characters may be dead (Alex in *The Big Chill*), imaginary (Keyser Söze in *The Usual Suspects*), elusive (the witch in *The Blair Witch Project*), or otherwise engaged (Rosaline in *Romeo and Juliet* or "Crazy Rhoda" Zimmerman in *The Odd Couple*). The absence of such characters may be conspicuous, as in *The Women*, where husbands, boyfriends, and other males are frequent topics of discussion among the all-female cast but never seen by the audience. Or their absence may have a subtle power, as in *Cat on a Hot Tin Roof*, where a suicide victim from the past exerts more influence on a troubled marriage than is readily apparent. Sometimes the importance of offstage characters is so significant that the story is named after them, as in *Rebecca*, where an insecure bride is tormented by the legacy of her husband's deceased wife.

ABOUT THE EXERCISE
You may have any number of offstage characters in a dramatic story. This exercise can help you explore those who matter most.

Examples are from *Doubt: A Parable* by John Patrick Shanley, recipient of a 2005 Pulitzer Prize for Drama and Tony Award for Best Play. Shanley later adapted the play to film for a 2008 release that earned an Academy Award nomination for Best Writing, Adapted Screenplay. This exercise focuses on the stage version.

The story is set in a 1964 Catholic elementary school in the Bronx and depicts the efforts of the principal to drive away a priest whom she suspects of child abuse, even though she has no factual evidence of his guilt. The offstage characters of this story are mainly the students and staff of the school.

Most are mentioned only briefly to create the ambience of a busy institution, but some play a critical role in the story.

Think about the offstage characters in your story and who among them might affect story events or at least deserve to be mentioned in dialogue. You are likely to find the most important offstage characters from the lives of your principal characters.

To begin, identify your two most important onstage or onscreen characters:

- *Character 1*, the main character of the story—for example, Sister Aloysius, the principal of St. Nicholas Church School
- *Character 2*, the second most important character in the story—for example, Father Flynn, the parish priest and basketball coach at St. Nicholas

■ CHARACTER 1'S UNSEEN LIFE

Who from your Character 1's unseen life, past and present, might influence the course of your story even though they never appear in it physically? Use the following questions to brainstorm possibilities. For each offstage character you name, describe a memorable detail. For example, one of the unseen characters in Aloysius's life is her coworker Mrs. Carolyn, the strange woman with the goiter who plays the portable piano.

Who's who in the unseen world

1. *Original family.* Think about your character's childhood family, such as parents, siblings, aunts, uncles, cousins, or grandparents. Identify and describe any unseen members of this family who are relevant to your story.
2. *Current family.* Identify and describe any members of your character's current family who do not appear in the script but are relevant to the story.
3. *Work associates.* The character's work life, past and present, may include many individuals whom the audience never meets, such as bosses, employees, coworkers, or customers. If any are relevant to your story, identify and describe them.
4. *Friends and lovers.* Among the unseen friends and lovers in your character's life, is anyone important enough to mention in the story? If so, who are they and how would you describe them?
5. *Others in the community.* Think about the communities in which your character has participated, such as schools, teams, clubs, churches, neighborhoods, or other social organizations. Identify and describe any unseen members of this larger social world who are relevant to your story.

■ CHARACTER 2'S UNSEEN LIFE

Now go back and answer the same five questions under "Who's who in the unseen world" with your Character 2 in mind.

■ FIRST UNSEEN CHARACTER

You have now identified a number of individuals who will not appear in your story but may be referenced in it for one reason or another. Some of these offstage characters matter more than others. In *Doubt* the most important offstage character is eighth-grader Donald Muller. In addition to being the first and only black student in a school full of warring Irish and Italians, Donald is gay, a fact that has led to beatings from his father at home and threats on his life from students at the public school he used to attend. Who is the most important unseen character in your story? Write a detailed description of him or her with a focus on what matters most.

1. **Why important.** In *Doubt* Donald Muller is not just important. He is pivotal to the story, since he is the boy whom Father Flynn may have abused. Donald is thus the catalyst for Aloysius's campaign to bring Flynn down. How is your unseen character important to the story?

2. **Why mentioned.** Because he is integral to the plot, Donald is mentioned many times as *Doubt* unfolds. In scene 4 he is the subject of a report that Sister James, an eighth-grade teacher, makes to Aloysius, her superior. In the here and now of the scene, James has a *feel bad* objective: she wants to warn Aloysius that Flynn may be having an inappropriate relationship with the boy. Imagine an important example of your unseen character being mentioned in your story. Who might make this reference, and why?

3. *Sample dialogue.* In scene 4 James tries to communicate her concerns about Donald by describing what happened after he visited the rectory. She says, "It's just the way the boy acted when he came back to class." Aloysius asks, "He said something?" James replies, "No. It was his expression. He looked frightened and . . . I think there was alcohol on his breath." Write a few lines of sample dialogue to show how and why your offstage character might be referenced during your story.

4. *Why unseen.* The fact that Donald remains offstage is core to our experience of *Doubt*: it forces us to focus on the reactions of the adults around the boy rather than on the boy himself. Donald's absence also adds to the uncertainty of Aloysius's allegations against Flynn, since we are never able to observe the boy's behavior or hear his version of what happened, such as how he acquired the wine. What is the main reason for keeping your offstage character physically absent from the dramatic action?

■ SECOND UNSEEN CHARACTER

Among the offstage population of *Doubt*, the second most important character is Monsignor Benedict. He is the one to whom Aloysius reports school problems that she cannot resolve on her own. However, Benedict is seventy-nine years old, a fan of Father Flynn, and so senile that he probably couldn't name the current president of the United States. At one point Aloysius describes the monsignor as "otherworldly in the extreme." Among your unseen characters, who is the second most important? Write a detailed description of him or her with a focus on what matters most.

1. **Why important.** Benedict is important because of his position in the hierarchy of the church and because he is the only one to whom Aloysius can officially report problems. It is because of Benedict's senility and alliance with Flynn that Aloysius decides not to go through regular channels to make her suspicions known. Though he never appears in the story, Benedict is thus essential to the plot, since he provides the motivation for Aloysius to take matters into her own hands. In effect, Benedict is the reason the play happens the way it does. How is your second unseen character important to the story?

2. **Why mentioned.** Aloysius refers to Benedict more than once in the story. In scene 4, after James has shared her concerns about Flynn, Aloysius begins to devise a plan to bring the priest down. In the here and now of the scene, she has a *convince* object: she wants James to understand that it would be futile to rely on Benedict for help. Imagine an important example of your unseen character being mentioned in your story. Who might make this reference, and why?

3. *Sample dialogue.* As Aloysius tries to figure out what to do about Flynn, James reminds her, "You're supposed to tell the monsignor!" Aloysius replies, "That you saw a look in a boy's eye? That *perhaps* you smelled something on his breath? Monsignor Benedict thinks the sun rises and sets on Father Flynn. You'd be branded an hysteric and transferred." Write a few lines of sample dialogue to show how and why your second unseen character might be referenced during your story.

4. **Why unseen.** Due to his senility and alliance with Flynn, Benedict has nothing to offer Aloysius in the way of assistance and support. This absence of help is underscored by his literal absence from the play. Since his dramatic function is only to exist as an obstacle, he is not necessary as an observable character. Why does your second offstage character remain physically absent from the dramatic action?

■ THIRD UNSEEN CHARACTER

Among the offstage characters of *Doubt*, the third most important is William London, another student in James's class whom Aloysius describes as a restless boy who is headed for trouble in life. William is sent by James to the principal's office because of a nose bleed that he experienced during the Pledge of Allegiance and that, in Aloysius's opinion, was self-induced with a ballpoint pen in order to escape school. Among your offstage characters, who is third most important? Write a detailed description of him or her with a focus on what matters most.

1. **Why important.** William matters in *Doubt* because he is the catalyst for scene 2—his nosebleed is the reason James comes to Aloysius's office—but mainly because of an interaction that Aloysius witnessed between him and Flynn in the backstory. On the first day of school, the priest reached out to touch William's wrist and William pulled away. It was a small incident, but it raised a question in Aloysius's mind about Flynn's relationship with children. William is thus the one who first sparks her mistrust of the priest. This makes him a central character in the backstory. How is your third unseen character important to the story?

2. **Why mentioned.** William gains his greatest importance during the showdown between Aloysius and Flynn in scene 8. Flynn has a *find out* objective: he wants to know why Aloysius is convinced of his guilt when she has no proof of wrongdoing. This is when she reveals what she witnessed between William and him on the first day of school. Imagine an important example of your unseen character being mentioned in your story. Who might make this reference, and why?

3. **Sample dialogue.** During their climactic duel in scene 8, Flynn demands to know why Aloysius refuses to trust him. She explains, "On the first day of the school year, I saw you touch William London's wrist. And I saw him pull away." Flynn says, "That's all?" Aloysius says, "That was all." Write a few lines of sample dialogue to show how and why your unseen character might be referenced during your story.

4. **Why unseen.** Because William is part of the circumstantial evidence against Flynn, his physical absence from the story adds to the uncertainty of Aloysius's allegations. As with Donald, we are not able to observe William directly or hear what he has to say about the priest. William thus gains the most power dramatically by remaining offstage. Why is your third offstage character physically absent from the dramatic action?

WRAP-UP

Even though the audience never meets them, offstage characters can serve the story in a number of ways. For best results, limit the number of unseen characters who will be mentioned in dialogue. When such characters must be discussed, keep the speaker's current objective in mind, and limit the reference to the details that matter most.

Related tools in *The Dramatic Writer's Companion.* For more about the power of unseen characters, go to the "Developing Your Character" section and try "The Dramatic Triangle." For more about exposition—the realm of the unobservable—go to the "Causing a Scene" section and try "There and Then."

SIDE BY SIDE

THE QUICK VERSION
Compare and contrast two characters from your story

BEST TIME FOR THIS
After you have a working sense of who the characters are

CHARACTER DIFFERENCES AND SIMILARITIES
It is a common assumption that the characters in a dramatic story each need to be distinct. Hamlet and Claudius, for example, are clearly different individuals. Each has a unique combination of traits that define his identity and fuel his need to accomplish something he views as important. It is because of such distinctions that these two men see the world in different ways, behave differently, and often find themselves in conflict. All of this makes for a good story.

The need for individuality, however, does not eliminate the importance of character similarities as well. If characters had no common ground, they could not be in the same story, just as Claudius could not have become part of Hamlet's life if he had lived in a different country or at a different time. Indeed, he might not have played a meaningful role in Hamlet's destiny if he had been born into a different family or class. The similarities among characters may extend into any area of their personalities or lives. It is through their common ground that they participate in the same events. In some cases, it is their similarities that force them to deal with each other in stressful situations where they would rather walk away.

ABOUT THE EXERCISE
Use this exercise to find out more about two of your characters by comparing and contrasting them. For best results, work in two columns, one for each character, so you can see your responses side by side.

Examples are from *Circle Mirror Transformation* by Annie Baker. Recipient of the 2010 Obie Award for Best New American Play, the story centers on interactions within an acting class at a Vermont community center.

Take these steps to begin your side-by-side character exploration:
- *Choose two characters* from your story to explore—for example, Schultz, age forty-eight, a carpenter, and Teresa, age thirty-five, a student of acupressure and Rolfing.
- *Choose a timeframe* for the exploration: beginning, middle, or end of

the story. Examples focus on Schultz and Teresa at the beginning of Baker's play.

- *Define the relationship* between your characters at this time. For example, Schultz and Teresa are students in an acting class who have just met.

■ HOW CHARACTERS COMPARE AND CONTRAST

In the following questions, "now" refers to the timeframe you chose.

1. *Unique trait.* Characters are made up of physical, psychological, and social traits that define who they are. Some of these traits are distinctive. One of Schultz's unique traits is his creativity with furniture. A carpenter by trade, he makes artistic chairs for a hobby, such as one that displays the sun and another that displays a cloud. One of Teresa's unique traits is her photographic memory. She can remember things from years ago in amazing detail, such as the name of the girl whom her ex-boyfriend first kissed in high school. For each of your characters, identify a distinctive trait.
2. *Universal trait.* Dramatic characters also have traits that are common. Such traits enable us to identify with the characters because they remind us of ourselves or people we know. One of Schultz's universal traits is his need for companionship. One of Teresa's universal traits is her desire to make a difference in the world. For each of your characters, identify an important trait that many others share.
3. *Key strength.* Schultz is a go-getter who is honest about his feelings and unafraid to pursue his desires. Teresa is a passionate person with confidence and poise, one of the best students in the class. For each of your characters, and without repeating a previous response, identify a key strength at this time in the story.
4. *Key weakness.* Schultz is needy. This makes him vulnerable with others and easily hurt. Teresa presents a cheerful exterior but is really a guarded person who fears emotional pain and thus tries to avoid problems. For each of your characters, and without repeating a previous response, identify a key weakness at this time in the story.
5. *Key backstory fact.* The past often has profound effects on the present. A key experience from Schultz's past was his divorce from his wife of twenty-seven years. This occurred about a year ago and has left him devastated. A key experience from Teresa's past was her decision five months ago to break up with her abusive boyfriend and move from New York City to Shirley, Vermont. The experience has made her hopeful for a better future. For each of your characters, identify a past experience that influences him or her in the present, and give an example of its impact.

6. *Most important relationship.* Dramatic characters have an array of relationships that affect who they are and what they do. The most important relationship in Schultz's life is his ex-wife, Becky. The most important relationship in Teresa's life is her father. Who is the most important person in each of your characters' lives now?

7. *Contradiction.* Fascinating characters often embody contradictions that reveal different sides of who they are. Schultz wants to start over and get married again, but he can't let go of his last marriage. Teresa also wants to be in a relationship, but she is attracted only to men who are not available. Identify a contradiction that each of your characters embodies now.

8. *Animal comparison.* Metaphors and similes are figures of speech in which something unfamiliar is described by comparing it to something familiar with similar attributes. Schultz might be described as a drooling cocker spaniel. Teresa might be a floating swan about to take flight. Think about the dominant traits of your characters. Find a comparison from the animal kingdom to imply something important about each.

9. *Values most.* Schultz most values romance and sex, and not necessarily in that order. Teresa most values caring for other people in a meaningful way and contributing to the welfare of society. What do each of your characters most value now?

10. *Values least.* Schultz least values his independence. He longs for the days when he was tied down to a safe, comfortable routine with his wife. Teresa least values big-city social life. She left New York because she felt that people there do not really care about one another. What do each of your characters least value now?

11. *Physical object.* Truths about characters are often revealed by the objects and elements in the physical world around them. One object that says a lot about Schultz is the wedding ring that he still wears though he has been divorced for a year. He clings to a past that made him feel secure. An object that reveals a lot about Teresa is the hula hoop she masters in a room of self-conscious acting students. She is graceful and well grounded. For each of your characters, identify an important object and what it reveals about him or her.

12. *Dominant emotion.* Characters usually experience a variety of emotions during a story, but some feelings dominate the mix. Schultz has been shoved out of nearly three decades of married life into a singular existence that does not suit him. His dominant emotion is loneliness. Teresa is an optimist who believes she can change not only herself but also the world. Her dominate emotion is hope. What is the dominant emotion of each of your characters?

13. *Burning desire.* Characters speak and act because they want something. Schultz's burning desire is to find a girlfriend. That's why he's taking an

acting class. Teresa's burning desire is to start life anew in a small town where people care about each other. What does each of your characters want most at this time in the story?

14. **Biggest secret.** Most characters have secrets that influence their thoughts, feelings, and behavior. Schultz's biggest secret is that he is addicted to Internet pornography. Teresa's biggest secret is that everything she does is motivated by a fear of being alone. What is the biggest secret influencing each of your characters now?

15. **Root action.** When you boil characters down to basic terms, you might see that each has a root action from which all of their other actions flow. Schultz's root action is *to build*. Just as he makes things as a carpenter, he is trying to construct new relationships and a new life for himself. Teresa's root action is *to touch*. Just as she massages clients physically through acupressure and Rolfing, she is trying to affect people emotionally: to nurture and comfort them. Think about what your characters say and do at this time in the story. For each one, define a root action.

16. **Likes most about the other.** Characters perceive each other in different ways as the story unfolds, and these perceptions affect their interactions. Schultz finds himself attracted to Teresa, though he barely knows her. What he likes most is her beauty, confidence, and agility in class. Teresa finds herself somewhat attracted to Schultz. What she likes most is the attention he gives her: he makes her feel important. Think about how your characters view each other now. From each one's perspective, right or wrong, what is the other character's most appealing trait?

17. **Likes least about the other.** Schultz is eager to start a new romantic relationship, so he doesn't like the fact that Teresa seems aloof. Teresa is put off by the needy look in Schultz's eyes, and though he seems nice, she finds him boring. (He's also wearing that wedding ring.) Think again about how your characters view each other now. From each one's perspective, right or wrong, what is the other character's worst trait?

18. **Most admirable trait.** Most characters have both positive and negative qualities. One of Schultz's most admirable traits is his willingness to take risks. As a carpenter in an acting class, he is a fish out of water, but in the pursuit of love, he's willing to give the class a try. One of Teresa's most admirable traits is her optimism in spite of her losses: she had to leave her boyfriend because he was abusive; her parents both may be dying; and her brother is getting married, making him less available for family support. What trait do you personally admire most in each of your characters?

19. **Least resembles the other.** Schultz and Teresa are social opposites. Schultz is eager for romance. This makes him socially outward, especially around women. Teresa is reluctant to rush into another

relationship that could cause more pain. This makes her socially inward, especially around men. How are your characters least alike now?

20. **Most resembles the other.** Schultz and Teresa have both suffered deep losses and are struggling to reinvent themselves. They both yearn for transformation. How are your characters most alike now?

WRAP-UP

Ideally, no two characters are alike. Yet no two characters are totally unalike. As you develop your script, continue to explore the differences that make each character unique and the similarities that motivate them to interact and often explain why they sometimes find themselves in the same situation.

Related tools in *The Dramatic Writer's Companion*. To continue exploring what makes each character unique, go to the "Developing Your Character" section and try "Characters in Contrast," "Finding the Character's Voice," or "Spinal Tap."

CHARACTER FACT SHEET

THE QUICK VERSION
Identify key facts about a character that could affect story events

BEST TIME FOR THIS
After you are well into the story

CHARACTER IS STORY
The process of building a dramatic story is closely related to the process of developing characters. To know what happens in the story is to know who the characters are, what they want, and why they behave the way they do.

Each character has a variety of traits that can be combined in a variety of ways. A key challenge of the dramatic writer is not only to identify the traits that a particular character embodies but also to determine which of these traits matter most in the story.

ABOUT THE EXERCISE
Use this exercise to identify important facts about one of your characters. As you step through the exercise categories, keep these suggestions in mind:

- *Choose facts that matter.* In each category you may find that different responses are possible. Always look for the fact that could have the greatest impact on the dramatic journey.
- *Don't repeat a fact you've already given.* Exercise categories are designed to prompt creative thinking. Some of them overlap and could generate similar responses. Always look for a new fact in each category.

Examples are from *A Streetcar Named Desire* by Tennessee Williams, with a focus on the character of Blanche Dubois. Recipient of the 1948 Pulitzer Prize for Drama, the play portrays Blanche's desperate efforts to find a safe refuge with her married sister after losing her own home and teaching job. The 1951 film adaptation received Academy Award nominations for Best Motion Picture and Best Writing, Screenplay.

◼ WHAT ARE THE FACTS?

A fact is something that is known to exist or to have happened. If you are creating a story from imagination, you are the one who decides what is true and not true for your characters. If you are developing a story based on actual people and events, you may need to do research to determine what the facts are. In either case, choose a character to examine and let the following categories help you determine what makes this character distinct and interesting.

1. *Physical fact.* When we first meet Blanche, she pretends to be a young southern belle, but she is actually much older than she appears. Aging is an issue that underlies many of her challenges throughout the dramatic journey. Identify an important physical fact about your character. It may relate to the character's age, race, appearance, health, agility, strength, or any other physical trait or condition.

2. *Psychological fact.* Blanche has learned to rely on the kindness of strangers for her well-being. Identify an important psychological fact about your character. This fact relates to the character's inner world: the realm of thoughts, beliefs, emotions, aspirations, needs, or any other psychological truths.

3. *Family fact.* Blanche is mostly alone in the world. Her parents are both dead, her sister is married, her husband committed suicide years ago, she has never remarried, and she has no children. Her lack of family increases her dependency on Stella, her only sister, who now lives with her husband in a one-room apartment. Identify an important fact about your character's family life.

4. *Work fact.* Blanche is a high school English teacher by profession but is currently unemployed. Her teaching background contributes to her image as a refined person, while her unemployment adds to her dependency on her sister for room and board. Identify an important fact about your character's work life.

5. *Social fact.* When Blanche first arrives in the French Quarter, she appears to be a woman of means, but she is secretly homeless and penniless. Without repeating a previous response, identify an important fact about your character's social status.

6. *Widely known fact.* When Blanche's parents died, the task of running the family estate, Belle Reve, fell on her shoulders since her sister, Stella, had moved to New Orleans and married. Identify an important fact about your character that many others know when the story begins. This fact may relate to any aspect of the character's identity or life, as long as it is public knowledge and could affect story events.

7. *Little-known fact.* After Blanche lost her family estate and her job, she had to resort to a life of prostitution in order to keep a roof over her head and food on the table. This is a history she conceals behind a prim and proper facade. Identify an important fact about your character that most others don't know when the story begins. This fact may have been intentionally hidden by the character—a secret—or it may be something that simply hasn't come to light yet.

8. *Fun fact.* Blanche likes to dress up in fancy evening clothes. She has a wardrobe trunk full of flowery dresses and colorful accessories,

including silver slippers and a rhinestone tiara. Identify a fun fact about your character.

9. *Haunting fact.* Years ago, after discovering her husband, Allan, having sex with an older man, Blanche told Allan that he disgusted her. It was because of her cruel reaction that he killed himself, and Blanche has never forgiven herself for her role in his death. Identify a fact from the past that haunts your character during the story.

10. **Shocking fact.** Blanche lost her teaching job when the school administration learned about an inappropriate relationship she had with a male student. Identify a shocking fact about your character from the backstory: something the character did or experienced at any time before the story begins. Look for a fact that could influence your character's beliefs, feelings, or behavior during the dramatic journey.

11. *Unfortunate fact.* Blanche is being courted by a quiet man named Mitch, who lives with his mother. Blanche does not view him as an ideal mate but pursues his affection because she believes he is her last chance for a happy future. Identify an important fact about your character that is sad but true.

12. *Dangerous fact.* Blanche has become a master of illusion, believing that it accounts for 50 percent of a woman's charm. For example, she places veils over the lamps at night to soften the light on her face and maintain the illusion that she is still young. Her flights of fancy eventually grow dangerous, however, and lead to a nervous breakdown. Identify a dangerous fact about your character.

13. *Fixed fact.* A "fixed fact" is an established truth that is virtually set in stone: it does not change as the story unfolds. By acting like a snob and trying to break up her sister's marriage, Blanche makes an enemy for life out of her sister's husband, Stanley. This is a fixed fact that will ultimately contribute to her downfall. Identify a fixed fact about your character that is important to the story because it is always true.

14. *Fleeting fact.* Whether positive or negative, some facts remain true only for a while. Blanche's relationship with Mitch appears to be marriage bound, but when her scandalous past catches up with her, she ends up alone again. The loss of Mitch is one of the final steps in her undoing. Think about how your character's life changes as story events unfold. Identify a fact about the character that is true at one time but not another. Look for a fact that is important because it ceases to be true.

15. *Fact to be proud of.* Blanche has been a darling of high society who once hobnobbed with the rich and cultured. Think about your character's greatest assets and accomplishments. What fact would he or she most enjoy bragging about?

16. *Fact to be ashamed of.* In her efforts to forget the guilt she feels over her husband's suicide, Blanche drinks too much, but only in private.

Identify a fact that makes your character feel ashamed. This fact may or may not be known by others.

17. *Recurring fact.* In addition to alcohol, Blanche repeatedly uses sex to dull the memory of her role in her husband's suicide. This has led her to have multiple sexual partners over the years and to seek intimacy only with strangers. Identify a fact about your character that is important because it keeps happening again and again.

18. *Brutal fact.* The truth is not always pretty. Blanche reaches the point in her life where the only "kindness of strangers" she can still find is the extended arm of a gentleman who will escort her to a mental asylum. Identify a brutal fact about your character.

19. *Fuzzy fact.* Like the meaning of an inkblot, the significance of some facts is hard to discern. Some people see this truth one way; others see it another way. Blanche has "highbrow" manners. Her brother-in-law, Stanley, sees her manners as a phony attempt to make herself look better than everyone else. Her suitor, Mitch, sees her manners as an attractive feature of her personality. Think about how others perceive your character. Identify a fuzzy fact about him or her—a truth that is interpreted in at least two different ways by others in the story.

20. *False fact.* Blanche believes that a wealthy southern gentleman named Shep Huntleigh will one day come to her rescue and take care of her for the rest of her life. The truth is that Shep once was her suitor but he has moved on and is now married to someone else. Identify something that your character perceives as a fact but is actually untrue.

■ WHICH FACTS MATTER MOST?

You have now collected twenty facts about your character. Though all are important, some matter more than others. Use the next set of questions to sum up what matters most. You may repeat whatever information is appropriate here or add any new information that occurs to you now.

1. *Positive facts.* Blanche is a complicated character who reveals many sides of herself as she searches for a safe refuge in a cruel world. Blanche, for example, has these strengths and assets:
   - she knows how to put her best foot forward and present herself well,
   - she is intelligent and resourceful, and
   - she has a sister who loves her.
   Identify the three positive facts about your character that matter most.

2. *Negative facts.* Blanche is a compelling dramatic character because she also has many weaknesses and vulnerabilities, including these:
   - she has lived with so much delusion that she often can't tell what's real and what isn't,

- she is a fragile person who must rely on others for almost everything, and
- she has a brother-in-law who wants to run her out of his home at any cost.

Identify the three negative facts about your character that matter most.

■ WHAT IF SOME FACTS WERE DIFFERENT?

You may gain new insights about your story by playing with the facts and imagining a few new possibilities for your character.

1. *Strength as liability*. Review the three positive character facts that you identified as most important, and begin to think about them in new ways:
   - Imagine that under certain circumstances, one of these strengths or assets could prove to be a liability. Mark one that could possibly get your character into trouble at some time in the story. For example, Blanche knows how to put her best foot forward.
   - Blanche's ability to present herself well turns against her as the story unfolds. Instead of impressing her brother-in-law, she alienates him by appearing phony and condescending. If she had been more honest about her problems, she might not have ended up in such dire straits at the end of the story. Suppose your story were to unfold in a slightly different way. How might the character strength you marked become a weakness?

2. *Weakness as strength*. Review the three negative character facts that you identified as most important, and begin to think about them in new ways:
   - Imagine that under certain circumstances, one of these weaknesses or liabilities could prove to be an asset. Mark one that could help your character accomplish something important at some time in the story. For example, Blanche is a fragile person who must rely on others for almost everything.
   - For Blanche, fragility becomes a powerful tool to manipulate others. By throwing herself helplessly into the arms of those around her, she acquires a free place to stay for now and a prospective husband for later. Suppose your story were to unfold in a slightly different way. How might the character weakness you marked become a strength?

WRAP-UP

Multidimensional characters have a complex mix of traits that define who they are and distinguish them from one another. As the dramatic journey unfolds scene by scene, the most important of these traits will be revealed through the actions of the characters as they pursue their goals and deal with obstacles.

As you develop your script, keep building on what you know about your characters to discover new physical, psychological, and social facts about them. Such discoveries can help keep you engaged in the characters as you write and often lead to new directions for the story, especially when you have reached a creative crossroads where you're not sure which way to proceed next.

Related tools in *The Dramatic Writer's Companion*. Any exercise in the "Developing Your Character" section can help you learn more about your character. For starters, try "Basic Character Builder," "What the Character Believes," "Where the Character Lives," and "Where the Character Works."

TWO VIEWS OF ONE CHARACTER

THE QUICK VERSION
Learn more about three characters by exploring how two of them view the third

BEST TIME FOR THIS
After you have a working sense of your principal characters

HOW CHARACTERS SEE THOSE AROUND THEM
As dramatic characters interact, they form certain impressions about one another. Whether accurate or not, these perceptions often affect character behavior. When the queen wiggles her finger, for example, minions rush to serve her because of their perceptions of her power. When a homeless man pleads desperately for money, passersby may not even glance his way because of their perceptions of his need.

How characters are viewed by others in the story often influences how the audience views them as well. We may be more likely to admire those whom others praise and find fault with those whom others criticize. When one character expresses an opinion about another, it is an opportunity to learn more about both of them. In some cases we learn more about the character offering the opinion than we do about the one being described. This is especially true when the opinion contradicts what we have observed. In Peter Shaffer's play *Amadeus*, for example, when Salieri criticizes Mozart, we understand that he feels jealous of the celebrated musician's talent.

ABOUT THE EXERCISE
This exercise can help you learn more about three of your characters by exploring how two of them view the third. Examples are from *The Lieutenant of Inishmore* by Martin McDonagh. Recipient of a 2006 Obie Award for Playwriting, the play centers on a cat named Wee Thomas that is mysteriously killed on a rural road on the island of Inishmore while the owner, an Irish National Liberation Army (INLA) enforcer, is in Northern Ireland torturing drug pushers. The enforcer's father must now figure out how to break the news to his violent son that the cat he cherished is gone.

To begin:
- *Choose one character to analyze*—for example, Padraic Osbourne, the cat-loving INLA enforcer. This will be your Character 1 for the exercise.

- *Identify two other characters* who believe they know Character 1 well. Define their relationship to him or her when the story begins. For example, Character 2 is Donny, Padraic's father, and Character 3 is Mairead, a teenage neighbor. If your story has only two characters, find the third in the offstage world.

Following are a series of questions about Character 1 at different times in the story. Answer each question twice—first from Character 2's perspective and then from Character 3's, with each response in the character's voice. For best results, record these opinions in two columns, one for each character, so you can easily compare them. Remember that not all responses may not be accurate and that each reveals something about the speaker as well as the subject.

■ IN THE BEGINNING

Imagine your Characters 2 and 3 as the dramatic journey begins. Ask each one separately the following questions about your Character 1:

1. *Length of relationship.* Donny has known his son, Padraic, for twenty-one years. Mairead has known her neighbor, Padraic, for five years. How long have you known Character 1?
2. *How relationship began.* Donny first saw Padraic wailing in his wife's arms a few hours after his son was born in their cottage. Mairead first noticed Padraic when she was in the fifth grade and he was in secondary school. He was with a group of boys throwing stones at sheep in a roadside field. How did you meet, or first become aware of, Character 1?
3. *Happiest memory.* One of Donny's happiest memories of his son was from a year ago, when Padraic asked him to take care of his cat while he was away. The request showed that a bond of trust still existed between father and son. One of Mairead's happiest memories of Padraic was from five years ago, when he complimented her ability to shoot out a cow's eyes from sixty yards away. What is your happiest memory of Character 1?
4. *Worst memory.* One of Donny's worst memories of his son was from nine years ago, when Padraic attacked his cousin for making fun of his "girlie" scarf. The cousin ended up in a wheelchair that Padraic later stole from him. That was the day Donny realized his son was a monster. One of Mairead's unhappiest memories was from five years ago, when Padraic first left Inishmore to fight for the freedom of Northern Ireland. She begged to go with him, but he refused because, first, she was a girl and, second, she was only ten. What is your unhappiest memory of Character 1?
5. *Relationship.* Donny's already fragile relationship with his son is now in jeopardy due to the death of Wee Thomas on Donny's watch. The

cat was Padraic's only friend. Mairead's relationship with Padraic is a distant one: she worships him from afar. How would you describe your relationship with Character 1 as the story begins?

6. *Emotional connection.* Donny sees Padraic as one to be feared. Mairead sees him as one to be admired and loved. What is your emotional connection to Character 1?

7. *Likes most.* What Donny likes best about Padraic is that he is far away in Northern Ireland. What Mairead likes best about him is his patriotism. What do you like most about Character 1 as the story begins?

8. *Likes least.* What Donny likes least about his son is his violent temper. What Mairead likes least about Padraic is his refusal to take her seriously as a warrior for Ireland. What do you like least about Character 1 as the story begins?

■ IN THE MIDDLE

Next, imagine your Characters 2 and 3 midway through the dramatic journey and ask each one these questions about your Character 1:

1. *Physical description.* To Donny, Padraic looks like an Osbourne—more like Donny's own father than himself—and has the strength of three men. To Mairead, Padraic is handsome and sexy. How would you describe Character 1 physically?

2. *Personal description.* Donny views Padraic as a mean sonofabitch with the anger of seven men. It was not by accident that he earned the nickname "Mad Padraic." Mairead sees him as a charming hero fighting for the liberation of Ireland. How would you describe Character 1 personally?

3. *Social description* Donny sees Padraic as a social misfit who never learned how to get along with anyone but his cat. That's why he is always in trouble. Mairead sees him as a born leader. How does Character 1 fit in socially with others, such as family, friends, or the community?

4. *Work life.* Padraic is an enforcer for the INLA. From Donny's perspective, it's a good job for Padraic because it gives him an outlet for his violent tendencies. It also gets him out of Donny's hair, since it often takes Padraic to Northern Ireland. From Mairead's perspective, being an INLA enforcer is the perfect job for Padraic because he is an Irish patriot who refuses to tolerate injustice. How well suited is Character 1 to his or her line of work, and why?

5. *Greatest delusion.* In Donny's opinion, Padraic suffers from the delusion that he is always right. In Mairead's opinion, Padraic suffers from the delusion that girls can't fight as well as boys. What is Character 1's greatest delusion?

6. **Key strength.** Donny believes that Padraic's greatest strength is his fearless commitment to his political beliefs. Mairead would agree. What is Character 1's greatest strength?

7. **Key weakness.** Donny believes that Padraic's greatest weakness is his inability to control his temper. Mairead believes that Padraic's greatest weakness is his narrow and rigid view of the world, which prevents him from being interested in anything but the freedom of Ulster. What is Character 1's greatest weakness?

8. **Surprising discovery.** Donny's most surprising discovery about Padraic is that he could actually torture, maim, and kill his own father. Mairead's most surprising discovery is that Padraic shot and killed her cat, Sir Roger. What is your most surprising discovery about Character 1?

■ IN THE END

Now ask your Characters 2 and 3 these questions about your Character 1 as the dramatic journey concludes:

1. **Relationship.** By the time the story ends, Donny's relationship with his son is over and without hope for reconciliation, since Padraic is now dead. Mairead's relationship with Padraic is also over. She just executed him for killing her cat. Think about how your relationship with Character 1 has changed and not changed since the story began. How would you describe this relationship now?

2. **Emotional connection.** Donny's current emotional connection to Padraic is one of grief. His son's life—as well as the lives of three other men and two cats—has ended in bloodshed. Mairead's current emotional connection to Padraic is also one of grief. She feels heartbroken that she had to kill him. What is your emotional connection to Character 1 as the dramatic journey ends?

3. **Likes most.** What Donny likes most about Padraic now is that he can no longer torture or kill anyone, including Donny. What Mairead likes best is that Padraic has been brought to justice for killing her cat. What do you like most about Character 1 as the dramatic journey ends?

4. **Likes least.** What Donny likes least about Padraic now is that he died in vain. As it turns out, the dead cat that triggered all of the violence was not actually Wee Thomas but another black cat that resembled him. Donny makes this painful discovery when the real Wee Thomas wanders home in search of food. What Mairead likes least about Padraic is that he committed an unforgivable crime—the murder of her cat—and can no longer be part of her dreams. What do you like least about Character 1 as the dramatic journey ends?

WRAP-UP

This has been a study of one character from two different perspectives and ultimately an examination of all three characters and their relationships. You may make further discoveries about them by comparing the responses at the end of the story to those at the beginning. How has Character 1 changed as a result of story events? How have the perceptions of Characters 2 and 3 changed? In what important ways have these relationships stayed the same?

Related tools in *The Dramatic Writer's Companion.* To continue exploring characters in relation to one another, go to the "Developing Your Character" section and try "Characters In Contrast" or "Three Characters in One."

NOTHING BUT THE TRUTH

THE QUICK VERSION
Explore a character's innermost thoughts and feelings

BEST TIME FOR THIS
After you have a working sense of the character

THE CHARACTER'S PRIVATE DOMAIN
A defining moment is a point in time in which the true nature of a character is revealed. It's when a struggling singer steps into the spotlight and emerges as an artist, or when a soldier flees from battle and is exposed as a coward. Revelations like these occur when conflict strips characters of their facades by forcing them to act under pressure.

To make such revelations truthful and logical, dramatic writers need to know the private realms of their characters: the innermost thoughts and desires that they guard from public view and rarely share with others, even those closest to them. These secret inner worlds offer a wealth of information about who the characters really are.

ABOUT THE EXERCISE
Use this exercise to learn the truth, the whole truth, and nothing but the truth about a character from your story. In each round, you are asked to imagine an actual or possible situation in the character's life and then to express his or her uncensored thoughts and feelings about it in a certain type of personal writing, such as a journal entry. Write each piece from your character's perspective and in your character's voice. For best results, work quickly and instinctively. Aim to complete each round in a few minutes. Then use the final set of questions to sum up key findings.

Regardless of how shy, secretive, or devious your character may be around others, he or she will have no reason to be anything but completely honest in these writings. This veracity will be fueled by the knowledge that no one else will ever actually read these words, particularly those who are the subject of them. As a result, the character can feel free to break through all inhibitions and fears. Even if the character is sometimes mistaken or deluded, these writings will thus reflect the full truth as he or she sees it.

To begin, choose a character to explore.

■ JOURNAL ENTRY

Imagine your character after a real or possible life-changing experience that he or she wants to keep hidden. Whether the experience was good or bad, the character feels the need the protect his or her feelings, or worries that this development could be misinterpreted by others, or fears what could happen if the truth were known.

1. Identify an actual or possible turning point, positive or negative, from any time in your character's life.
2. When and where in the character's life did this occur?
3. Suppose your character's only way to deal with this experience was to write about it in a private journal: to seek relief by telling the truth, the whole truth, and nothing but the truth about what happened. This is a page that no one else will ever read. It will be torn out later and burned. Write the journal entry in your character's voice.

■ LOVE LETTER

Think about the loves, past and present, in your character's life. Some may have blossomed into meaningful romances. Others may have ended in failure or heartache. Whether long-term or short-lived, each romance is an opportunity to learn more about the character's ability to deal with emotions and manage relationships.

1. To whom will your character's love letter be addressed?
2. How and when did this relationship begin?
3. Imagine a love letter that tells the truth, the whole truth, and nothing but the truth about your character's romantic affection for this individual as well as any hopes or fears about the future of the relationship. This flood of honesty can be uncensored and even reckless because this letter will never actually be mailed or read. Write the love letter in your character's voice.

■ WISH LIST

One key to understanding characters is to know what they want. Think about your character's greatest desires. Whether they relate to health, physical achievements, personal relationships, spiritual fulfillment, career, wealth, fame, travel, or other rewards, these wants reflect your character's values, beliefs, and view of the world.

1. Identify an actual or possible time, past or present, when your character feels needy or unsatisfied.
2. What development contributed most to the character's feelings of deprivation?

3. Imagine a wish list that tells the truth, the whole truth, and nothing but the truth about what would make your character happy. Some items on this list might be desires that are commonly seen as worthwhile. Others might be unusual wants that most others would not understand or approve of. Either way, your character doesn't need to worry about how the list will be judged since it will never be seen by anyone else. List at least three uncensored wishes in your character's voice.

■ LETTER OF REPROACH

Suppose that someone close to your character did something that really upset him or her. The culprit may have been a family member, spouse, lover, friend, coworker, or anyone else of importance in the character's personal life. Far from trivial, this offense was the kind that can leave emotional scars.

1. Who upset your character?
2. When and where did this offense occur?
3. What exactly did this person do or fail to do?
4. Imagine a letter of reproach to the offender about what happened. The purpose of this letter might be to make the culprit feel guilty, or to learn something important, or to deliver a warning or ultimatum. Whatever the objective, this letter tells the truth, the whole truth, and nothing but the truth about your character's thoughts and feelings now. It is, however, a letter that will never actually be mailed or read. Write the letter of reproach in your character's voice.

■ PERSONAL AD

Suppose your character felt extremely lonely at some time, past or present, and decided to seek romance by writing a personal ad. If your character lives in a time or place when such advertisements do not exist, try a "what if" to see what you can discover.

1. When in your character's life does this lonely period occur?
2. What experience triggered your character's need for companionship now?
3. Imagine a personal ad that will tell the truth, whole truth, and nothing but the truth about two things: who your character really is and whom your character really wants for romance. This ad can be unabashedly honest since it will never actually be submitted or published. Write the personal ad in your character's voice.

■ CONFESSION

Suppose your character committed a bad deed and wanted now to come clean and confess. This wrongdoing might have been immoral, illegal, or both. It might have been something the character did alone or with others. It might have occurred at any time in the character's life, past or present, and the need for confession may have arisen from hours, to days, to decades after that. Regardless of what happened or when it occurred, this bad deed is probably not known to most others.

1. What was the bad deed, and who else, if anyone, was involved?
2. When and where in your character's life did this occur?
3. What has prompted your character to confess this wrongdoing now?
4. To whom will this confession be addressed?
5. Imagine a confession that will tell the truth, the whole truth, and nothing but the truth about what happened. The purpose might be to purge the soul, to seek forgiveness, or to restore justice by revealing the sordid details of this terrible act and your character's thoughts and feelings about it now. Not one word of this outpouring, however, will see the light of day. Write the confession in your character's voice.

■ EULOGY

Think about those who have made a difference in your character's life. Whether good or bad, these important influences may have been family members, friends, rivals, neighbors, classmates, work associates, mentors, or anyone else who has contributed to the character's knowledge and experience of the world. Then imagine that one of them has just died. This death may have occurred at any time before the story begins, during the story, or after the story ends.

1. Who died, and what was his or her relationship to your character?
2. What was the cause of death, and when did this occur?
3. Imagine a eulogy that will tell the truth, the whole truth, and nothing but the truth about the deceased. Since this is a final statement that will never actually be read or heard by anyone else, it can dispense with all the things one is supposed to say at a memorial and get down to the nitty-gritty of uncensored memories and conclusions. Write the eulogy in your character's voice.

■ KEY INSIGHTS

Use the following questions to sum up the key insights you gained from exploring your character's private domain. Answer each question from your perspective as the writer.

1. Of the character relationships that surfaced during these personal writings, which one is most nurturing?
2. Which relationship is most damaging?
3. What strengths do these writings reveal in your character?
4. What weaknesses or flaws do they expose?
5. Whether positive or negative, what is the most defining character trait that emerged from these writings? The most unusual trait?
6. Think about the wants and needs that these writings uncovered. What was the strongest desire at work? The most surprising desire?
7. What is the biggest problem or challenge that emerged for your character?
8. What is your character's biggest delusion?
9. Think about personal themes—positive and negative—that can run through one's life, such as putting family first, trying to do the right thing, looking for the easy way out. What is the strongest recurring personal theme in your character's life?
10. What is your character's greatest secret?

WRAP-UP

Not all of your character's innermost thoughts and feelings will be revealed to the audience during the story. Exploring this private realm is, nevertheless, an important part of script development that can help you flesh out character needs and motivations, understand the character in more profound ways, and make writing choices that feel truthful and logical for this character in this story.

Related tools in *The Dramatic Writer's Companion*. To sum up your findings and identify what matters most, go to the "Developing Your Character" section and try "Defining Trait." To learn more about what your characters are hiding, try "The Secret Lives of Characters" in the same section.

WHAT IS THE CHARACTER DOING NOW?

THE QUICK VERSION
Use action and image to explore revealing moments in a character's life

BEST TIME FOR THIS
After you have a working sense of the character

ACTIONS SPEAK LOUDER THAN WORDS
While dialogue is an important part of a dramatic script, what matters most in the end is not what the characters say but what they do—in each scene, in each act, and in the story overall. This doing does not refer to arbitrary physical actions, such as "gazes out the window" or "rolls her eyes and takes another sip of her martini." Rather, it is the essential behavior of the characters as they work strategically to overcome obstacles and achieve objectives. Such actions are greater and more important than dialogue: they fuel it, bring meaning to it, and sometimes even contradict it. He says that he wants to help her, for example, but he is really fishing for information to get her money.

Here are six warning signs that a dramatic writer may be paying too much attention to what the characters say and not enough to what they do:

- *The character is talking too much.* When writers focus on dialogue more than behavior, they have a tendency to exercise this love of words without restraint. As a result, the dramatic action slows to a snail's pace. Or there is so much information that it's hard to follow or know what matters most. Or we get what's going on but don't really care. Beware of characters who speak in paragraphs or sit around passively and allow others to do so.
- *The character is talking too brilliantly.* Some lines of dialogue exist in a script only because the writer adores them. These darlings are often masterful displays of language, psychological insight, or retrospective elucidation. The bad news is that they bring the story to a halt by spinning off tangents that lead nowhere. The good news is that you can kill darlings easily without changing the story.
- *The character isn't really doing anything.* If words matter more than actions, a character may be nothing more than an information device to explain story developments or to preach the author's message. In effect, the character becomes a living encyclopedia who does little except talk. The dramatic action has stopped because something important is missing, such as an objective or conflict.

- *The character is doing something, but it's the same thing over and over.* In a one-beat scene the character uses one strategy to achieve one objective. That can work dramatically if it's a short scene, such as the first witches scene in *Macbeth*, which is one beat driven by one objective and only ten lines long. However, if writers find themselves writing long scenes with few or no beat changes, it may be a sign that they have forgotten about behavior and are too preoccupied with words. It may also be a sign that the scene has become monotonous and predictable.

- *The character feels remote or absent.* We tend to learn the most about characters by watching how they act under stress. If they don't do enough, we end up with insufficient information to make inferences about them and get more involved in their world. Even if they tell us their life stories, they feel like strangers who have failed to capture our interest because our knowledge of them is intellectual rather than emotional. We have "heard" them but not "lived" them.

- *What's happening is not interesting to watch.* When heading to the theater, we say that we are going to "see" a show—not "hear" one. This reflects the fact that we get most of our information about the world though sight. Writers who are preoccupied with speeches tend to forget that we in the audience expect to see something interesting. When characters actively try to affect one another and use different strategies to do so, they most likely create a variety of images for us to watch. On the other hand, if the characters are speechifying and listening to each other passively, we may be stuck with nothing to watch but talking heads.

ABOUT THE EXERCISE

This exercise can help you use action and image to deepen your understanding of a principal character from your story. Each round focuses on a different time in the character's life and includes three steps:

1. *Describe an image* that focuses on your character doing something significant at a given time. For example, Lewis is seven years old as he sits at his desk in the classroom of a rural schoolhouse with paper and pen in front of him. An arithmetic test is in progress. While the teacher at the front of the room reads her book, he secretly leans over to inspect the test paper of the girl beside him.

2. *Find an interesting detail* in the image that you didn't notice at first. For example, the numbers on Lewis's test paper are identical to those of the girl beside him even though many of her answers are wrong.

3. *Write a caption* for the image that adds meaning. For example, "Lewis discovers cheating."

Some of your images may depict the character acting alone, but you will get the most from the exercise by finding examples of interactions with others. Look for images that reveal important character information. Whenever you are focused on the here and now of the story, try to find images that are not already in your script.

To begin, choose a character to explore.

■ CHILDHOOD

Think about your character's childhood, and imagine him or her doing something that suggests what those early years were like. Complete steps 1 to 3.

■ TEENAGE YEARS

Think next about your character's teenage years. As life has gone on, he or she has had an array of new relationships and experiences—some good, some bad. The character has changed in some ways and stayed the same in others. What is your character doing now? Complete steps 1 to 3.

■ A YEAR BEFORE THE STORY BEGINS

Time has continued to march on, and it is now about one year before the story begins. Certain things have happened and not happened in your character's life. Certain things have changed and not changed. A stream of decisions, discoveries, experiences, and relationships have been shaping the character into whom we will meet when the story begins. What is your character doing now? Complete steps 1 to 3.

■ A FEW DAYS OR WEEKS BEFORE THE STORY BEGINS

The beginning of the story is now only a few days or weeks away. Your character is somewhere doing something. Whether routine or usual, it is an activity that reveals important information about the character at this particular time in his or her life. Complete steps 1 to 3.

■ A FEW MINUTES OR HOURS BEFORE THE STORY BEGINS

The character is now very close to embarking on a dramatic journey that will in some way be transformative. Think backwards from how this story begins. Imagine your character doing something only a few minutes or hours before. This doing may or may not relate to what will happen in scene 1. Either way, it's an activity that provides an insight into the character whose world will soon be shaken up. Complete steps 1 to 3.

■ START OF THE JOURNEY

A dramatic journey is set into motion by an experience, positive or negative, that upsets the balance of the character's life and arouses the need that will drive most of his or her behavior as the rest of the journey unfolds. This inciting event typically happens early on. It may take the form of a decision, discovery, or revelation. Or it may be an event caused by outside forces. Imagine your character either during or immediately after this life-changing experience. Complete steps 1 to 3. Remember to look for an image that is not already in your script now.

■ MAJOR TURNING POINT

Ideally, your character's dramatic journey will unfold from beginning to end in a way that is not predictable. Its unexpected directions will be due to reversals—some good, some bad—that will keep taking the character into unexplored territory where new challenges must be faced. In a full-length script, each act typically ends with such an experience. Imagine your character either during or immediately after a major turning point in the dramatic journey—for example, at the end of the first act. Complete steps 1 to 3. Look for contrast between this image and the one you found for the start of the journey.

■ END OF THE JOURNEY

Move forward now to the final destination of the dramatic journey. For better or for worse, this is where the events of the story have led. Your character has succeeded or failed in fulfilling the need that was aroused by the inciting event. Either way, something fundamental about the character has changed. Imagine your character doing something now. Complete steps 1 to 3. Look for contrast between this image and the previous two that you described, especially the image for the start of the journey.

■ A FEW DAYS OR WEEKS AFTER THE STORY ENDS

From a creative perspective, the lives of most dramatic characters continue after their onstage or onscreen story comes to an end. Some live happily ever after. Others suffer the painful consequences of their wrongdoings. What happens to a character after the final scene is sometimes called the *afterstory*. Knowing this future can help you flesh out your character more fully and understand what needs to happen during the dramatic journey. Imagine your character doing something a few days or weeks after the story ends. Complete steps 1 to 3.

■ A FEW YEARS AFTER THE STORY ENDS

What are the long-term effects of the dramatic journey? Leap ahead into the afterstory to find a telling action from your character's life a few years after the story ends. Complete steps 1 to 3. Look for an image that provides insight into whom your character will eventually become.

WRAP-UP

You've been exploring the doings of your character and what they reveal. The first five images suggest the roots of action for the dramatic journey. They help explain the character whom we meet as the story begins.

The next three images show how your character contributes to story events and suggest his or her overall arc of action. Knowing this arc can help you make better decisions at the scenic level.

The final two images show the ultimate consequences of all this. Your understanding of this future can help you see story events from a new perspective and uncover truths about the character that you might have otherwise overlooked.

> Related tools in *The Dramatic Writer's Companion.* You may better understand your character's behavior by finding a root action from which all other actions flow. To learn more, go to the "Developing Your Character" section and try "Spinal Tap."

Causing a Scene

Scenes are the steps of a dramatic journey. Ideally, each scene centers on one main event that reveals new information about the characters, changes the world of the story, and brings the dramatic journey closer to its destination. Use the following scene-development exercises during writing or revision to flesh out the elements of dramatic action, add power and depth to scenic events, and refine your dialogue.

While any number of characters may be present in a scene, each exercise focuses on the two most important ones to help you get started. Character 1 in any scene is the character who most actively makes it happen. This role is usually filled by the main character of the whole story, but others may serve as Character 1 in a scene if the main character is absent or not driving most of the scenic action. Character 2 is the second most important character in the scene.

THE REAL WORLD

THE QUICK VERSION
Explore the physical life of a scene and use it to find new story ideas

BEST TIME FOR THIS
During scene planning

PHYSICAL LIFE: THE LANDSCAPE OF TRUTH
The world of a story has a physical realm that grounds the characters in a certain reality, reveals important truths about them, and influences story events. This physical life includes the settings in which the action occurs, material elements that make up these settings, and objects that can be found here. It also includes the characters themselves: their health, their appearance, and other physical traits and conditions. Much can be learned from the physical realm of a story if you take the time to explore it.

ABOUT THE EXERCISE
This exercise can help you discover new ideas for a scene by fleshing out its physical life. Examples are from *In the Next Room (or the vibrator play)* by Sarah Ruhl. Nominated for a Tony Award for Best Play and selected as a finalist for the Pulitzer Prize for Drama in 2010, the play shows what happens when a New York doctor in the 1880s begins to use a new invention—the vibrator—to treat "hysteria" in women and occasionally men. The story focuses on the doctor's wife, the limited social status of women in the Victorian era, and the nature of marriage and love.

In an early scene in act 2, Character 1—who drives most of the action and makes the scene happen—is Catherine Givings, in her twenties, the lonely wife of a doctor and frustrated mother of a newborn infant whom she is unable to nurse. Character 2 is Leo Irving, in his twenties or thirties, an English painter who has been emotionally and artistically blocked since the failure of a romance nine months ago. Their relationship: Leo is a new patient of Catherine's husband. She and Leo now meet by accident for the first time. The main event of the scene: she develops a secret crush on him.

To prepare for the exercise, choose a scene you wish to develop, identify the two most important characters—Characters 1 and 2—and define their relationship. Then sum up the main event of the scene as you see it now: what happens overall.

■ HERE AND NOW

A dramatic scene unfolds in a certain place at a certain time.

1. **Setting.** Ruhl's scene takes place in the living room of the Givings house, located in "a prosperous spa town outside of New York City, perhaps Saratoga Springs." The living room is adjacent to the doctor's private room, also known as an "operating theater." Identify the setting for your scene.

2. **Time.** Ruhl's play takes place in the 1880s, which she describes as "the dawn of the age of electricity and after the Civil War." The exercise scene occurs on a late-winter afternoon during doctor visiting hours. Outside it has begun to grow dark. Define when your scene takes place.

3. **Objects.** In the front matter of her play, rather than provide a narrative description of the set, Ruhl offers a list of items that can be found here:

   > A piano.
   > Closed curtains.
   > Knick knacks.
   > One chaise.
   > A birdcage.
   > A pram/bassinette.
   > A rocking chair.
   > Sumptuous rugs, sumptuous wallpaper.
   > Many electrical lamps, and one particularly beautiful one, with green glass.

   List at least nine objects or physical elements that can be found in your setting now.

4. **Most interesting objects.** Three of the most interesting items on Ruhl's list are (a) the closed curtains, (b) the birdcage, and (c) the beautiful electrical lamp. Review your list of objects, and mark the three that you find most interesting for any reason.

5. **Details.** In Ruhl's scene, (a) the closed curtains create a feeling of claustrophobia (the outside world is literally shut out); (b) the birdcage is a symbol of imprisonment, which adds to the enclosed feel of the room and of Catherine's life; and (c) the beautiful electrical lamp is not only a sign of the opulence that the Givings enjoy but also a reminder of the new power—electricity—that has entered their lives. For each of your three most interesting objects, identify an unusual or telling detail.

6. **Color.** If one were to stand alone in the Givingses' living room and look around, a color that might suddenly stand out is green. Imagine yourself alone in the setting of your scene. What color might suddenly catch your eye?

7. **Where color resides.** The green that stands out in the Givingses' living

room is the glass of the electrical lamp, which is on and seems bright in this otherwise dim room full of shadows. Think about the color that caught your eye. What were you looking at?

8. *Sounds.* In the Givingses' living room now, one might hear a muffled sound of two men talking in the next room. Listen to your setting. What do you hear now, either in this place or from somewhere nearby?

9. *Smells.* There is a faint aroma in the Givingses' living room of herbal tea brewing in a teapot. What do you smell now in your setting or from somewhere nearby?

10. *Feeling.* Sealed by closed doors and curtains, this room feels like a sumptuous cage: comfortable but confining. Use a simile or metaphor to describe your setting.

11. *Object in action.* After his treatment in the next room, Leo will be distracted by the light of the electrical lamp, and Catherine will turn it off for him. This will lead to an unexpected moment of intimacy in which he compares the light bulb—a "light without a flame"—to "relations with a prostitute." Both, he says, are only the "outer trappings of the act." In the Victorian era, even the mention of prostitution is scandalous, so for Catherine the moment is awkward and, in a naughty way, exciting. Identify an object or physical element in your setting that could influence your scene, and describe how.

12. *Another object in action.* The closed curtains also will play a role in Ruhl's scene. After the electrical light in the room is turned off, Leo will part those curtains to show Catherine the world outside as darkness falls and distant windows of neighbors begin to light up in the darkness. "Little squares of light, other people's lives," he says, "sheltered against the night, so hopeful . . ." Find another object or physical element in your setting that could play a role in your scene. Describe its use or purpose.

13. *Social context.* Most places have a code of conduct—a set of rules and expectations—that people here are expected to observe. If you wish to speak in a library, for example, you are supposed to whisper. If you wish to speak in a classroom, you are supposed to raise your hand. Here is an important code of conduct for the Givingses' living room: when patients arrive at the front door, Catherine is supposed to hide so they do not see her. Think about the codes of conduct that govern your setting. Identify a rule or expectation that is relevant to your scene because a character will either obey it or rebel against it.

14. *Impact on action.* Catherine is supposed to hide when patients arrive. This rule is important because it is a restriction she will choose to ignore when she accidentally meets Leo in the living room. The forbidden nature of their encounter adds to the excitement she feels in talking with him. Think about the code of conduct you identified for your setting. Describe how it might influence your scene.

15. *History.* Every setting has a history of events that may influence what happens here and now. In the history of the Givingses' living room, the parade of patients who come and go have mostly been women. The presence of a male patient now is a rare phenomenon that sparks Catherine's decision to break the household rules and entertain Leo over tea. Identify a fact from the history of your setting that could influence your scene.

■ CHARACTER 1: HERE AND NOW

Focus next on Character 1 in this place at this time.

1. *Relationship to setting.* Catherine's relationship to the living room is personal. This is her home. What is the nature of your Character 1's relationship to the setting when your scene begins—for example, personal, professional, social, economic, religious, academic, or accidental?

2. *Why here now.* Catherine enters the living room now because the wet nurse is in the nursery with the baby and her husband is in the operating theater with a patient. Alone and bored, she has nowhere else to go. Why is your Character 1 here now?

3. *Appearance.* Catherine is dressed in formal Victorian clothing that includes a floor-length multilayered dress, a bustle, a corset, a hoop, many underthings, including bloomers, and numerous buttons and ties, all of which serve to seal her inside the dress and also to disguise her female form. Her hair is bound in an elaborate bun to keep it from flowing freely. In short, she is a vision of containment. Describe your Character 1's physical appearance here and now. Include an unusual or telling detail.

4. *Last significant experience here.* Over the past two weeks, animated by the presence of the wet nurse in the house and her feelings of failure as a mother, Catherine has been secretly breaking household rules, the biggest of which is to keep out of her husband's operating theater, especially when he's not there. Two weeks ago, using a hatpin to pick the lock on the door, Catherine sneaked in with one of her husband's patients, Mrs. Daldry, and explored the mystery of vibrators while he was at his club. If your Character 1 has been in your setting before, recount his or her last significant experience here. If the character has never been here before, go to the next question.

5. *Likes most.* What Catherine likes most about her living room is the social life it offers: the opportunity to meet the patients who come to see her husband. However, she can visit with them only when her husband is in the next room working or away from home so that he is not aware of what she's doing. What does your Character 1 like most about your setting here and now?

6. *Likes least.* What Catherine likes least about her living room is the stale air that hangs within the walls and compels her occasionally to run outside for fresh air, even if it is raining, What does your Character 1 like least about your setting now?

■ CHARACTER 2: HERE AND NOW

Focus next on Character 2 in this place at this time.

1. *Relationship to setting.* Leo's relationship to the Givingses' living room is professional. He is a patient of Catherine's husband and must pass through the living room to reach the doctor's office and then again to exit from it. What is your Character 2's relationship to the setting when your scene begins?

2. *Why here now.* After feeling emotionally and artistically blocked for nine months due to a failed love affair, Leo has reached the point in his life where he must take drastic measures to start painting again. He has thus come here today to be treated by the renowned Dr. Givings, who observes that "hysteria" is very rare in men, except for artists. In your scene, why is Character 2 here now?

3. *Appearance.* Leo is handsome and wild-eyed. He detests modernity, so he is dressed in an old-fashioned coat that his father had thrown away. Having just received electrical therapy in the next room, Leo glows with health and vitality. Describe your Character 2's physical appearance here and now. Include an unusual or telling detail.

4. *Last significant experience here.* This is Leo's first visit to Dr. Givings, so he has no history in this place other than the electrical therapy he just received in the next room. That treatment has inspired him to be unusually honest and passionate with Catherine, and this will, in turn, lead her to develop a secret attraction to him. If your Character 2 has been in your setting before, sum up his or her last significant experience here. If the character has never been here before, go to the next question.

5. *Likes most.* What Leo likes most about the Givingses' living room is the growing darkness here as evening falls with the lamp turned off. This is his favorite time of day, and he enjoys sitting here in the dark with Catherine. What does your Character 2 like most about the setting here and now?

6. *Likes least.* What Leo likes least about the Givingses' living room are the electrical lamps that surround him, products of the modernity that he despises. What does your Character 2 like least about your setting now?

■ KEY FINDINGS

As you explored your scene's physical life and the truths it reveals, you may have found many new possibilities for dramatic action. Focus on those that matter most.

1. *Pivotal object.* In the physical life of Ruhl's scene, the most important object is the green electrical lamp. What object or physical element in your setting feels most important to you now?

2. *Impact on action.* The light from the green lamp will lead Leo to compare electric light to relations with a prostitute. By triggering a moment of intimacy and opening Catherine's eyes to the possibility of Leo as a romantic partner, the lamp thus triggers the main event of the scene. Think about the pivotal object in your scene. What role might it play in the dramatic action?

WRAP-UP

As you develop your story, it is important to know the physical realm your characters inhabit and to understand how it affects, and is affected by, story events. Physical life is the real world of the story: the concrete reality that keeps the characters grounded and roots the dramatic action in the here and now.

Related tools in *The Dramatic Writer's Companion.* To learn more about the physical life of a scene, go to the "Causing a Scene" section and try "Where in the World Are We?" or "In the Realm of the Senses."

WHAT'S NEW? WHAT'S STILL TRUE?

THE QUICK VERSION
Explore the given circumstances for a scene

BEST TIME FOR THIS
During scene planning

SOME THINGS CHANGE, SOME DON'T
We typically enter the world of a dramatic story when something new happens in the lives of the characters. To experience something new is to find out that your sister tried to kill her husband (*Crimes of the Heart* by Beth Henley). Or it is to fall in love with your computer operating system (*Her* by Spike Jonze).

Dramatic characters tend to encounter many events they have never experienced before, and it is often the unfamiliarity of these developments that leads to conflict and drama. Something may be *new* because it never happened before—for example, you enroll in law school to win back the boyfriend who dumped you (*Legally Blonde* by Amanda Brown, Karen McCullah, and Kirsten Smith). Or something may be considered new because even though it has been true for some time, you are just discovering it now—for example, that your lover is transgender (*The Danish Girl* by Lucinda Coxon based on a novel by David Ebershoff).

What's new in the world of your story may be a good thing: you become the protégé of an acclaimed fiction writer (*Collected Stories* by Donald Margulies). Or it may be a bad thing: you find a strange man's hat in your girlfriend's apartment (*The Motherfucker with the Hat* by Stephen Adly Guirgis). Dramatic action is the result of how the characters deal with the new situation.

A dramatic story is also about what is *not new*: what is still true in spite of the events that have taken place up to now. It may be good that a certain truth has endured: your great love for someone survives all obstacles, even death (*Romeo and Juliet* by William Shakespeare). Or it may be bad: you can't overcome your addiction to war (*The Hurt Locker* by Mark Boal).

Sometimes what isn't new is the point of a scene—for example, your mother is still a morphine addict (*Long Day's Journey into Night* by Eugene O'Neill). And sometimes what isn't new is even the point of the whole story—for example, you will always be in love with someone who is in love with someone else (*No Exit* by Jean-Paul Sartre).

ABOUT THE EXERCISE

This exercise can help you flesh out the given circumstances for a scene and how they might influence the dramatic action. The goal is to explore the present in relationship to the past, especially the recent past, in order to understand what has changed and not changed in the world of the story as your scene unfolds.

Examples are from act 2, scene 2, of *Anna in the Tropics* by Nilo Cruz, recipient of the 2003 Pulitzer Prize for Drama. The story is set in Florida in 1929 at the start of the Great Depression. The setting is a Cuban American cigar factory where workers are both educated and entertained by lectors who read aloud to them while they hand-roll cigars. Readings range from newspaper articles to literature. When a new lector from Cuba begins to read from Tolstoy's *Anna Karenina*, however, he arouses discontent and dreams of a better life among his listeners.

Character 1 in the exercise scene is Palomo, age forty-one, a cigar roller in the factory. Character 2 is Conchita, age thirty-two, daughter of the factory owner and also a cigar roller. Their relationship: husband and wife in a passionless marriage. The main event of the scene: Palomo rekindles his passion for his wife by getting her to tell him the salacious details of her marital infidelity so that he can experience it vicariously.

To prepare for the exercise, choose a scene you wish to develop, identify the two most important characters—Characters 1 and 2—and define their relationship. Then sum up the main event of the scene as you see it now: what happens overall.

■ SCENIC CONTEXT

Define where and when the dramatic action occurs.
 1. *Setting.* Cruz's scene takes place in a Florida cigar factory where workers sit at tables and hand-roll cigars. Identify the setting for your scene.
 2. *Time.* It is the end of a workday after most of the other factory workers have left. Conchita has recently turned her flirtation with the new lector, Juan Julian, into a sexual affair. She has done this to substitute for the lovemaking she no longer receives from her husband. Identify when your scene take place.

■ WHAT'S NEW?

The given circumstances for a scene reflect what is happening in the world of the story as the scene begins. These circumstances may be physical, psychological, social, economic, political, or spiritual.
 1. *Setting.* The exercise scene occurs in the second act of the play in a setting we have seen before. What's new about the setting now is not so much how it looks to the workers or the audience but rather

how it is perceived by Conchita. This factory for her is no longer just a workplace. It is also where she secretly meets her lover, Juan Julian, for steamy encounters in the back room. This new dimension of the setting will add to the passion with which she speaks about her lover during the scene.

Think about the setting for your scene in relation to the given circumstances. Is there anything new about this place at this time that could influence the dramatic action? Compared to the past, for example, has the physical environment changed in any way for better or worse? Does it look different? Or sound different? Or does it smell or feel different? Perhaps there is an important object here now that wasn't here before. Or perhaps your characters view this place differently because of something that happened here or elsewhere. This is a discovery exercise. What's new about your setting when the scene begins, and how might this affect the dramatic action?

2. *Character 1.* Palomo has ended up in a passionless marriage with the factory owner's daughter. What's new for Palomo when the scene begins is the realization that his wife has changed since the new lector from Cuba arrived and that she is probably having an affair with him. This conclusion will arouse Palomo's need to confront his wife and find out what she's been up to.

Think about what's been happening in your Character 1's life just before your scene begins. Are there any new physical, psychological, or social developments that might influence his or her behavior now? If so, what's new for Character 1 when the scene begins, and how might this affect the action?

3. *Character 2.* Conchita's affair with Juan Julian started a few days ago. What's new now is that in her last encounter with him, she experienced a passion so profound and so engulfing that it terrified her—in a good way. This experience will enable her to open up and admit the truth about the affair when her husband confronts her. She has been liberated from the chains of secrecy and guilt.

Think about what your Character 2 has been up to recently. Are there any new developments that might influence his or her behavior in the scene? If so, what's new for Character 2 when the scene begins, and how might this affect the action?

4. *World of the story.* There has been a disturbing change recently in the world of the cigar factory. One of the owners, Conchita's unpopular half-uncle, Cheché, in response to low sales, has introduced a new cigar-rolling machine that he wants the factory to adopt. The workers see this as a threat to their jobs. The resulting tension in the factory adds to the go-for-broke honesty between Palomo and Conchita in the scene. What's at risk is not only their marriage but also their livelihood.

Think about the world of your story. Life is happening. Certain physical, psychological, and social developments are taking place. What's new in this world when your scene begins, and how might this affect the action?

5. *Event.* You've been exploring what's new in the lives of your characters when the scene begins. Shift your focus forward now to the dramatic event that will unfold here and now. Something new will happen. In the scene between Palomo and Conchita, a secret will be exposed, and he will connect with his wife sexually by imagining her with her lover. What's new about what will happen between your characters in your scene?

■ WHAT'S STILL TRUE?

A dramatic story is about not only what has changed in the lives of the characters but also what has *not* changed. Look next for enduring truths in the world of your story.

1. *Setting.* Many important truths endure in the cigar factory where Palomo and Conchita work. This factory is what brought them together in the first place: he was a worker who married the owner's daughter. It's also what brought Juan Julian into their lives: he came here from Cuba to work as a lector. In addition, the factory is what keeps them trapped together as they struggle through the challenges of a romantic triangle. Because of the factory, they must deal with each other every day. Palomo has to roll cigars here while his wife's lover reads aloud to her and the other workers. This physical trap adds urgency and importance to Palomo's need in the scene to confront his wife about what's going on when Juan Julian isn't reading.

   Think about the setting for your scene in relation to the given circumstances. As the scene begins, what is an important enduring truth about this place at this time—something that has not changed—and how might this influence the action?

2. *Character 1.* Palomo still loves his wife, is possessive of her in the factory, and feels jealous of her new sex life. However, he enters the scene with the same lack of sexual interest in her that has kept them emotionally distant for some time. The secret truth is that Palomo is sexually attracted to his wife's lover. This desire will fuel the intensity with which Palomo will interrogate Conchita about her sex life, and it will be the real reason that he becomes so excited that he makes love with her.

   Think about your Character 1 when your scene begins. What is an enduring truth about him or her that will influence the scene, and how might it do so?

3. *Character 2.* In spite of her infidelity, Conchita still loves Palomo and wishes they could have a happy marriage. These feelings will lead to her brutal honesty in the scene and her willingness to engage in a role

play where she makes love with her husband as if he were her and she were Juan Julian. It is ultimately her enduring love of Palomo that enables the characters to make a sexual connection.

Think about your Character 2 when your scene begins. What is an enduring truth about him or her that will influence the scene, and how might it do so?

4. *World of the story.* Palomo and Conchita live in a world where family is revered and family ties must not be broken. The cigar factory itself is family owned, with Conchita's father, mother, and half-uncle running it and her sister and husband working in it alongside her. Once a man and woman marry in this world, they are husband and wife for the rest of their lives. Anything that threatens the family unit, therefore, is a problem that must be solved. This enduring truth will influence Palomo and Conchita to confront the fact that their marriage is in jeopardy and find a way to save it.

Think about the world of your story when your scene begins. What is an enduring truth in this world that might influence the scene, and how might it do so?

5. *Event.* While certain changes may occur during a scene, certain facts will still be true when it draws to a close. As the scene between Palomo and Conchita ends, they are moving to the back room to have sex. The fact remains, however, that they are still trapped in the same factory where each day the handsome Juan Julian will read to them and provide a lingering distraction for both husband and wife. This enduring truth will lead to continuing problems between Palomo and Conchita and contribute to the rising tensions in the factory.

Think about what happens in your scene. What is an important fact that will not be changed by this event, and how might this enduring truth affect future action?

WRAP-UP

Every dramatic scene has a unique set of given circumstances that reflect what's currently happening in the world of the story. You can learn a lot by fleshing out these roots of action, with a focus on what has changed and not changed in the lives of your characters at this particular time in the story. Such factors often explain character thoughts, feelings, and needs as a scene begins and thus contribute in important ways to the dramatic event that takes place.

> **Related tools in *The Dramatic Writer's Companion.* To continue exploring the given circumstances for a scene, go to the "Causing a Scene" section and try "The Roots of Action."**

THE PAST BARGES IN

THE QUICK VERSION
Explore how the past affects the present

BEST TIME FOR THIS
During scene planning

THE POWER OF THE PAST
Drama is a storytelling art that focuses on the here and now of the characters. We watch what happens and make inferences about what we have observed. Most characters come to their stories, however, with a lot of baggage from the past: personal experiences that have affected them in lasting ways. Some of these experiences may need to be revealed during the story so we can better understand what's happening. Sometimes revelations about the past can be major turning points, as in John Patrick Shanley's *Doubt: A Parable* when a teaching nun at a Catholic elementary school informs the principal that one of her eighth-graders had alcohol on his breath when he returned to her classroom after a meeting with the parish priest.

When writers are unable to master the power of the past, they have to find excuses to drag it into the present so that everything else comes to a stop while the audience listens to what happened back then. These explanations often come in the form of memories, dreams, readings of diaries and letters, interviews, news bulletins, and whatever other devices the writer can find to insert information into the story.

A key challenge of the dramatic writer is to figure out how not to drag the weight of the past into the present but rather to force the past to barge in on the present—like an intruder who shows up at the door and demands attention. This is the kind of past that cannot wait and cannot be still. It is a woman who was abused by an adult neighbor when she was twelve years old (*Blackbird* by David Harrower). It is a married couple whose young son has died after a drowning accident (*God's Ear* by Jenny Schwartz). It is a man who had an affair with his best friend's wife (*Betrayal* by Harold Pinter).

ABOUT THE EXERCISE
Use this exercise to explore the backstory of two important characters and how it might influence the dramatic action of a scene. "Backstory" refers to what has happened in the lives of the characters prior to the scene. Whether the events of the past were positive or negative, and whether they occurred

recently or long ago, they become important if they affect character behavior here and now.

Examples are from *Fences* by August Wilson. Recipient of the 1987 Tony Award for Best Play and Pulitzer Prize for Drama, the play is set in the 1950s and is one of ten plays by Wilson exploring the African American experience in the twentieth century. *Fences* was later made into a 2016 film from the screenplay he wrote before his death in 2005. The film earned him a post-humous Academy Award nomination for Best Writing, Adapted Screenplay.

The exercise focuses on act 1, scene 3, of the play. Character 1—who drives most of the action and makes the scene happen—is Troy Maxson, a fifty-three-year-old married black ex-con who now works as a garbage col-lector in a big city. Character 2 is Cory Maxon, age seventeen, a high school student who is being actively recruited for a college football scholarship. Their relationship: father and son. The main event of the scene: Troy tries to convince his son to give up football so he can meet his responsibilities at home, at school, and at work.

To prepare for the exercise, choose a scene you wish to develop, identify the two most important characters—Characters 1 and 2—and define their relationship. Then sum up the main event of the scene as you see it now: what happens overall.

■ SCENIC CONTEXT

Define the context for the dramatic action.
1. *Setting.* Wilson's scene takes place in the small dirt yard of "an ancient two-story brick house set back off a small alley in a big-city neighborhood." Define the setting for your scene.
2. *Time.* The action occurs on a Saturday afternoon in 1957 after Cory returns home from football practice. Much to his father's consternation, Cory ran out early that morning without doing his household chores. Define when your scene occurs.

■ HOW THE PAST AFFECTS CHARACTER I

Fences is a story in which the past keeps barging in on the present. The fences that Troy builds between himself and the rest of the world grow out of a hard life that included an abusive father, fifteen years in prison for robbery and murder, and the loss of his dreams. A key experience from this past is Troy's former baseball career. Though an accomplished player with a stellar batting average, he was rejected from the major leagues because of his race. This experience is important dramatically because it changed Troy's life, and it is relevant to scene 3 because it fuels his need to discourage his son's dream of professional football.

Think about your Character 1's backstory in relation to the scene you are developing. Look for past experiences that could influence the character's thoughts, feelings, or behavior in the present. Identify the fact from the past that feels most important and relevant to your scene—even if this fact is not revealed at this time in the story.

1. *Positive impact.* Troy's whole life has been scarred by the racism that led to his rejection from professional baseball. However, just as every cloud has a silver lining, even the worst experience can have positive outcomes. For example, the rejection that Troy suffered has made him a stronger and more responsible man, determined to protect himself and his family. Think about your Character 1's backstory fact. What is an example of its positive impact?

2. *Negative impact.* Troy's rejection has also affected him negatively. He has become bitter and resentful because of it. He also tends to live in the past and to disregard any social changes that have taken place since. Think again about your Character 1's backstory fact. What is an example of its negative impact?

3. *Impact on self-perception.* Troy's rejection in the past affects how he perceives himself in the present. Because of his failure to realize his greatest dream, Troy now sees himself as a pragmatist with his feet on the ground and the weight of the world on his back. How might your Character 1's backstory fact affect his or her self-perception at this time in your story?

4. *Perception of other character.* Because of his rejection from professional baseball, Troy sees his son as another potential victim of racism who will suffer a broken heart if he tries to follow his dream of playing professional football. How might your Character 1's backstory fact affect his or her perception of Character 2 during your scene?

5. *Impact on feeling.* Troy's rejection long ago influences how he feels here and now. Physically, he's keyed up for battle as he tries to command his son to do as his says. Emotionally, he feels enraged and anxious. How might your Character 1 be affected physically or emotionally during your scene as a result of what happened in the past?

6. *Impact on need.* Troy's rejection directly affects what he wants here and now: to convince Cory to quit the football team so that he can avoid the type of emotional pain that Troy suffered. Whether directly or indirectly, how might your Character 1's backstory fact influence his or her scenic objective?

7. *Impact on behavior.* Troy's rejection also affects what he does here and now. At different times in the scene, he demands Cory's respect and obedience, scares him into doing what he wants, scolds him for being irresponsible, mocks him for questioning his father's love and loyalty, justifies his own actions by flaunting his sense of duty to his family, and berates his son for not living up to his personal responsibilities.

Identify at least three examples of how your Character 1's backstory fact might affect his or her actions during your scene. Look for strong verbs, such as *demands*, *scares*, *scolds*, *mocks*, *justifies*, and *berates*.

8. **The past barges in.** Sometimes a character is influenced more by what happened in the past than by what is happening now. When this occurs, the past has barged in. It has forced its way into the present to affect the character a certain way—for example, to shape the character's perceptions and feelings, motivate an objective, or trigger certain behavior. Troy's rejection by the major leagues is a subject that is not dragged in arbitrarily as a topic of discussion while a father and son build a fence. Rather, it is a fact from the past that barges in and demands attention. Troy has to bring up the loss of his own dream in order to convince his son to avoid the same kind of heartbreak. Sum up your exploration of Character 1's backstory fact by describing how and why it will barge into the present of your scene and demand attention.

■ **HOW THE PAST AFFECTS CHARACTER 2**

Cory's past is dominated by the fact that he has been raised by Troy in the way Troy was raised by his father: in an often cold, abusive way. This up-bringing has created a brooding feeling in Cory that his father doesn't like him. It has also driven him to the football team, where he has performed so well that he recently received the offer of a college football scholarship. This opportunity is important dramatically because it has aroused a dream of becoming a professional football player, and it is relevant to scene 3 because it fuels his need to get his father's signature on the scholarship papers.

Think about your Character 2's backstory in relation to the scene you are developing. Identify the fact from the past that feels most important and relevant to your scene.

1. **Positive impact.** The offer of a football scholarship has had a strong positive impact on Cory. It has given him hope for a better future. Think about your Character 2's backstory fact. What is an example of its positive impact?

2. **Negative impact.** The offer of a football scholarship also has had a downside. Cory has neglected his responsibilities: his schoolwork, his household chores, and his after-school job. This has put him in a precarious position with his father. Think again about your Character 2's backstory fact. What is an example of its negative impact?

3. **Impact on self-perception.** Cory's big chance affects how he perceives himself during the scene. Receiving positive reinforcement outside of home has boosted his self-esteem: he's not as bad or as weak as his father has led him to believe. How might your Character 2's backstory fact affect his or her self-perception during your scene?

4. *Perception of other character.* As a result of Cory's scholarship offer, he sees his father as a growing threat to his dreams and his future. This turns out to be a perceptive insight, since his father will later go to the coach and have Cory removed from the team. How might your Character 2's backstory fact affect his or her perception of Character 1 during your scene?

5. *Impact on feeling.* The opportunity of a football scholarship has made Cory feel anxious. He has never wanted anything so much, and the possibility of losing it is devastating. How might your Character 2 be affected physically or emotionally during the scene as a result of what happened in the past?

6. *Impact on need.* Cory's opportunity directly affects what he wants in the scene: to get his father's blessing for the football scholarship. This need has become urgent since a recruiter will be here soon from a North Carolina college with paperwork that his father must sign. Whether directly or indirectly, how might your Character 2's backstory fact influence his or her scenic objective?

7. *Impact on behavior.* Cory's opportunity also affects what he does in the scene. At different times, for example, he pleases his father by being obedient, persuades his father to buy a television so he can watch football, challenges his father's negativity, celebrates how the sports world has changed, prods his father into signing the scholarship papers, and figuratively stabs his father in the heart by making him feel rotten ("why ain't you never liked me?"). Identify at least three examples of how your Character 2's backstory fact might affect his or her actions during your scene. Look again for strong verbs, such as *pleases, persuades, challenges, celebrates, prods,* and *stabs.*

8. *The past barges in.* The offer of a football scholarship is a fact from the recent past that is not dragged into scene 3 arbitrarily. It is the reason for scene 3. It barges in on the building of a fence and demands that both son and father deal with it. For Cory, the scholarship is a goal to be won. For Troy, it is a problem to be resisted. Sum up your exploration of Character 2's backstory fact by describing how and why it will barge into the present of your scene.

WRAP-UP

The secret of a great story is a great backstory that is rarely explained but often implied.

As you develop your script, keep exploring the past experiences of your characters to help you understand who they really are, what they bring to each scene, and why they may feel compelled to act in certain ways under the rising pressure of dramatic events.

Related tools in *The Dramatic Writer's Companion.* To dig deeper into a character's backstory, go to the "Developing Your Character" section and try "Into the Past." To explore scenic elements that may reflect past experiences, go to the "Causing a Scene" section and try "Basic Scene Starter."

LEVELS OF DESIRE

THE QUICK VERSION
Explore character objectives at three levels: story, scene, and beat

BEST TIME FOR THIS
During scene planning, writing, or revision

WHY CHARACTERS ACT: THEY WANT SOMETHING
In drama, desire operates on three levels: story, scene, and beat. Knowing character wants at each level can help you understand who characters are and how they will behave at any given time.

At the story level, a character typically has a burning desire that is difficult to fulfill. Whether it is a man's desire to be a television wrestling star (*The Elaborate Entrance of Chad Deity* by Kristoffer Diaz) or a woman's need to break free of the economic and social ties that bind her (*A Doll's House* by Henrik Ibsen), this superobjective tends to be aroused early in the story and not get achieved, if at all, until the end. Though it may not always be top of mind, the superobjective underlies most of what the character says and does. It's what makes the story happen.

Each scene in the story is a step toward trying to achieve the superobjective either by reaching for it directly or by tackling obstacles that stand in the way. Desire at this level translates into a scenic objective: a need to accomplish something important here and now that, if successful, will move the character closer to the overall goal. The scenic objective may be aroused prior to the scene or during it. Either way, it drives most of the character's actions during the scene and causes a dramatic event to occur.

Just as a story is made up of scenes, a scene is made up of beats, or units of action. Desire at this level translates into the strategies and tactics that the character tries in pursuit of the scenic objective. Whether successful or not, these beat actions bring variety to the scene and keep it from growing stale.

Most character objectives, particularly at the scene and beat level, are behavioral. They reflect a desire to affect another character in an important way and fall into four general categories: to make the other character feel good; to make the other character feel bad; to find out something important; or to convince the other character of something important. At the beat level, some objectives may be physical—for example, to complete a physical task, such as finding a house key that has been misplaced.

ABOUT THE EXERCISE

Use this exercise to identify what a character wants in the story, in a scene, and in two beats of the scene. Then explore how these levels of desire affect the scenic action.

Examples are from scene 9 of *Water by the Spoonful* by Quiara Alegría Hudes, recipient of the 2012 Pulitzer Prize for Drama. The story focuses on a returning Iraq War veteran's search for meaning. His dramatic journey runs parallel to that of four recovering drug addicts who connect through an online chat room. All of the characters are trying to heal from something that has harmed them.

Scene 9 focuses on two of the recovering addicts. Character 1—who drives most of the action and makes the scene happen—is Orangutan, an Asian American teacher in her thirties who was born in Japan and adopted in infancy by an American family. Character 2 is Chutes&Ladders, an African American man in his fifties who has worked a low-level job at the IRS for two decades. Their relationship: online friends who have never met in person. The main event of the scene: Chutes&Ladders derails Orangutan's plan to find her birth parents, a potential stressor that could trigger a drug relapse.

To prepare for the exercise, choose a scene you wish to develop, identify the two most important characters—Characters 1 and 2—and define their relationship. Then sum up the main event of the scene as you see it now: what happens overall.

■ **SCENIC CONTEXT**

Begin by fleshing out the context for the dramatic action.
  1. *Setting.* The Hudes scene takes place in two locations connected by the Internet: an IRS office in San Diego, California, where Chutes&Ladders works, and a train station in Sapporo, Japan, where Orangutan waits for a train. Define where your scene occurs.
  2. *Time.* The year is 2009. In the IRS office in San Diego, it is late afternoon. At the train station in Sapporo, it is early morning, twenty minutes before the train departs for Kushiro, the city where Orangutan was born. Define when your scene takes place.
  3. *Given circumstances.* Though Orangutan and Chutes&Ladders have been online friends for three years at recovertogether.com, she recently disappeared from the site for three months and then returned with the news that she is now sober and living in Japan. Her absence from the site has deepened her friendship with Chutes&Ladders to the extent that she has asked him to join her—in person—in Japan, but that has not happened because he is averse to taking risks that could lead to a drug relapse. Think about what's happening in the world of your story when your scene begins. Identify any given circumstances—

physical, psychological, social, economic, political, or spiritual—that might influence the dramatic action of your scene.

■ DESIRE AT THE STORY LEVEL

Now that you have a working sense of how the scene fits into the through-line of the story, begin to explore the wants and needs of your Character 1 at the story level.

1. *Superobjective.* Orangutan's quest—her superobjective—is to feel connected to humanity. Think about the desire that drives most of your Character 1's dramatic journey. What is the character's superobjective, or quest?

2. *Measure of success.* The more specific the character's objective, the more focused the character's actions will be. Objectives tend to work best dramatically when their outcome is measurable—that is, when a specific sign will indicate whether the objective has been achieved. This sign might be a certain statement, action, event, or other outcome that would signal success. For example, Orangutan wants to feel connected to humanity. She will know this has happened if she can develop a meaningful, in-person relationship with Chutes&Ladders without smoking crack. How will your character know if the superobjective has been achieved? Identify the measure of success.

3. *Trigger.* Orangutan's desire to feel connected to humanity stems back to her adoption at the age of eight days by an American family. She has never known her birth parents or, until now, seen her birth country of Japan. What experience triggered your character's superobjective, either during the story or prior to it?

4. *Contributing factor.* Orangutan's need for connection has been reinforced by years of feeling like an outsider. Japanese by birth, she grew up in Cape Lewiston, Maine, where there was only one other Asian American. She chose the cyber name Orangutan because, unlike other great apes, orangutans do not live in groups and thus symbolize solitude. Think about your character's superobjective. What is a contributing factor from his or her life that has reinforced this desire?

5. *Conflict.* Orangutan wants to feel connected to humanity. Her biggest obstacles are internal: her feelings of alienation, an impulsive nature that often gets her into trouble, and her relentless desire to smoke crack. At the story level, what are the main obstacles that will make your character's superobjective difficult to achieve?

6. *Motivation.* At stake for Orangutan are her survival and well-being. What is at stake for your character overall?

■ DESIRE AT THE SCENIC LEVEL

Focus next on Character 1 in the scene you are developing.

1. *Objective.* The main event of the scene will occur here and now because Character 1 will pursue an important objective and either succeed or fail. Orangutan has a *feel good* objective. She wants Chutes&Ladders to approve her emotionally risky decision to find her birth parents. What does your character want most in your scene? Choose a general behavioral objective: *feel good, feel bad, find out,* or *convince.* Then translate it into the specific terms of your scene.

2. *Measure of success.* Orangutan wants to get Chutes&Ladders' blessing. The measure of success would be certain words appearing on her computer screen—for example, his telling her that he supports what she's doing. How will your character know whether the scenic objective has been achieved?

3. *Trigger.* Orangutan made a vow to find her birth parents in Japan if she could stay sober for three months. Having reached that milestone, she is now in Sapporo, waiting for the train to Kushira with the address of her birth parents in her pocket. Her need for Chutes&Ladders' approval is triggered by the fear that she cannot accomplish this feat without his support. This fear is heightened by the fact that the train is about to depart. What triggers your character's scenic objective during the scene or prior to it?

4. *Contributing factor.* Orangutan's participation in an online community of addicts—the family she found—has fueled her desire for connection to the family she was born into. Chutes&Ladders is the closest member of her online family, so his support matters most. He's also older and wiser than her, and that adds to the value of his approval. What contributing factor has fueled your character's scenic objective?

5. *Relation to superobjective.* By involving Chutes&Ladders in a critical decision, Orangutan is taking steps to strengthen her friendship with him. This action directly supports her superobjective: to feel connected to humanity though a meaningful, in-person relationship. It is thus a sound, logical step for her to take. How does your character's scenic objective relate to his or her superobjective?

6. *Conflict.* Orangutan wants to get Chutes&Ladders' blessing for her trip to Kushira. Her main problem is that he wants her to stay off that train. What obstacles will make it difficult for your character to achieve the scenic objective?

7. *Motivation.* For a recovering addict, any major stress can trigger a relapse. As Orangutan tries to get a friend to support her at an emotionally difficult time, her sobriety is at stake. What is at stake for your character?

■ DESIRE AT THE BEAT LEVEL

Now look more closely at the scene to see what your character wants at the beat level. Ideally, each beat is a unit of action that centers on one topic, one behavior, or one emotion. Working together, beats bring variety to the scene and determine its structure and rhythm.

1. *Early beat action.* One of Orangutan's early tactics in scene 9 is to amuse Chutes&Ladders by telling him a funny story about how the Japanese, in an effort to create jobs in the early 1980s, had all of the rivers in Hokkaido straightened out and how now, to create more jobs, they plan to put all the rivers back to the way they were, starting with the Kushiro River. This is a *feel good* tactic. Identify a tactic that your character might try early in the scene as a step to achieve the scenic objective.

   • *Measure of success.* Orangutan wants to make Chuter&Ladders feel good. She will know she has succeeded if she can get him to respond online with a happy-face emoji or words that show he finds her story amusing. How will your character know whether his or her early tactic has succeeded?

   • *Why this.* Orangutan chooses to tell a funny story because she thinks that Chutes&Ladders will be more open to her risky scheme if he is in a good mood. The story also provides a way to get the name of her birth city, Kushiro, into the conversation so she can get to the subject she really wants to discuss. Think about your character's early tactic. Right or wrong, why might he or she try this?

   • *Relation to scenic objective.* Putting Chutse&Ladders in a good mood is a smart step toward bonding with him and getting his approval. Orangutan's tactic thus supports her scenic objective. How does your character's early tactic relate to the scenic objective?

2. *Later beat action.* Orangutan tries a number of tactics to get Chutes&Ladders' approval. Later in the scene, after he has learned her plan and condemned it, she tries to make him feel guilty about not supporting her. This is a *feel bad* action and quite different from her earlier tactic. Identify another tactic your character might try later in your scene. Look for an example that is clearly different from the earlier one.

   • *Measure of success.* Orangutan wants to guilt-trip Chutes&Ladders for not supporting her. She will know she has succeeded if she can get him to apologize. How will your character know if the later tactic has succeeded?

   • *Why this.* Attacking Chutes&Ladders is an impulsive act of retaliation. Think about your character's later tactic. Right or wrong, why might he or she try this?

   • *Relation to scenic objective.* Antagonizing Chutes&Ladders runs counter to Orangutan's objective and is thus a bad tactic that leads to her failure to win his approval. How does your character's tactic relate to his or her scenic objective?

■ SUBCONSCIOUS NEED

Some characters at the scenic level have a subconscious need that is different from the conscious one. Orangutan wants to get a friend's approval for her plan to find her birth parents. Her behavior suggests, however, that she might subconsciously want him to talk her out of this plan because of the risks it involves. The deeper desire to be defeated could explain why her tactics work against her and why she ends up not getting on the train after she fails to get his blessing. If your character had a subconscious desire in the scene, what would it be, and how would that affect the dramatic action?

WRAP-UP

Different levels of desire work together to drive character behavior as a dramatic story unfolds. As you write and revise, keep in mind that each character's scenic objective is not only a step toward an overall goal in the story but also a source of beat actions that can reveal different sides of the character and bring more variety to the scene.

> **Related tools in *The Dramatic Writer's Companion*. For more about character objectives, go to the "Causing a Scene" section and try "What Does the Character Want?" For more about dramatic action at the beat level, try "How It Happens" or "Thinking in Beats" in the same section.**

MOTHER CONFLICT

THE QUICK VERSION
Explore sources of conflict for a scene

BEST TIME FOR THIS
During scene planning, writing, or revision

PROBLEMS, PROBLEMS
To understand conflict in drama is to know what characters want and why they are having a hard time getting it. Objectives and conflict thus go hand in hand. Suppose that a man has no food in his kitchen. If he just returned home from a restaurant and wants to sleep, the lack of food is currently not an issue. However, if he just woke up hungry and wants to eat, the lack of food becomes a conflict. It is precisely his objective *to eat* that establishes it as such. And if the man is not just hungry but starving, the lack of food becomes an urgent problem that cannot be ignored.

When we think of conflict, we may think of characters arguing: the bigger the argument, the more dramatic the scene. However, character objectives and motivations can turn anything into a problem. It is the objective that defines what the problem is and the motivation that determines how urgently it must be addressed.

ABOUT THE EXERCISE
Use this exercise to explore potential conflicts that your character may face while pursuing an objective in a scene. Examples are from scene 3 of *Bent* by Martin Sherman, nominated for a 1980 Pulitzer Prize for Drama and Tony Award for Best Play. The story deals with the persecution of gays in Nazi Germany. Sherman later adapted the story to film for a 1997 release.

Character 1—who drives most of the action and makes the scene happen—is Freddie, a middle-aged gay man who pretends to be straight in order not to alienate his wealthy family, on whom he relies for money. Character 2 is Max, in his early thirties, an openly gay man who, with his lover, is being pursued by the Gestapo after a raid of his Berlin flat. The character relationship: Freddie is Max's uncle and the only family member with whom Max has had contact over the past ten years. The main event of the scene: Freddie and Max make a deal to get Max and his partner out of Nazi Germany.

To prepare for the exercise, choose a scene you wish to develop, identify the two most important characters—Characters 1 and 2—and define their relationship. Then sum up the main event of the scene as you see it now: what happens overall.

As you proceed, keep the main focus on your Character 1.

■ SCENIC CONTEXT

Define the context for the dramatic action.

1. *Setting.* Sherman's scene takes place in a park in Cologne, Germany, near a forest where Max and his lover are currently hiding from the Gestapo. Define the setting for your scene.
2. *Time.* The action occurs in 1936 a few days after Max called Freddie and asked for his help in escaping the country. Their meeting now is the first time they have seen each other since Max fled Berlin two years ago. Define when your scene takes place.

■ SCENIC OBJECTIVE AND MOTIVATION

Before you can identify possible conflicts for a scene, you need to know what your character wants and why the character wants it now.

1. *Scenic objective.* Ideally, the main event of the scene will occur here and now because Character 1 wants something important and will either succeed or fail in getting it. Freddie has a *convince* objective: to persuade Max to accept a set of fake identification papers and a train ticket to Amsterdam so he can escape the Gestapo before it's too late. Think about how your Character 1 wants to affect whoever else is here now. For example, is Character 1 trying to make the other character *feel good* or *feel bad*? Or is Character 1 trying to *find out* something or *convince* the other character of something important? Pick a general behavioral objective and translate it into a specific need.
2. *Trigger.* The character's scenic objective may be incited before the scene or during it. Freddie's objective was incited prior to the scene when he received Max's call for help. Freddie has now come to a park in Cologne for the express purpose of giving his nephew the means to get out of Nazi Germany. Think about your Character 1's scenic objective. When is this objective incited, and what triggers it?
3. *Motivation.* If difficult obstacles stand in the way of what characters want, they need compelling reasons to deal with that trouble instead of walking away from it. What's at stake for Freddie is his nephew's life. Identify what's at stake for your Character 1. This is what will be gained if the objective succeeds or lost if it fails.

■ SOURCE OF CONFLICT: SELF

A character's pursuit of an objective generates dramatic action when it is difficult to achieve. The problems that contribute to this difficulty can come in many different forms and arise from many different sources. In some cases, characters are their own worst enemy. They defeat themselves as they struggle to satisfy their desires. Their problems may stem from any of the following:

1. *Personal traits.* Whether positive or negative, a character's own physical, psychological, or social traits can be a source of conflict. Freddie wants to help his nephew but is without much gravitas. He lives on the purse strings of others and hides his true nature. This has made him a weak character who has trouble asserting himself. Think about what your Character 1 wants in your scene. What personal traits could make this objective hard to achieve?

2. *Emotional state.* Whether positive or negative, a character's emotions can also create conflict. Freddie is nervous about meeting Max in a public place to help him escape the Nazis. This anxiety makes it difficult for Freddie to act effectively and authoritatively. What emotions could hamper your Character 1 during the scene?

3. *Mental state.* Ideas, beliefs, and memories running through a character's mind can be another source of conflict. As he meets with Max, Freddie is aware of a man with a mustache watching him from across the park. Is that a gay man flirting with him or a police officer tailing him? Freddie's preoccupation with such questions makes it hard for him to concentrate now. How might your Character 1's mental state interfere with the scenic objective?

4. *Behavior.* A character's own actions can sometimes be self-defeating. Freddie wants to convince Max to accept new identity papers and a train ticket to Amsterdam, but his fear of being caught prevents him from doing so openly. Instead he poses as someone who came to the park to read the newspaper and happened to meet a friendly stranger. This ruse gets in the way of what he really came here to do. How might your character's behavior make the scenic objective difficult to achieve?

■ SOURCE OF CONFLICT: THE OTHER CHARACTER

The most common source of conflict in drama is the other character.

1. *Personal traits.* Character 2's physical, psychological, or social traits often contribute to Character 1's conflict in a scene. Freddie wants to help save his nephew's life, but Max is a headstrong man who tends to leap before he looks. This makes him unwilling to consider an offer that does not immediately meet his expectations. Think about what

your Character 1 wants now. What personal traits of Character 2 could make this objective difficult to achieve?

2. *Emotional state.* Character 2's feelings can be another source of conflict for Character 1. Max has been on the lam with his partner, Rudy, for two years and has come to this meeting filled with anxiety. That emotional state will make it difficult for Freddie to get through to him. How might Character 2's emotional state make it difficult for your Character 1 to achieve the scenic objective?

3. *Mental state.* Character 2 may also have ideas, beliefs, and memories that spell trouble for Character 1. Max is more attached to his partner than he would admit and came to this meeting expecting *two* tickets to Amsterdam. That expectation will create a problem for Freddie, who has arrived with only one ticket. How might Character 2's mental state make it difficult for your Character 1 to achieve the scenic objective?

4. *Behavior.* In many dramatic scenes, conflict results because Character 2 wants something contrary or contradictory to what Character 1 wants. Upon learning that Freddie has brought only one train ticket to Amsterdam, Max refuses to accept anything but two tickets. How might Character 2's actions make your Character 1's scenic objective difficult to achieve?

■ SOURCE OF CONFLICT: PHYSICAL LIFE

Conflict in a scene can arise from the setting and what's in it. Keep your Character 1's objective in mind as you consider physical life as a potential source of conflict.

1. *Setting.* The scene between Freddie and Max takes place in a public park in Cologne in broad daylight. The public nature of this park adds to the tension between them. Anyone could be watching, and that includes the man with the mustache nearby. Freddie's goal is to give his nephew the envelope in his pocket, but doing so could put both of their lives in danger if that man is a Gestapo agent. How might the setting for your scene add to the conflict your Character 1 faces here and now?

2. *Object or physical element.* The envelope in Freddie's pocket is itself a source of conflict, because it contains only one ticket to Amsterdam instead of two. Max refuses to leave the country without his partner. Think again about the setting for your scene. What object or physical element here could add to Character 1's conflict?

■ SOURCE OF CONFLICT: THE PAST

You've been exploring the here and now of a scene and how it might create problems for your Character 1. The past also can be a source of conflict. Max decided long ago to make his sexual orientation public and live a lifestyle that led his conservative parents to disown him. His only family now are Rudy, his partner, and Freddie, his uncle. It is Max's attachment to Rudy that prevents him from accepting only one ticket to Amsterdam. And it is his sole reliance on Freddie that makes his need for a second ticket urgent. All of this adds to the conflict Freddie faces as he tries to save his nephew's life. How might the past create conflict in the present for your Character 1?

■ SOURCE OF CONFLICT: THE FUTURE

The future may also play a role in creating dramatic tension. For Freddie, the threat of getting arrested by the Gestapo adds to the difficulty of coming to his nephew's rescue. If he is not extremely cautious, both he and Max could end up dead. How might future possibilities contribute to the conflict your Character 1 faces here and now?

■ CENTRAL CONFLICT

You've been exploring potential sources of conflict for a scene. Some of your findings are more important than others. Focus now on what matters most.

1. *Central conflict.* Freddie wants Max to accept the train ticket that could save his life. Of all the obstacles standing in the way, the biggest is Max's refusal to accept an envelope that contains only one ticket. This, then, is the central conflict of the scene. Think about the conflict possibilities you've explored for your scene. What is the biggest hurdle that your Character 1 must overcome to achieve the scenic objective?

2. **Why difficult.** Max's resistance to Freddie's offer is a big problem because it is fueled by high stakes. If Max were to accept only one train ticket, he could be sacrificing either his own life or his partner's. What makes the central conflict of your scene a difficult problem that cannot be easily solved?

3. **Why urgent.** Freddie wants to give Max a train ticket that he refuses to accept. If this transaction were a routine matter, Freddie might shrug it off and continue on his way, feeling disgruntled about his nephew's ingratitude. However, this isn't business as usual, and Freddie can't ignore the problem. His nephew's survival is at stake, and this may be Freddie's last chance to save him. Think again about the central conflict of your scene. Why can't this problem be avoided or put off until later?

WRAP-UP

In drama nothing important happens except through conflict. There is always a problem to be solved. For each scene of your script, know what your characters want, what problems they face, and why these problems must be tackled here and now. It is through a character's struggle with conflict that we see how important an objective really is. Without such struggle, the dramatic action of a scene may seem flat, and any successful outcome of that action may feel unearned or inconsequential.

Related tools in *The Dramatic Writer's Companion.* To explore dramatic conflict further, go to the "Causing a Scene" section and try "What's the Problem?" or "Heating Things Up." Or go to the "Developing Your Character" section and try "Adversaries: Then and Now."

WHY DID THE CHARACTER CROSS THE ROAD?

THE QUICK VERSION
Explore different levels of motivation for character behavior

BEST TIME FOR THIS
During scene planning, writing, or revision

THE WHY OF ACTION
Motive is a key ingredient in almost everything that characters do, from buying groceries to choosing a career to finding a romantic partner. For behavior to make sense, there must be a reason to act—even if it is a faulty or illogical reason or one that the character will later regret. This motive may be noble or base, healthy or unhealthy, profound or petty. It may arise spontaneously or after much deliberation.

Regardless of its nature, motivation can exist on two levels: the *apparent* reasons that drive a certain behavior (she works overtime because she is ambitious) and the *hidden* reasons that drive a behavior (she works overtime because she is lonely). Whether apparent or hidden, motivation reflects the fact that in the eyes of the character, something important is at stake.

ABOUT THE EXERCISE
Use this exercise to do an in-depth exploration of a character's motivation in a scene. Examples are from scene 6 of John Patrick Shanley's play *Defiance*, which explores racial tensions at a Marine Corps base in North Carolina during the Vietnam War. Character 1—who drives most of the action—is Chaplain White, age thirty-five, white, the smarmy and unpopular new chaplain at the base. Character 2 is Lee King, age twenty-seven, black, a captain who was recently appointed executive officer to Lieutenant Colonel Littlefield. The relationship between the chaplain and King: fellow Marines stationed at the same base, with King outranking the chaplain. The main event of the scene: the chaplain tries to convince King to file a report that Littlefield slept with the wife of a man down his chain of command, a disclosure that would ruin Littlefield's military career.

To prepare for the exercise, choose a scene you wish to develop, identify the two most important characters—Characters 1 and 2—and define their relationship. Then sum up the main event of the scene as you see it now: what happens overall.

■ SCENIC CONTEXT

Define the context in which the dramatic action occurs.

1. *Setting.* Shanley's scene takes place in a park on a Marine Corps base, Camp Lejeune, in North Carolina. Away from the offices and barracks, this is where two men dealing with sensitive issues can talk privately. Define the setting for your scene.

2. *Time.* It is lunchtime. The year is 1971, when the Vietnam War and the civil rights movement have divided the world both on and beyond the base. Issues of race and authority are rocking the Marine Corps. This social framework will be a key factor in a black captain's decision about whether to destroy a white colonel's career. Define when your scene takes place.

3. *Given circumstances.* Private First Class Davis, a young man from the poor South, recently told Chaplain White in confidence that Lieutenant Colonel Littlefield had slept with Davis's wife. Davis is so upset by the betrayal that he wants to be transferred to Vietnam so he can die in battle. To avoid Littlefield, he went to King for the transfer, but King denied it when he learned why Davis wanted to go. Davis then said he would ask Littlefield directly for the transfer, but King convinced him to wait and is now trying to figure out how to handle this potentially explosive situation. Think about the world of your story as your scene begins. Identify any physical, psychological, social, economic, political, or spiritual circumstances that could affect the dramatic action.

■ OBJECTIVE AND CONFLICT

To explore a character's motivation in a scene, you need to know what the character wants and what obstacles stand in the way. Focus on your Character 1.

1. *Scenic objective.* Dramatic characters tend to have four basic types of behavioral objectives: to make the other character *feel good*, to make the other character *feel bad*, to *find out* something important, or to *convince* the other character of something important. The chaplain has a *convince* objective: to persuade King to do the right thing and report the colonel's wrongdoing to the general. What is your Character 1's scenic objective?

2. *Central conflict.* The character's pursuit of the objective will generate dramatic action if obstacles stand in the way. These conflicts may arise from within the character, from others with opposing needs, from the situation at hand, or from all of these sources. The chaplain wants King to report Littlefield. His biggest problem is King's resistance to doing so because it would destroy the colonel's career and put King in jeopardy as well. What is your Character 1's central conflict in the scene?

■ MOTIVATION

Characters deal with conflict because they have something at stake. At the scenic level, their motivation needs to be strong enough to keep pushing them forward until success or failure is reached. Two types of motivation may drive such behavior.

1. *Apparent motivation.* Sometimes the reason to act seems obvious. It's what one would expect from this character in this situation. The chaplain wants to convince King to file a damaging report against his commanding officer. Why does the chaplain want this? Here are some apparent reasons:

   • he believes that the colonel should be punished for what he did
   • he cannot report the wrongdoing himself since it was revealed to him in confidence
   • he believes it is his duty to fight evil within his flock
   • he promised to help the victimized young man
   • the young man could die if the situation is not resolved correctly

   Think about what Character 1 wants in your scene. Why does he or she want that? List as many apparent reasons as you can.

2. *Hidden motivation.* Reasons for pursuing a certain course of action are not always obvious. In some cases characters have ulterior motives that lead them to behave in deceitful ways. In other cases they have hidden motivations that even they themselves are not aware of. They may be influenced unknowingly by experiences from their past or by subconscious forces. These hidden factors can be among the most powerful motivators of what characters do.

   The chaplain wants King to file a report that would destroy the colonel's career and possibly King's as well. Why does the chaplain want that? Here are some hidden reasons:

   • he wants revenge on Littlefield for humiliating him in the past
   • he wants revenge on King for disrespecting him as well
   • he needs to establish his moral authority in a place where most people don't seem to take him seriously
   • he feels insecure about his ability to administer his vocation and needs a success to boost his own confidence

   Think again about what your Character 1 wants. Why does he or she want that? List as many possible hidden reasons as you can.

■ WHAT'S AT STAKE

What really motivates your Character 1 in the scene you are developing now? The following random list of motivators can help you explore possibilities for what will be gained if your character's objective is achieved and what will be lost if it's not. Use a simple 0-1-2-3 scale to rate each motivator, with 0 meaning that it has no relevance for Character 1 in this particular scene and 3 meaning that it is highly relevant.

- *Love.* From romance to friendship to spiritual bonding, love often motivates characters to act. Love has little relevance now for the chaplain, though he does feel some loyalty to the young man he promised to help. Love thus earns a low rating of 1. How would you rate love as a motivator for Character 1 in your scene?
- *Truth.* Sometimes it is knowledge that motivates characters to pursue objectives. For the chaplain, the airing of the truth is a key factor in his desire to expose Littlefield, so it earns a high rating of 3. How relevant is truth for Character 1 in your scene?
- *Freedom.* Freedom of choice, expression, or movement can be at risk in many situations but not for the chaplain now. Rating: 0. How relevant is freedom for Character 1 in your scene?
- *Justice.* As the chaplain tries to right a wrong, justice is a very strong motivator. Rating: 3. How relevant is justice for your character now?
- *Security.* The chaplain's safety is not in question, but the young private's survival could be at risk. Rating: 2. How relevant is security for your character now?
- *Wealth.* Money is a strong motivator for many dramatic characters but not for the chaplain. Rating: 0. How relevant is wealth for your character now?
- *Pleasure.* From sex to gluttony to aesthetic appreciation, pleasure is another strong motivator for many characters but not for the chaplain. Rating: 0. How relevant is pleasure for your character now?
- *Power.* The quest for power drives almost everything the chaplain does. Rating: 3. How relevant is power for your character now?
- *Self-esteem.* The need to achieve, protect, or restore one's self-esteem, or sense of honor, is often what drives characters to act. For the chaplain, who is new on the base and has been humiliated by both Littlefield and King, self-esteem is a strong motivator. Rating: 2. How relevant is self-esteem for your character now?
- *Salvation.* Many believe that redemption is the paramount value. Factored into this belief are notions of morality, God, and the afterlife. The chaplain's need to right a wrong may be driven partly by heavenly aspirations, but this is hardly what concerns him most. Rating: 1. How relevant is salvation for your character now?

■ KEY FINDINGS

Sum up your findings and what they reveal.

1. *Motivators by rating.* Think about the ten values you've been exploring and how much or how little they motivate Character 1 in your scene. Group these values now by the ratings you assigned to them.

- *Rating: 0.* For Chaplain White, freedom, wealth, and pleasure were each rated 0 because they have no relevance to the scene. Look at your 0 ratings to see which values you can dismiss for your scene. For any of these, is it surprising that the value doesn't matter, and if so, what does that tell you?
- *Rating: 1.* Love and salvation both received a 1. While they may motivate the chaplain's behavior to some degree, they are minor influences. The chaplain's disregard for love and salvation is a telling factor. One might expect more from a man of the cloth pleading the case of a victimized young man. Look at your 1 ratings. What do they suggest about your character? For any of these, is it surprising that it matters or that it doesn't matter more?
- *Rating: 2.* In a rating system where 3 is tops, 2 is a weighty factor. Self-esteem and security received this rating because they both motivate the chaplain in significant ways. His need to restore his own honor suggests that his motives may have more to do with himself than with the young man he is trying to help, though his concern about someone else's security indicates some altruism. Look at your 2 ratings. What do they say about your character? For any of these, is it surprising that it doesn't matter more or that it matters so much?
- *Rating: 3.* Justice, truth, and power each received a 3, making them the most powerful motivators of the chaplain's behavior now. Since a serious wrong has been committed in secret, the values of justice and truth are logical motivators in his efforts to convince King to file the damaging report. Power is a more surprising motivator for this man of the cloth, yet he seems as determined to build up his own power as he is to destroy the colonel's. Look at your 3 ratings. What do they tell about your character? For any of these, is it surprising that it matters so much, and if so, what does that suggest?

2. *Primary motivator.* As he tries to convince King to file the damaging report against Littlefield, the value that matters most to the chaplain is justice. Look again at the values you rated 3. Which is the single most important value at risk now?

3. *Key conclusions.* By looking at justice in relation to the other factors, especially the competing importance of power (rated 3) and the strong importance of self-esteem (rated 2), one might reach a surprising conclusion: the justice the chaplain seeks is not so much for the young man as for himself. His justice is his revenge against the colonel who humiliated him. Think again about your character's primary motivator in relation to the other factors in his or her motivational palette. What insights can you gain from this comparison?

WRAP-UP

Motivation is an essential ingredient of dramatic action. It explains why characters pursue nearly impossible dreams and why they go to the trouble of tackling problems that will not be easy to solve. For such efforts to make sense, the character must have something vital at stake. This is what will be gained if the character's goal is achieved and what will be lost if it fails.

> **Related tools in** *The Dramatic Writer's Companion.* **To learn more about a character's reasons for acting, go to the "Causing a Scene" section and try "Good Intentions."**

THE STRATEGICS OF THE SCENE

THE QUICK VERSION
Explore strategies a character might try to achieve a scenic objective

BEST TIME FOR THIS
During scene planning

HOW CHARACTERS GET WHAT THEY WANT
Strategics is the art of using certain methods to bring about a desired outcome. Dramatic writers draw from this art every time they write a character who wants something important and takes different steps to get it. Sometimes these steps, or strategies, are planned in advance. Other times they arise spontaneously.

Character strategies are the stuff of the scene: the dialogue we hear and physical action we see. Each time a character tries a new strategy, a new unit of action, or beat, begins. Strategy is thus a tool that can bring variety to a scene and keep pushing the story forward. A common dramaturgical problem in new scripts is a conflict that has grown stale because the character has been trying the same strategy for too long and failed to recognize what the audience figured out long ago: that this strategy doesn't work and the character needs to try something else.

The character who drives a scene typically wants one thing but has to try different ways to get it. Changes in strategy occur because of the obstacles that stand in the way (conflict) and the importance of achieving the objective now (motivation). One objective can thus trigger many topics and behaviors. As a result, the strategic approach tends to be dynamic: it keeps changing as the character is forced to manage conflict.

ABOUT THE EXERCISE
Use this exercise to explore different strategies a character might try to achieve a scenic objective. Examples are from the opening scene of *Ruined* by Lynn Nottage. Recipient of the 2009 Pulitzer Prize for Drama, the play explores life in a rundown brothel during a civil war in the Democratic Republic of Congo. This is a world where money is king and murder, rape, and torture are common. The term *ruined* refers to a woman who has been genitally mutilated during rape. The victims of such crimes are often viewed as pariahs to be banished from their homes and villages.

Character 1—who drives most of the action—is Christian, in his forties, a traveling salesman who is "perpetually cheerful." Character 2 is Mama

Nadi, also in her forties, a shrewd businesswoman who runs a brothel. Their relationship: business associates. He supplies what she needs to run her establishment, such as soap, cigarettes, condoms, and girls. The main event of the scene: Christian persuades Mama Nadi to purchase two teenage homeless girls.

To prepare for the exercise, choose a scene you wish to develop, identify the two most important characters—Characters 1 and 2—and define their relationship. Then sum up the main event of the scene as you see it now: what happens overall.

■ **SCENIC CONTEXT**

Define the context for the dramatic action.
1. *Setting.* The setting for Nottage's scene is a rundown café, bar, and brothel in a rain forest on the outskirts of a small mining town in the Democratic Republic of Congo. Identify the setting for your scene.
2. *Time.* It is a hot early afternoon during a war between the Congolese government and rebel soldiers. Identify when your scene takes place.

■ **ELEMENTS OF ACTION**

Define the basic elements of dramatic action for your Character 1.
1. *Objective.* Mama Nadi is the main character of *Ruined*, but Christian is the main character of the first scene because he drives most of the action. He does this because he wants something: to convince Mama Nadi to buy two homeless girls, Sophie and Salima, whom he has brought here on his truck full of merchandise. The scene is thus driven by his need to make a sale. Think about how your Character 1 wants to affect your Character 2. Identify a general behavioral objective: to make the other character *feel good* or *feel bad*, to *find out* something, or to *convince* the other character of something important. Then translate the objective into the specific terms of your story.
2. *Conflict.* Character objectives do not cause scenes to happen unless they are difficult to achieve. Christian knows that Mama Nadi is a tough, practical, and unsentimental businesswoman and that she will not want the girls he has brought for a number of reasons. She already has enough prostitutes in the brothel. And even if she did need more, she would not want these particular girls because neither will be good for business: one is plain and the other is ruined. Mama Nadi's resistance to buying the girls is the main obstacle that Christian faces. What will make it difficult for your Character 1 to achieve the scenic objective here and now?
3. *Motivation.* If difficult problems stand in their way, characters must be motivated to tackle them. In *Ruined*, the lives of two girls are at

risk. With a civil war raging and no parents to protect them, Sophie and Salima need a new home, and in this brutal world, Mama Nadi's brothel is one of the safest places they can be. Though Christian presents himself as a trafficker of human lives, the transaction is not only about money. It's also about a pledge he made to the families of the girls to find them a safe home. This pledge is particularly important because one of the girls—the ruined one—is his niece. What is at stake for Character 1 in your scene?

■ **POSSIBLE STRATEGIES**

Christian tries many strategies to get Mama Nadi to buy the two girls on his truck. His diverse behavior creates a rich, multi-beat scene that reveals a lot about the characters and the world they inhabit. Use the following four general types of behavioral action to explore possible strategies for Character 1 in your scene.

1. *Feel good.* Christian tries to make Mama Nadi feel good in different ways. He presents her with gifts: first a new tube of red lipstick and later a rare box of Belgian chocolates that he knows she will savor. He also recites a poem that he wrote for her. Think about what your Character 1 wants. If one strategy was to make Character 2 feel good, how specifically would Character 1 try to do so?

   • *Rationale.* From Christian's point of view, it makes sense to give Mama Nadi things she likes. She's a hard woman who is not used to being pampered, so his gifts are likely to throw her off guard and make her receptive to his proposition. Think about your Character 1's possible *feel good* strategy. From the character's point of view, right or wrong, why might this strategy make sense?

   • *Summary.* How characters act is more important than what characters say, and the words in our language that express action are verbs. Christian's strategy of presenting gifts to Mama Nadi could be summed up literally by the verb phrase *to gift* or figuratively by the verb phrase *to caress.* Think about the *feel good* strategy you chose for your character. Sharpen your understanding of this action by summing it up in two verb phrases: one that describes the action literally and one that describes it figuratively.

2. *Feel bad.* Christian also tries to make Mama Nadi feel bad in different ways. He lays a guilt trip on her: he had to go to a lot of trouble and risk to get here on roads that are now dangerous because of the war. He also tries to arouse her sympathy for two abused homeless girls. Think about what your Character 1 wants. If one strategy was to make Character 2 feel bad, how specifically would Character 1 try to do so?

   • *Rationale.* From Christian's point of view, trying to elicit guilt and sympathy from Mama Nadi makes sense because he knows there is a soul lurking beneath her hard exterior. He also believes that she secretly loves him and that he has the ability to stir the humanity within her. Think about your Character 1's possible *feel bad* strategy. From the character's point of view, right or wrong, why might this strategy make sense?

- *Summary*. Christian's attempt to make Mama Nadi feel guilty could be summed up literally by the phrase *to guilt* or figuratively by the phrase *to stab*. Think about the *feel bad* strategy you chose for your character. Learn more about this action by summing it up in two verb phrases: one literal, one figurative.

3. **Find out.** Faced with Mama Nadi's resistance to his proposal, Christian tries to figure out how to swing the deal his way. Would Mama Nadi be willing to give the girls a trial period to see how they work out? Would she take the ruined girl as part of a special package with the plain girl: two for the price of one? What's the most Mama Nadi would pay? Think about what your Character 1 wants. If one strategy was to find out something important, what specifically would the character want to know?

- *Rationale.* From Christian's point of view, it makes sense to bargain with Mama Nadi and find common ground. They've had many business dealings in the past, and he knows that he can get her agreement if he is persistent and flexible. Think about your Character 1's possible *find out* strategy. From the character's point of view, right or wrong, why might this strategy make sense?
- *Summary*. As Christian tries to make a sale, his efforts to get favorable terms for himself and the girls could be summed up literally by the phrase *to negotiate* or figuratively by the phrase *to dig*. Think about the *find out* strategy you chose for your character. Sum it up in two verb phrases: one literal, one figurative.

4. **Convince.** To convince others is *not* to explain something to them. It is to persuade them to adopt new beliefs or agree to new actions. Christian tries to convince Mama Nadi that the girls will be good for her business because they can cook, clean, and do other chores to keep the brothel running. He also stresses that because of the rich red dirt of the region, good times will come to the mining town soon and Mama Nadi will need extra help to handle the increased business this will bring. Think about what your Character 1 wants. If one strategy was to convince Character 2 of something important, what would be the specific topic?

- *Rationale.* From Christian's point of view, it makes sense to focus on the girls as good business investments, because business is Mama Nadi's chief concern. Think about the *convince* strategy you chose for your character. From the character's point of view, right or wrong, why might this strategy make sense?

- *Summary*. Christian's attempt to convince Mama Nadi of the merits of his business proposition could be summed up literally by the phrase *to sell* or figuratively by the phrase *to bedazzle*. Think about the *convince* strategy you chose for your character. Sum it up in two verb phrases: one literal, one figurative.

■ SAMPLE ACTION PLAN

Now that you've explored possible strategies that Character 1 might try in your scene, begin to think about how these strategies could work together to form an action plan that the character either formulates in advance or devises from moment to moment.

1. **Early strategy.** The opening scene of *Ruined* centers on a transaction. Christian begins his strategic approach to this transaction not by presenting the two girls he wants to sell but by flirting with Mama Nadi and reciting a poem he has written. The girls meanwhile are hidden outside on the truck, and it will not be until later that their presence is revealed. Christian's action plan is unique to him but illustrates an approach that is typical in dramatic scenes. The first actions tend to be what the character sees as the least demanding or most timely steps. It is much easier to flatter Mama Nada and recite poetry than it is to sell her something she doesn't want.

   Think about the possible strategies you identified for your Character 1 as well as any new strategies that come to mind now. Some of these steps would be easier for your character than others. From the character's point of view, right or wrong, what would be the least demanding or most timely step to try? This might be one of the character's first strategies in the scene.

2. **Late strategy.** One of Christian's final strategies is to reveal the truth: the ruined girl, Sophie, is his niece, and he promised her sister he would find her a safe home. This is the last card he can play, because it reveals how vulnerable he really is. The transaction is not about business as usual. It is about his family and himself, and he cannot get more personal than this in his strategic approach.

   The steps between the first action and the final action often reflect the transition that takes place in a scene, with each new strategy requiring greater effort or risk than the one before. As a result, more and more is demanded of the character as the scene unfolds. Of the strategies you identified so far or can think of now, what would be the most difficult or risky step for your Character 1 to try? If this is one of the character's last strategies, it might be the one that leads finally to success or failure.

WRAP-UP

We learn a lot about characters by how they try to achieve their objectives: what strategies they choose and don't choose, how well they execute these strategies, how they manage the unexpected, and how they think and act under rising pressure. If you give two characters the same objective and put them into the same situation, you will most likely end up with two different action plans, since each will draw from a unique set of personal resources and life experiences.

> Related tools in *The Dramatic Writer's Companion*. To continue exploring character strategies and tactics, go to the "Causing a Scene" section and try "How It Happens."

THE SCENES WITHIN THE SCENE

THE QUICK VERSION
Explore the nature and function of French scenes

BEST TIME FOR THIS
During scene planning, writing, or revision

WHEN CHARACTERS COME AND GO
Named after a seventeenth-century French system for identifying scenes in a dramatic script, a "French scene" is a unit of dramatic action demarcated by the entrance or exit of a character. Each time someone comes or goes, a new combination of characters forms and a new French scene begins. If there are a number of such comings and goings, one scene can be made up of several French scenes. Some may be as short as a few lines. Others may extend for pages. Ideally, something important happens in each of these character combinations that contributes to the scene as a whole.

Originally used for rehearsal scheduling, French scenes enable the director to plan which actors rehearse in which groups and on what material. This is important from a writer's perspective because it implies that in each French scene there is something worth rehearsing: an event that, however small, is significant enough to move the whole scene forward.

French scenes affect the tempo of dramatic action, which may feel fast paced if they are abundant and slow paced if they are not. French scenes also reveal key information about relationships, since they enable us to see how mood and behavior can change as characters come or go. When a new character arrives after a scene has begun, for example, a friendly gathering may turn hostile. Or when a character departs before the scene ends, a professional meeting may suddenly turn romantic.

ABOUT THE EXERCISE
Use this exercise to develop a scene with two or more French scenes. The model has four French scenes but can be tailored to your needs. Examples are from act 1, scene 13, of *The Clean House* by Sarah Ruhl. Recipient of the 2004 Susan Smith Blackburn Prize and a finalist for the 2005 Pulitzer Prize for Drama, the play centers on three women from different walks of life who reach across class boundaries to find a common bond.

The model features the three main characters: Lane, a married doctor bent on perfection; her maid, Matilde, who would rather be a comedian; and her sister, Virginia, who uses cleaning to distract herself from her failures.

The main event of the scene: Lane has a breakdown after revealing that her husband has left her for another woman.

To prepare for the exercise, choose a scene you wish to develop that consists of two or more French scenes. Identify the characters who populate the scene and define their relationships. Then sum up the main event of the scene: what happens overall.

■ SCENIC CONTEXT

Define the context for the dramatic action.

1. *Setting.* Ruhl's scene takes place in Connecticut in the all-white living room of a house owned by married doctors Lane and Charles. Define the setting for your scene.
2. *Time.* The action begins in the middle of the afternoon on a day when Lane would normally be at the hospital. Define when your scene takes place.
3. *Given circumstances.* Lane's maid, Matilde, stopped cleaning the house because it made her sad. She would rather think up jokes and be a comedian. Lane's sister, Virginia, came to Matilde's rescue two weeks ago and has been cleaning the house for her without Lane's knowledge. Think about what's happening in the world of your story when your scene begins. Identify any physical, psychological, social, economic, political, or spiritual circumstances that could affect the dramatic action.

■ FRENCH SCENE I

The first French scene begins with certain characters doing something, routine or unusual, that is in some way important to the story.

1. *Who's doing what.* Virginia is ironing the clothing of her sister, Lane, and her brother-in-law, Charles. Matilde is watching her while thinking up a joke. Identify who is present when your scene begins, and describe what each is doing.
2. *Why here now.* Virginia is here now because her sister is at work and thus won't see her doing Matilde's job. Matilde is here now because this is where she lives and because she enjoys Virginia's company. Why is each character here now?
3. *Mood.* As Matilde watches Virginia iron, the mood is friendly. What is the emotional atmosphere when your scene begins?
4. *What happens.* The event of this first French scene is a discovery: Virginia and Matilde find red women's underwear in the laundry and conclude that it belongs to someone other than Lane. Large or small, what event occurs in your French scene 1?
5. *What's revealed.* As the two women react to the strange underwear, we

see that Virginia is worried about her sister's marriage and that Matilde relishes a good scandal. What does your French scene reveal about each character?

6. *Dramatic function.* This French scene foreshadows the news of Charles's infidelity and shows that the conspiratorial pact between Matilde and Virginia has deepened. What is the dramatic function of your French scene 1?

■ FRENCH SCENE 2

The second French scene begins when someone new arrives or when someone who was here leaves. A different combination of characters is now present.

1. *Who's doing what.* A new French scene begins when Lane unexpectedly arrives home. As she enters, Virginia hides the red underwear and rushes to the couch as if she had not been ironing. Matilide rushes to the ironing board as if she had. Identify who is present when your French scene 2 begins, and describe what each is doing now.

2. *Why the entrance or exit.* Lane is here now because this is where she lives and because she was too upset to stay at work. She did not appear in the first French scene because she was still en route from the hospital. If someone new just entered your scene, explain why the character is here now and why the character did not appear in the previous French scene. Or if someone just left, explain why.

3. *Mood.* As the three women suddenly find themselves in the same room, the mood grows tense. What is the emotional atmosphere when your French scene 2 begins?

4. *What happens.* The event of this French scene is a revelation: Lane announces that she is going to shoot herself. Large or small, what event occurs in your French scene?

5. *What's revealed.* Lane's announcement shows that she is extremely upset and that neither Virginia nor Matilde know how to respond. These dynamics also reveal how dysfunctional Lane's relationships have become with everyone around her. What does your French scene reveal about each character?

6. *Dramatic function.* This French scene foreshadows that Lane has bad news, raises concerns about her mental health, and escalates the tension between her and the rest of the world. What is the dramatic function of your French scene 2?

■ FRENCH SCENE 3

If your scene includes a third French scene, it begins with another character entrance or exit so that the combination of characters changes again.

1. *Who's doing what.* The third French scene begins after Lane exits to the kitchen. Matilde begins to iron underwear, as if she had been doing this all along. Virginia compulsively stands and sits, stands and sits. Identify who is present when your French scene 3 begins, and describe what each is doing now.

2. *Why the entrance or exit.* Lane left the living room because she was too upset to remain in the presence of others. If someone new just entered your scene, explain why the character is here now and why the character did not appear in the previous French scene. Or if someone just left, explain why.

3. *Mood.* Though Matilde and Virginia are alone again, the mood has grown even more tense. What is the emotional atmosphere when your French scene 3 begins?

4. *What happens.* The event of this French scene is a physical action: Virginia compulsively rearranges the objects on Lane's coffee table. Large or small, what event occurs in your French scene?

5. *What's revealed.* Virginia's rearrangement of objects shows how she uses obsessive-compulsive housecleaning to deny problems. Matilde's rush to the ironing board shows that even though she hates housework, she doesn't want to lose her job. What does your French scene reveal about each character?

6. *Dramatic function.* This French scene reinforces Virginia's neurotic personality and sets the stage for Lane's discovery in the next French scene of who has really been cleaning her house. What is the dramatic function of your French scene 3?

■ ANY ADDITIONAL FRENCH SCENE(S)

If your scene has a fourth French scene, it begins with another character entrance or exit. This is true for any additional French scenes that may follow. If your scene has more than four French scenes, repeat the following set of questions as needed.

1. *Who's doing what.* The fourth French scene begins when Lane returns from the kitchen with a bloody towel over her wrist. Matilde and Virginia stare at her in horror. Who is present when your new French scene begins? What is each one doing now?

2. *Why the entrance or exit.* Lane has returned to the living room because she was afraid of what she might do if she remained alone. She did not appear in the previous French scene because she was in the kitchen cutting her wrist. If someone new just entered your scene, explain why the character is here now and why the character did not appear in the previous French scene. Or if someone just left, explain why.

3. *Mood.* The sight of Lane's blood has now raised tension in the room to

the level of crisis. What is the emotional atmosphere when your new French scene begins?

4. *What happens.* This French scene centers on Lane's nervous breakdown, which includes evidence of a botched suicide attempt, her revelation about her husband's infidelity, her realization that Virginia has been secretly cleaning her house, and her decision to fire Matilde. Large or small, what event occurs in your new French scene?

5. *What's revealed.* Lane's bloodied wrist and news of her failed marriage reveal how messy her life has become after years of striving for impossible perfection. Virginia's reaction to the crisis shows how much she cares for her sister but also how much Lane resists her help. Matilde's silent relegation to the ironing board shows that in Lane's eyes she is still only a maid. This is reinforced when Lane fires her for not doing her job. What does your new French scene reveal about each character?

6. *Dramatic function.* This new French scene introduces a major turning point for all three women, reveals the depth of Lane's distress and denial, escalates the conflict between her and the other women, and opens the door to the new territory of act 2. What is the dramatic function of your new French scene?

■ MAIN EVENT

The main event of Ruhl's scene is Lane's breakdown, which consists of slitting her wrist, screaming at her sister, and firing her maid. This outcome is triggered by her discovery of her husband's infidelity earlier but is fueled by the odd behavior of the other women now. Their behavior is due, in turn, to the strange underwear in the laundry (French scene 1) and Lane's unexpected arrival home (French scene 2). Lane's breakdown is further fueled by Virginia's compulsive rearrangement of the coffee table (French scene 3), which leads Lane to realize that her sister and maid have also betrayed her (French scene 4). How do your French scenes work together to produce the main event of your scene?

WRAP-UP

French scenes offer the opportunity to present different combinations of characters in the same setting and to show how their individual presence or absence can affect the dynamics of the whole scene. For best results, try to motivate each character entrance or exit with an emotional need rather than a utilitarian one, such as leaving to get another cup of coffee from the kitchen. French scenes can add a lot of power to dramatic storytelling when the comings and goings of the characters are not arbitrary.

Related tools in *The Dramatic Writer's Companion*. French scenes break down into smaller units of action known as beats. To do a beat analysis of a scene, go to the "Causing a Scene" section and try "Thinking in Beats."

THE COLOR OF DRAMA

THE QUICK VERSION
Use color associations to flesh out a scene instinctively

BEST TIME FOR THIS
During scene planning, writing, or revision

COLOR AS A TOOL FOR SCENE DEVELOPMENT
Dramatic writers face the challenge of how to externalize the inner worlds and past experiences of their characters. The physical life of the story offers opportunities to translate character information into concrete terms that the audience can observe and interpret. *Physical life* here refers to the setting for a scene and what's in it.

Color is a key component of this domain. It not only contributes to how the world of the story looks but also has the power to evoke emotions and ideas—in the writer, in the characters, and ultimately in the audience. Color can thus be a powerful means of creating, experiencing, and understanding a story at a gut level.

ABOUT THE EXERCISE
This exercise focuses on color as a tool to flesh out the physical life of a scene and explore new possibilities for dramatic action. As you proceed, try to work instinctively and remember that important discoveries may lie where you least expect them.

Examples are from the opening scene of my play *Love and Drowning*, which explores near-death experience and its impact on people's lives. Character 1—who drives most of the action—is Ella Harding, in her forties, a middle-class housewife who lives in a suburban ranch house and teaches piano lessons in her living room. Character 2 is Hank Harding, also in his forties, an insurance salesman. Their relationship: married for thirteen years. The main event of the scene: Ella fails to engage her husband in lovemaking.

To prepare for the exercise, choose a scene you wish to develop, identify the two most important characters—Characters 1 and 2—and define their relationship. Then sum up the main event of the scene as you see it now: what happens overall.

■ SCENIC CONTEXT

Define the context for the dramatic action.

1. *Setting.* The opening scene of *Love and Drowning* takes place in Ella and Hank's private room at Jonah Harbor, a remote seaside institute that caters to people who have had near-death experiences. Define the setting for your scene.

2. *Time.* The action begins in late afternoon of a rainy autumn day. It is one week after Ella began to hear Hank talking intimately in his sleep to another woman. Define when your scene takes place.

3. *Given circumstances.* The Hardings were recently in a catastrophic boating accident that resulted in clinical drowning: neither had vital signs until rescuers resuscitated them. While Ella was down, she saw the classic "tunnel of light" reported through the ages by many others who have experienced near death. Hank, however, saw nothing. Their different responses to near death has put a strain on their already troubled marriage. Think about what's happening in the world of your story when your scene begins. Identify any physical, psychological, social, economic, political, or spiritual circumstances that could affect the dramatic action.

■ COLOR EXPLORATIONS

Use the following questions to tap the power of color and brainstorm new possibilities for your scene. Look for responses that seem important even if you don't know why.

1. *Red.* Hank is wearing a red cardigan sweater that Ella gave him for Christmas years ago. He wears it often, especially when he feels anxious. That explains why there are now holes forming in the elbows. If there were something red in your scene or something that had red in it, what would it be? How would you describe it?

2. *Blue.* Ella and Hank have blue pills that they get from Dr. Schroeder and take when they feel distressed. They don't know that these pills are placebos and that the person dispensing them is not really a physician. If there were something blue in your scene or something that had blue in it, what would it be?

3. *Green.* As in many institutions, the walls of Ella and Hank's room have been painted green to induce feelings of peacefulness and growth. If there were something green in your scene or something that had green in it, what would it be?

4. *Yellow.* The reading lamp beside Hank's chair has a yellow lampshade. The inside fabric is ripped and torn. If there were something yellow in your scene or something that had yellow in it, what would it be?

5. *Black.* The medical journal that Hank is reading has a black cover. He

never used to read books like this before the accident. Now he can't stop reading anything he can get his hands on, even highly scientific and technical manuals. If there were something black in your scene or something that had black in it, what would it be?

6. **White.** The sheets on Ella and Hank's bed are white. Unlike the linens at home, they are scratchy old hospital-style sheets that have no decorative pattern and smell musty. It is on these sheets that Ella lies each night listening to her husband making love to someone else in his dreams. If there were something white in your scene or something that had white in it, what would it be?

7. **Another color.** If I could move around freely in this setting and watch my characters as the scene unfolds, another color that might catch my eye is gray. It's the blown-out light bulb from the reading lamp. Ever since Ella's "tunnel of light" experience, her electromagnetic field blows out light bulbs and appliances when she gets upset. Look for one more color in your scene, and describe what you find.

■ **COLOR ASSOCIATIONS**

We each have associations, positive or negative, with certain colors: emotions, memories, or ideas that influence our perception of a color and the meanings we bring to it under different circumstances. Such associations have come into play as you used color to explore the physical life of your scene. Continue to work instinctively as you address the next set of questions.

1. **Color of the scene.** Imagine that the scene itself has a color—one color—that somehow encompasses not only the physical life but also the characters and the dramatic action. For me, the scene between Ella and Hank is blue. This is not a literal description. There may be no actual blue pigment in sight during a production. The choice reflects only what I personally associate with blue as I think about my characters in this particular situation. If your scene had a color, what would it be?

2. **Emotional response.** We each have different emotional associations with color, depending on where we are, what we're looking at, whom we're with, and how we feel. A color that seems pleasant at one time may seem unpleasant at another. When I think of my scene as blue, I feel sadness. Though Ella and Hank have been married for thirteen years, they live in separate worlds now. Think about the color of your scene. What emotion does it stir in you, and why?

3. **Physical response.** When I think about my scene as blue, the physical sensation that comes to mind is dampness and cold. I imagine that Ella and Hank's room feels that way now. Maybe that's why Hank is wearing that sweater. Perhaps Ella has a sweater on, too. The warm days of summer are over, but the furnace in the building is not yet on

for the fall. The sea is nearby, so the air is full of moisture, and it's been raining for days. This is not a comfortable place to be now. Think again about the color of your scene. What physical response does it produce in you, and why?

4. *Free associations.* Color also can stir up thoughts and memories. When I think about my scene as blue, it makes me think of water, the ocean, a swimming pool, trembling lips, turning blue all over after swimming too long in cold water, death, freezing, bloating, silence, paralysis, the bathtub, imprisonment, an inability to speak, heavy bodies. Feel the color of your scene. With your characters in mind, identify at least a dozen random thoughts or memories that come to mind now.

5. *Three most powerful associations.* Among my personal associations for blue, the three that feel most powerful are paralysis, turning blue after swimming too long in cold water, and heavy bodies. Review your color associations. Choose the three that feel most powerful for any reason and could somehow be integrated into your scene.

■ COLOR IN ACTION

Imagine that the three choices you made are more important than you realize. They are rooted in the personal experiences of your life and reflect desires, beliefs, and values that have in some way mattered to you. Keep working instinctively as you now use these color associations to learn more about your scene.

1. *Characters.* Focus first on the two most important characters in the scene and what your color associations might reveal about them.

   • *Character 1* in my scene is Ella. Of my three most powerful color associations, the one that feels strongest for her is "heavy bodies." This could be a figurative description of her at this time in her life. She has had an ethereal "tunnel of light" experience that she did not want to leave. As she sits in this room now with her husband on a rainy day, she feels heavy, weighed down in gravity, trapped in a physical state that no longer suits her. She is a "heavy body" yearning for flight. This describes her emotional state as the scene begins, and it will fuel her need in the scene to rekindle her marriage by making love to her husband. Of your three most powerful color associations, which feels strongest for your Character 1? Describe the connection, literally or figuratively, and how it might influence the dramatic action.

   • *Character 2* in my scene is Hank. My strongest color association for him is "paralysis." This again is a figurative description. What Ella doesn't know is that, ever since the boating accident, Hank has lived with the belief that he is responsible for her drowning. Ella believes she was trapped under the water by a reef, but it was actually

Hank's hand holding on to her in an attempt to save himself. His feelings of guilt and betrayal have left him in an emotional paralysis that prevents him having an honest relationship with his wife. This fact will contribute to Ella's failure in the scene to rekindle their marriage. Of your three most powerful color associations, which feels strongest for your Character 2? (If appropriate, you can repeat the association from before.) Describe the connection literally or figuratively and how it might influence the dramatic action.

2. *Scenic event.* The main event of the scene between Elle and Hank is her failure to reestablish intimacy with him. My strongest color association for this event is "turning blue after swimming too long in cold water." This figuratively describes what happens in the scene. The cold here is the isolation and neglect in which they have lived too long. Ella's frustrated attempt to warm things up leaves them feeling even more isolated than before. Of your three most powerful color associations, which feels strongest for the main event of your scene? (If appropriate, you can repeat an association from before.) Describe the connection, literally or figuratively, and how it might affect the scene.

WRAP-UP

The physical life of a setting can be a rich source of story ideas as well as a tool to reveal characters and advance the dramatic action. Color is a powerful component of this realm because of the personal associations, memories, and emotions it can stir. As you develop your script, keep looking for new opportunities to use places, objects, and physical elements to root your characters in the reality of their world and embody important truths about them and the dramatic journey that is taking place.

Related tools in *The Dramatic Writer's Companion*. To explore physical life in more detail, go to the "Causing a Scene" section and try "Where in the World Are We?"

THE EMOTIONAL ONION

THE QUICK VERSION
Explore how different layers of emotion can affect character behavior

BEST TIME FOR THIS
During scene planning, writing, or revision

THE COMPLEXITY OF HUMAN EMOTION
The thoughts, decisions, and actions of dramatic characters are influenced by how they feel. This inner life can be complex, since emotions tend to occur not in isolation but in layers—like the skins of an onion.

If one could peel away the outer layers of an emotional onion, one might find many different feelings underneath. Characters thus may be affected not only by the emotions they sense but also by deeper feelings at a subconscious level. During an argument with his supervisor, for example, a desperate salesman might be aware of only one emotion, such as anger, but other feelings, such as fear or sadness, may contribute to his behavior as well. As you prepare to write a scene, you may benefit from taking the time to explore the mysterious realm of human emotions.

ABOUT THE EXERCISE
Use this exercise to flesh out the emotional life of a scene. You will be working with primary emotions, such as these:

Love	Happiness	Anger	Disgust
Hate	Sadness	Fear	Surprise

Each primary emotion can lead to secondary emotions that reflect different degrees of that basic feeling. For example, love can range from affection to lust to longing, anger can range from irritation to frustration to rage, and fear can range from uneasiness to anxiety to horror.

Examples are from an early scene in *The Curious Incident of the Dog in the Night-Time*, a play by Simon Stevens adapted from a novel by Mark Haddon. Recipient of seven Olivier Awards, including Best New Play, it centers on an autistic teenager from Swindon, England, who investigates the killing of a neighbor's dog.

Character 1—who drives most of the action—is Christopher Boone, a remarkably intelligent teenager who has trouble interpreting everyday life due to his Asperger syndrome. He has never ventured alone beyond the end of his street. Character 2 is Mrs. Alexander, an elderly widow who is hard of hearing. Their relationship: neighbors who have spoken only once before. The scenic event: Christopher learns why his mother left home—she was having an affair with a married man who lived nearby.

To prepare for the exercise, choose a scene you wish to develop, identify the two most important characters—Characters 1 and 2—and define their relationship. Then sum up the main event of the scene as you see it now: what happens overall.

■ SCENIC CONTEXT

Define the context for the dramatic action.

1. *Setting.* *The Curious Incident of the Dog in the Night-Time* has a fluid, impressionistic style that enables the audience to experience the world through Christopher's unusual mind. The scene between Mrs. Alexander and him stretches across two settings in the town of Swindon: Christopher's front yard and a nearby park. Define where your scene occurs.

2. *Time.* The action takes place in the afternoon a few days after the mysterious killing of a neighborhood dog. Define when your scene occurs.

3. *Given circumstances.* Christopher's neighbor Mrs. Shears had him arrested after discovering him in her front yard with her dead dog. When a policeman took his arm to escort him away, Christopher—who does not like to be touched—hit him and was subsequently charged with assaulting a police officer. The boy received a "caution," or warning, which disturbs him because he believes it could affect his future. To find out who did kill the dog, Christopher has begun to interrogate his neighbors. This led him to Mrs. Alexander's house yesterday, but when she left him at her front door to fetch some biscuits (cookies), he ran away in fear that, like Mrs. Shears, she might have him arrested. Think about what's happening in the world of your story when your scene begins. Identify any physical, psychological, social, economic, political, or spiritual circumstances that could affect the dramatic action.

■ EMOTIONAL ONION: CHARACTER 1

Peel away the layers of emotion that could affect your Character 1 during your scene.

1. *Outer emotion.* As Christopher interacts now with a woman he barely knows, the outermost layer of his emotions is fear. What primary emotion will be most observable in your Character 1 as your scene unfolds?

   • *Examples.* Emotions have different triggers, take different forms, and exist with different degrees of intensity. Many fears affect Christopher during his encounter with Mrs. Alexander. He feels nervous around strangers; worries that she might call the police on him; dreads what would happen if he got arrested again with a caution on his record; fears living in a neighborhood where a killer is still on the loose; and feels anxious about breaking his promise to his father that he would not interrogate any more neighbors. What are at least three specific examples of your Character 1's outer emotion at this time in the story?

- *Key feeling.* Of the fears that Christopher experiences now, the most powerful is his fear of living in a neighborhood where a killer is still on the loose. This will motivate his decision to interrogate Mrs. Alexander in spite of the promise he made to his father. Of the specific outer feelings you identified for your Character 1, which will most affect the dramatic action of your scene, and how?

2. *Underlying emotion.* If Christopher's fears could be peeled away like an onion skin, one might discover underneath a layer of love. Though his capacity for love is not foremost on his mind now, it influences his behavior and adds another dimension to his fears. Think again about your Character 1 at this time in the story. If there were another primary emotion underneath the first one, what would it be?

- *Examples.* Christopher may not be focused on love now, but it is nevertheless relevant to the scene. He loves his father; loves his missing mother; feels affection for his pet rat, Toby; enjoys mathematics more than any other subject—he knows all of the prime numbers up to 7,507—and is proud of the fact that he will be the first in his school to take the high-level tests known as "maths level A." These are all different types of love that influence his interaction with Mrs. Alexander. What are at least three specific examples of your Character 1's underlying emotion at this time in the story?

- *Key feeling.* Of the loves affecting Christopher now, the most powerful is his love of his mother. When he discovers that Mrs. Alexander knows why his mother deserted him, his love of her will drive him to learn as much as possible in spite of the painful truths that might be exposed. Of the specific underlying feelings you identified for your Character 1, which will most affect the dramatic action of your scene, and how?

3. *Deep emotion.* If Christopher's fears and loves could be peeled away, one might discover a layer of anger underneath. He does not act angry here and now, but his capacity for anger affects a number of his choices as the scene unfolds. Think again about your Character 1 at this time in the story. If there were a third primary emotion lurking under the other two, what would it be?

- *Examples.* Because Christopher's anger is more buried than his other feelings, he may not be aware of its influence. Yet it is there at work in many forms. He feels angry about being different from other people; angry about not having a mother; angry about being accused of killing a dog when he did no such thing and of telling lies when he is incapable of saying anything but the truth. What are at least three specific examples of your Character 1's deep emotion here and now?

- *Key feeling.* Of the angers that influence Christopher during the scene, the most powerful is his anger at not having a mother. This will motivate him to pry the truth out of Mrs. Alexander when she lets it slip that she knows why his mother ran away from home. Of the specific deep feelings you identified for your Character 1, which will most affect the dramatic action of your scene, and how?

4. *Dominant emotion.* You've been exploring Character 1's emotional life with the premise that at any given time, more than one primary emotion may be present to some degree, even if the character is not aware of this. Of all the feelings that affect Christopher in the scene, the one that dominates the mix may be anger. It does not manifest itself directly now—he never yells or fights—but it may be what pushes him through his fears to find out why his mother deserted him. Think about your scene and the layers of emotion you've uncovered. What single emotion dominates the mix?

■ EMOTIONAL ONION: CHARACTER 2

Now do a similar exploration for the second most important character in the scene.

1. *Outer emotion.* Mrs. Alexander feels surprise as she interacts with the autistic boy from across the street who inexplicably fled from her door yesterday. What primary emotion will be most observable in your Character 2 as your scene unfolds?

- *Examples.* Mrs. Alexander feels astonished by the discovery that Christopher ran away yesterday because he thought she might call the police on him; feels amazed by his display of math genius; and feels shocked by the realization that no one has told him why his mother left home two years ago. What are at least three specific examples of your Character 2's outer emotion here and now?

- *Key feeling.* Of the surprises Mrs. Alexander experiences during the scene, the most powerful is the shock of learning that Christopher does not know why his mother deserted him. This will motivate Mrs. Alexander to reveal the truth: his mother was having an affair with Mr. Shears, who used to live down the street. Of the specific outer feelings you identified for your Character 2, which will most affect the dramatic action of your scene, and how?

2. *Underlying emotion.* Mrs. Alexander may also be affected by some

degree of love as she interacts with this young and vulnerable autistic boy. Think again about your Character 2 at this time in the story. If there were another primary emotion underneath the first one, what would it be?

- *Examples.* Mrs. Alexander feels amused by Christopher's earnest and innocent approach to life; feels compassion because of the difficulties his autism creates; and feels protective of his well-being. What are at least three specific examples of your Character 2's underlying emotion at this time in the story?
- *Key feeling.* Of the loves that affect Mrs. Alexander now, the most powerful is her protectiveness. This will lead her to be cautious when Christopher grills her about why his mother deserted him. Think about the underlying emotion you chose for your Character 2. Of the examples you identified, which will be most powerful during the scene, and how might this affect the dramatic action?

3. *Deep emotion.* If Mrs. Alexander's surprises and loves were to be peeled away, one might discover a layer of fear underneath. For your Character 2, suppose there were another primal emotion lurking under the other two. What would it be?

- *Examples.* Mrs. Alexander frets about missing out on things because of her poor hearing; fears she might say the wrong thing and scare Christopher away again; worries about his emotional well-being, especially after she lets it slip that she knows why his mother left home; fears that Christopher's father will be upset if she tells Christopher the truth about his mother; and fears that the neighbors will disapprove if she interferes with the boy's personal life. What are at least three specific examples of your Character 2's deep emotion here and now?
- *Key feeling.* Of the fears that influence Mrs. Alexander during the scene, the most powerful is her concern about Christopher's well-being. This is what motivates her to overcome her other fears and tell Christopher the truth about his mother. Of the specific deep feelings you identified for your Character 2, which will most affect the dramatic action of your scene, and how?

4. *Dominant emotion.* Of all the feelings that affect Mrs. Alexander in the scene, the one that dominates the mix may be love. Her caring for Christopher and her concern about his well-being drive most of her behavior and lead to the scene's main event: her revelation to him about his mother's marital infidelity. What emotion dominates the mix for your Character 2?

WRAP-UP

When you are developing any dramatic scene, it is important to know how the characters feel in order to understand how they might act in the present circumstances. Keep in mind, however, that characters may be influenced simultaneously by different layers of emotions, including some in the subconscious. To learn more about characters at any given time, and especially at critical moments in the story, try peeling away their obvious emotions to see what deeper forces also may be affecting them.

Related tools in *The Dramatic Writer's Companion*. To continue exploring character feelings, go to the "Developing Your Character" section and try "Getting Emotional." To examine emotion at the scenic level, go to the "Causing a Scene" section and try "Character Adjustments" or "The Emotional Storyboard."

WHY THIS? WHY NOW?

THE QUICK VERSION
Explore the importance and urgency of a dramatic event

BEST TIME FOR THIS
During scene planning, writing, or revision

WHAT MAKES A SCENE "DRAMATIC"
Importance and urgency are basic ingredients of dramatic storytelling. If a scene has *importance*, it is worthwhile. Something meaningful occurs and affects the dramatic journey in either a good or a bad way. If a scene has *urgency*, it centers on a course of action that cannot be put off until later; it has to happen now.

Importance and urgency are distinct elements that can exist without each other. Something can be important but not urgent. For example, he needs to go to the dentist to have his teeth cleaned. That's important, but he doesn't need to do it this instant. He'll schedule an appointment for next week.

Urgency implies importance, but something can require immediate action—the pressure of necessity—without being significant. For example, she is playing tennis with a friend. The ball heads her way. There is an urgency to swing the racket and hit the ball, but not much is at stake other than a point in a friendly game.

In a dramatic story, some scenes have more importance and urgency than others. What happens during the climax, for example, is usually more important and more urgent than what happens in the middle of act one. However, each scene—if it is indeed a *dramatic* scene—has some degree of both importance and urgency.

ABOUT THE EXERCISE
Use this exercise to flesh out why a dramatic event matters and why it happens now. Examples are from an early scene in *Joe Turner's Come and Gone* by August Wilson, which received the 1988 New York Drama Critics' Circle Award for Best Play and is part of his ten-play cycle about the African American experience in the twentieth century. Set in Pittsburgh in 1911, the story was inspired by a blues song with the same name. It was once sung by black women after the men in their lives had been illegally enslaved by a notorious plantation owner named Joe Turner.

A few characters are present in Wilson's scene, but the exercise focuses on the two who matter most. Character 1—who drives most of the action—is Herald Loomis, age thirty-two, an African American man who was once enslaved by Joe Turner's men and is now searching for his missing wife. Character 2 is Rutherford Selig, a white man in his fifties with greasy hair and two occupations: he is a door-to-door peddler of pots, pans, and other metal goods and also a People Finder who, for one dollar, helps locate missing persons. The relationship between Loomis and Selig: strangers. The scenic event is a transaction: Loomis hires Selig to find his wife.

To prepare for the exercise, choose a scene you wish to develop, identify the two most important characters in it—Characters 1 and 2—and define their relationship. Then sum up the main event of the scene as you see it now: what happens overall.

■ SCENIC CONTEXT

Define the context for the dramatic action.
1. *Setting.* Wilson's scene takes place in the kitchen of a Pittsburgh boarding house run by Seth and Bertha Holly. This is where Loomis and his daughter have been staying for the past week. Define the setting for your scene.
2. *Time.* The action occurs on a Saturday morning in August, 1911, after the owner, Seth, has finished his weekly business with the traveling salesman Selig. Define when your scene occurs.

■ WHY THIS?

The importance of a scenic event can be measured by what it reveals about the past, what it reveals about the characters in the present, and how it affects the future.
1. *Evidence of the past.* Loomis hires Selig to find his wife. This scenic event matters dramatically because of what it reveals about the history of the story. Eleven years ago, Loomis was enslaved by Joe Turner's men and forced to work on a chain gang. When he finally returned home seven years later to reunite with his family, he found only his young daughter still living with his mother-in-law. His wife, Martha, had left home to seek work elsewhere. For the past four years, Loomis and his daughter have been traveling the country in search of Martha. The transaction between Loomis and Selig is a consequence of that previous chain of events and thus evidence that they happened. What important information does your scene reveal about the past?
2. *Information about Character 1.* Loomis has become desperate after searching for his wife for years. The prospect of getting help from a professional People Finder is now so important to him that he will spend his last dollar to make it happen. To put that dollar in

perspective, the cost of lodging and food for a entire week in the boarding house is two dollars. And Loomis is unemployed. What's at stake is not only a reunion with his wife but also a mother for his daughter and the means to become a new man: Loomis believes that he cannot know who he is until he sees his wife's face again. What important information does your scene reveal about your Character 1?

3. *Information about Character 2.* While the deal between Loomis and Selig is vitally important to Loomis, it is a routine matter for Selig, who is actually a fraud. The only people he finds are those whom he has previously transported to other places on his sales route after charging them a dollar for a lift in his wagon. This information is revealed later when Bertha learns that Loomis has hired Selig to find his wife. "This old People Finding business is for the birds," she says. "[Selig] ain't never found nobody he ain't took away. Herald Loomis, you just wasted your dollar." What important information does your scene reveal about your Character 2?

4. *Impact on the future.* The scene between Loomis and Selig is a key stepping stone in the plot of Wilson's play. If it weren't for the deal with Selig, Loomis would have no reason to stay and wait in the boarding house, which he cannot afford and where he is not welcome. It is because of this deal that the rest of the story will take place here. It is also because of this deal that Loomis will ultimately be reunited with Martha. She will be returned here by Selig, who will find her by chance in a town on his sales route. The transaction between Loomis and Selig is thus critical to the rest of the story. How and why is your scenic event essential to your story? Describe its impact on the future.

■ WHY NOW?

Ideally, there are reasons for a dramatic event to occur at a particular time in the lives of the characters and at a particular point in the story. These reasons translate into given circumstances that bring some degree of urgency to the dramatic action.

1. *Physical circumstances.* Sometimes the urgency of a scene is due to the physical state or condition of a character or to circumstances surrounding the setting and what's in it. On Saturday mornings Selig meets in the kitchen with Seth, the boarding house owner, to do business: Selig delivers sheet metal, which Seth then uses to make pots and pans, which Selig in turn sells to his customers from door to door. It is now Saturday morning, and Selig has just finished up with Seth in the kitchen. If Loomis wants to meet with Selig, this is the only time and place he can do so. What physical circumstances, if any, contribute to the need for your scene to happen now?

2. *Psychological circumstances.* The urgency of a scene also may be due to

the inner world of a character: the realm of emotions, thoughts, beliefs, and desires. All of Loomis's efforts to find his wife have failed. He has now reached the end of his rope and feels exhausted. The discovery of a People Finder is a renewal of hope and creates the psychological imperative to meet with this professional as soon as possible. What psychological circumstances might contribute to the urgency of your scene?

3. *Social circumstances.* The necessity for dramatic action may also be the result of social factors related to a character's family, workplace, or life in the community. Society is a powerful influence in Wilson's play. Though slavery legally ended decades earlier, the sons and daughters of those freed now find themselves lacking in cultural identity and social status as they struggle to start new lives in the North. Loomis's lack of identity and low social standing add to his need to find outside help now. What social circumstances might contribute to the urgency of your scene?

4. *Economic circumstances.* Most of the characters in Wilson's play are economically deprived, especially Loomis, who has no job and so little money in his pocket that he must offer up his young daughter as a household servant to cover part of the week's rent. This boarding house is the only place he can find Selig, but Loomis cannot afford to stay here longer than a week. He must meet with Selig now, while the People Finder is still in the kitchen. What economic factors, if any, could add urgency to your scenic?

5. *Political circumstances.* Power—or lack of it—often explains why a dramatic event must happen now. As a white man in the racially imbalanced world of Wilson's play, Selig has the most money, mobility, and power. His personal stature is increased by the fact that he is a lifeline to the boarding house: he brings business here. Loomis, however, as a black man in 1911, is a second-class citizen with limited control over his life and destiny. He also has the lowest status in the boarding house because he is new here and without many resources. These dynamics feed his desperation to hire Selig and thus acquire a powerful ally in the search for his wife. What political circumstances— personal or societal—might add urgency to your scene?

6. *Spiritual circumstances.* Sometimes the pressure of necessity is created by spiritual factors: beliefs or practices related to higher powers, religion, the supernatural, the afterlife, miracles, psychic phenomena, or anything else above and beyond the material plane. When we first meet Loomis, he rejects spiritual matters. His lack of faith may contribute to his decision to rely on a People Finder rather than prayers to realize his goal. What spiritual circumstances, if any, might add urgency to your scene?

■ KEY FINDINGS

Sum up your key findings about the importance and urgency of your scene.

1. *Importance.* While many factors contribute to the significance of the transaction between Loomis and Selig, the scene is important mainly because it establishes three critical story facts: how desperate Loomis has become in the search for his wife, why he will remain here at the boarding house for the rest of the play, and how Martha will eventually be found and brought back to him. What makes your scene important?

2. *Urgency.* Wilson's scene must happen here and now because of the high stakes involved for Loomis and because this is the only place and time that he can meet with Selig, his last hope for finding Martha. Why does your scene have to happen here and now in the lives of your characters?

WRAP-UP

As you enter any new scene, know why it is essential to your story and why it must happen now. If you run into trouble writing a scene, you may need to make the scenic event a bigger and more meaningful turning point for the character. Or you may need to find new reasons why it cannot be put off until later.

> **Related tools in *The Dramatic Writer's Companion.* For more about given circumstances, go to the "Causing a Scene" section and try "The Roots of Action." For more about a scenic event, try "Scene in a Sentence" in the same section.**

RELATIONSHIP STORYBOARD

THE QUICK VERSION
Use the dynamics of a character relationship to map out a scene

BEST TIME FOR THIS
During scene planning, writing, or revision

HOW CHARACTERS CONNECT
In most dramatic stories, we come to know the characters in relationship to one another. Their connections may be personal or professional, friendly or unfriendly, distant or close. Or one relationship may be all of these things as the story unfolds. The changing dynamics of a relationship can reveal a lot about the characters involved and how they affect, and are affected by, the dramatic journey. A principal character relationship can thus be a tool to understand the causes and effects of a scenic event.

ABOUT THE EXERCISE
This exercise can help you map out the structure of a scene by developing a simple storyboard for it. Unlike a traditional storyboard, which uses visual images to portray action, you will be using words to describe the relationship between the characters at three points in the scene: the beginning, middle, and end.

Examples are from act 2, scene 5, of *Becky Shaw* by Gina Gionfriddo. A finalist for the 2009 Pulitzer Prize for Drama, the comedy explores the crisis that ensues when a newlywed couple arranges a blind date for two romantically challenged friends, who get robbed at gunpoint after their first dinner together.

Character 1—who drives most of the action—is Becky, in her thirties, a needy temp secretary with few friends and a family that shuns her. Character 2 is Max, also in his thirties, a successful money manager who cannot keep a girlfriend for more than three months. Their relationship: they met five days ago on a disastrous blind date. The scenic event is a showdown over the future of their relationship: he wants to end it, she doesn't.

To prepare for the exercise:
- *Choose a scene* you wish to develop, identify the two most important characters in it—Characters 1 and 2—and define their relationship. Then sum up the main event of the scene as you see it now: what happens overall.
- *Set up the storyboard* by creating a row of three panels labeled

"Beginning," "Middle," and "End." Each needs to be large enough to allow a few words to be added.

■ SCENIC CONTEXT

Define the context for the dramatic action.

1. *Setting.* Gionfriddo's scene takes place in a café in Providence, Rhode Island. Identify the setting for your scene.
2. *Time.* The action begins on a Thursday afternoon, five days after the blind date on which Becky and Max were robbed. Identify when your scene takes place.
3. *Given circumstances.* When Becky and Max were at the police station after the robbery, Max let it slip that he had slept with Suzanna, the wife of Becky's coworker and only friend, Andrew, who arranged the blind date. On the way home, Becky was still so upset by the robbery that Max let her come up to his hotel room, where they ended up having sex. He wouldn't let her spend the night, however, and instead gave her cab fare to go home. Becky has tried many times since then to reach Max, but he has not returned her calls. He is here now only as a favor to Suzanna. Think about the world of your story as your scene begins. Identify any physical, psychological, social, economic, political, or spiritual circumstances that could affect the dramatic action.

■ BEGINNING OF SCENE

Imagine what happens in the beginning of your scene, and complete the following steps before filling in the first panel of your storyboard.

1. *Description.* When the scene between Becky and Max begins, they have different views of their relationship. Becky sees it as a romance with a promising future. Max sees it as a mistake he wants to forget. Their relationship is extremely imbalanced. How would you subjectively describe the relationship between your Characters 1 and 2 as your scene begins? This is your interpretation of the facts.
2. *Emotional connection.* Becky feels attracted to Max but worries about his failure to return her many calls. Max feels annoyed about sitting here now with a woman whom he considers pushy and not up to his standards. How do your Characters 1 and 2 feel about each other as your scene begins?
3. *Subtext.* At any given time, the relationship between two characters has a subtext that reflects what they are thinking but not actually saying. Becky's subtext now might be "Poor Max feels embarrassed about looking like a fool during the robbery, and that's why he was afraid to return my calls." Max's subtext might be "I wish this freak

would leave me alone." What is the subtext for each of your characters as your scene begins? Write each subtext in the character's voice.

4. *What matters most.* When all is said and done, the relationship between Becky and Max at the beginning of the scene might be summed up as "emotionally imbalanced." How would you sum up the relationship between your Characters 1 and 2 as your scene begins? You can repeat any of your previous responses or find a new one. Write your summary in the "Beginning" panel of your storyboard.

■ END OF SCENE

If something important happens in a scene, the character relationship will likely be affected in important ways. The changes that occur may be positive or negative, long term or short term, and the characters may or may not be aware of these effects and their significance. Skip ahead now to what might happen at the end of your scene. Complete the following steps before filling in the third panel of your storyboard.

1. *Description.* Becky and Max are now in a confrontation that borders on violence. She is threatening to tell her friend Andrew that Max slept with his wife. Max knows that this could ruin not only Suzanna's marriage but also his own relationship with her. He is now grabbing Becky's arm as if he might hurt her. Their relationship has thus become adversarial and threatening. How would you subjectively describe the relationship between your Characters 1 and 2 as your scene ends?

2. *Emotional connection.* Becky and Max are now both in a rage. Her anger is controlled. His is on the verge of exploding. How do your Characters 1 and 2 feel about each other as your scene ends?

3. *Subtext.* The subtext of the relationship between Becky and Max has changed significantly. Hers now might be "You're going to be sorry you treated me this way." His might be "I wish I had never met you." What is the subtext for each of your characters as your scene draws to a close?

4. *What matters most.* With Becky threatening to blackmail Max and with his nearing the threshold of physical violence, their relationship has grown "scary." What matters most about the relationship between your Characters 1 and 2 as your scene ends? Write your summary in the "End" panel of your storyboard. Look for as much contrast as possible between this and your summary in the "Beginning" panel.

■ MIDDLE OF SCENE

If a character relationship changes in a significant way, the transition probably begins well before the scene ends. Focus now on the middle of your scene as the breeding ground for the change that occurs. Imagine what happens, and complete the following steps before filling in the second panel of your storyboard.

1. *Description.* In the middle of the scene between Becky and Max, she begins to realize that he never intended to have a serious relationship with her, even when they were having sex. Her discovery of his cold-heartedness is the catalyst for the threatening changes in their relationship later. For now, they have become brutally honest. How would you subjectively describe the relationship between your Characters 1 and 2 in the middle of your scene? Think of this as a transition point between the beginning and the end.

2. *Emotional connection.* Becky's attempts to woo Max not only fail but also make his rejection of her increasingly blunt. Their relationship is now cold and unfriendly. How do your Characters 1 and 2 feel about each other in the middle of your scene?

3. *Subtext.* While Becky and Max confront the truth, the subtext of their relationship moves into new territory. Hers might be "You're a pig who used me for sex." His might be "I want to get out of here." Think about how your character relationship is changing in the middle of the scene. What is each character's subtext now?

4. *What matters most.* As they interact in the café, Becky and Max come to terms with how poorly they fit together as a couple. What matters most now is how "brutally honest" they have become. What matters most about the relationship between your Characters 1 and 2 in the middle of your scene? Write your summary in the "Middle" panel of your storyboard.

■ WHAT THE STORYBOARD REVEALS

The storyboard for Gionfriddo's scene shows that the relationship between Becky and Max evolves from "extremely unbalanced" to "brutally honest" to "scary." In other words, two characters start out as mismatched losers and end up as enemies because of brutally honest exchanges between them. Review your relationship storyboard now in chronological order:

1. Is there a significant difference between the "Beginning" and "End" panels? If they seem too similar, it may mean that not enough has happened in the scene. How can you increase the importance and impact of the dramatic action?

2. Is the "Middle" panel a clear link between the "Beginning" and "End"? If not, you may need to rethink how the scene unfolds so that it focuses more on one main event.

3. What story does your storyboard tell? Is this right story for this scene?

WRAP-UP

Dramatic stories are about character relationships under stress. When starting a new scene between characters who know each other, be sure to consider the nature, history, and power structure of their relationship. Know what impact recent events have had on them and what developments could occur as a result of how they feel about each other now. Whether the characters are currently on good terms or bad, their relationship provides a context for their interaction and is likely both to influence and to reflect the dramatic action as the scene unfolds.

Related tools in *The Dramatic Writer's Companion*. For another way to map out the structure of a scene, go to the "Causing a Scene" section and try "Seeing the Scene" or "The Emotional Storyboard." To explore relationships further, go to the "Developing Your Character" section and try "Allies: Then and Now" or "Adversaries: Then and Now."

CLASSIFIED INFORMATION

THE QUICK VERSION
Explore how character secrets can affect dramatic action

BEST TIME FOR THIS
During scene planning, writing, or revision

GREAT CHARACTERS HAVE GREAT SECRETS
How characters behave is often influenced by the secrets they bring to the dramatic action. These hidden truths can take many forms. Characters may be hiding

- who they are (I am your father: Darth Vader, *The Empire Strikes Back*)
- who someone else is (he's your brother, not your cousin: Violet, *August: Osage County*)
- what they did in the past (I forged my father's signature to get a loan: Nora, *A Doll's House*)
- what they plan to do in the future (I will run away from home and start a new life elsewhere: Tom, *The Glass Menagerie*)
- how they really feel now (I wish I were you: both Austin and Lee, *True West*)
- what they know about the world around them (the water in the town's new municipal baths is contaminated: Peter, *Enemy of the People*)

Secrets may center on something positive (I'm a superhero: Clark, *Superman*) but often have a negative aspect that explains why information is being withheld (all I really want is your money: Fay, *Loot*). Some secrets are meant to protect the secret keeper (it was I who robbed the office: Levene, *Glengarry Glen Ross*). Some secrets are meant to protect someone else (I don't want you to know I'm pregnant while you're mourning the death of your child: Izzy, *Rabbit Hole*).

ABOUT THE EXERCISE
Use this exercise to uncover character secrets that could affect the dramatic action of a scene—even if those secrets are not revealed at this time. Examples are from an early scene in *The Sixth Sense* by M. Night Shyamalan, recipient in 2000 of an Academy Award nomination for Best Writing, Screenplay Written Directly for the Screen. The story centers on the relationship between a child psychologist and a disturbed eight-year-old boy who can see and talk to dead people.

Character 1—who drives most of the action—is Dr. Malcolm Crowe, in his thirties, a once-successful child psychologist who has lost confidence in his ability to help patients. Character 2 is Cole Sear, an anxious, socially isolated eight-year-old boy who suffers from possible mood disorders and communication difficulties. Their relationship: Cole is Malcolm's first patient in two years. What happens in the scene: Malcolm meets Cole and takes a first step toward gaining the frightened boy's trust.

To prepare for the exercise, choose a scene you wish to develop, identify the two most important characters in it—Characters 1 and 2—and define their relationship. Then sum up the main event of the scene as you see it now: what happens overall.

■ SCENIC CONTEXT

Define the context for the dramatic action.

1. *Setting*. The meeting between Malcolm and Cole takes place among the pews of an empty church. Define the setting for your scene.
2. *Time*. The action begins in the afternoon, after church services for the day have ended. Define when your scene takes place.
3. *Given circumstances*. It has been two years since a former child patient named Vincent Gray, now an adult, resurfaced in Malcolm's home as an armed intruder. High on drugs, he accused Malcolm of failing to help him, then shot Malcolm and killed himself. This incident left Malcolm so shaken that he has been unable to resume his practice until now. The notes that Malcolm received about the new patient, Cole, are identical to the notes he originally received about Vincent. Think about the world of your story when your scene begins. Identify any physical, psychological, social, economic, political, or spiritual circumstances that could affect the dramatic action.

■ CHARACTER 1'S SECRET

Explore what your Character 1 is hiding when the scene begins.

1. *Secret*. When he first meets Cole, Malcolm has a secret: he feels like a failure and is not sure he still has the ability to help others professionally, particularly this frightened boy. The case feels like a last chance for Malcolm to redeem himself—or utterly fail. Suppose your Character 1 had a secret that was relevant to your scene. This might be a secret you are already aware of or one you are just realizing now. Identify what your Character 1 is hiding at this time.
2. *Reason for secrecy*. Malcolm will eventually let down his guard and reveal his secret, but for now he feels compelled to keep his insecurity hidden. He might otherwise lose the boy's confidence, jeopardize the case, and ruin his last chance to save his career. Think about your

Character 1's secret. Why is he or she hiding this? Identify what's at stake.

3. *Impact.* From a dramatic storytelling perspective, the secrets of characters matter only if they influence the action. Malcolm's hidden insecurity will result in a cautious approach to his new patient. It also will motivate Malcolm's objective in the scene: to break through Cole's resistance and gain his trust—no matter what. How might your Character 1's secret influence him or her during your scene?

■ CHARACTER 2'S SECRET

Focus next on what your Character 2 may be hiding.

1. *Secret.* Cole has a secret, too. It is a hidden truth that will not be revealed until the end of the story and that will provide the final ironic twist that leaves Malcolm—and many in the audience—stunned. Cole's secret is that Malcolm is a ghost who doesn't realize he's dead. The gunshot wound inflicted by his former patient was actually fatal. Suppose your Character 2 also had a secret that was relevant to your scene. Identify what he or she is hiding at this time in the story.

2. *Reason for secrecy.* For most of the story, Cole conceals the knowledge that Malcolm is a ghost who doesn't know he's dead. In this early scene, Cole's motivation for keeping this news secret is the uncertainty of how this stranger might respond to such news and the fear that something violent could occur. What's at stake for Cole is his safety. Think about your Character 2's secret. Why is he or she hiding this? Identify what's at stake.

3. *Impact.* Cole's secret has a profound impact on him not only because Malcolm is a ghost—Cole is used to seeing dead people—but also because Malcolm is a stranger. Experience has taught the boy that strangers, whether living or dead, can be violent. His secret makes him so fearful that he refuses to speak until halfway through the scene. His secret thus sparks the scene's central conflict: Cole's mistrust of Malcolm. How might your Character 2's secret influence him or her in your scene?

■ SECRETS AND PHYSICAL LIFE

Character secrets are often rooted in the physical realm of the story. Settings, objects, and physical elements can help explain the nature of a secret, contribute to its importance, and ground it in the world of the story.

When Malcolm finds him in the church pew, Cole is playing with a set of green and beige toy soldiers. Uncommon in a church, these objects suggest that he comes to this church for reasons other than prayer. We will learn later that he views the church as a refuge from ghosts where he can relax and play. Another object gains importance after the meeting ends. As Cole leaves the church, in a move that suggests fear and need for protection, he pockets a small statue of Jesus from a table near the door.

Certain objects in the scene thus embody Cole's secret: his ability to interact with dead people who sometimes do frightening things. The same objects also suggest an arc of action in the scene, as he moves from toy soldiers at the beginning to the Jesus statue at the end. Think about the secrets of your characters. With one of these secrets in mind, identify anything physical that relates to this secret, and describe the connection.

■ SECRETS AND SUSPENSE

When characters have secrets, they may say unexpected things or act in unusual ways. Such behavior can create suspense by raising questions in the minds of the audience about what's really going on and what might happen next. When the audience asks questions and waits for answers, they are engaged in the dramatic journey.

1. *Unanswered question.* Most scenes end with at least one unanswered question that creates the need for more story. By the time the church scene ends, the odd encounter between a boy and child psychologist has stirred up a number of questions, such as *what's wrong with Cole?* and *will Malcolm be able to help him?* Think about the secrets of your characters and how they affect the dramatic action. What is the most important question that either secret might raise during the scene but not answer?

2. *Triggers.* Our questions are triggered by what we see and hear as we watch a scene. In the church scene, our curiosity may be aroused by such factors as a boy who plays alone in a church with toy soldiers, who speaks in Latin while doing so, who acts terrified and refuses to speak, and whose arms are covered with tiny cuts and bruises. Noticed by Malcolm but not mentioned, these unusual wounds may contribute most to the suspense generated. Think about the unanswered question at the end of your scene. What specific elements might trigger this question in the minds of the audience?

3. *Answer.* In some cases the question raised by a scene gets answered in the next scene or soon afterward. In other cases it doesn't get answered until much later in the story, if at all. In *The Sixth Sense*, the question *what's wrong with Cole?* gets answered about halfway through the story when he utters the now-famous line: "I see dead people." The second question—*will Malcolm be able to help him?*—doesn't get answered until the end of the story, when Cole finally reestablishes a union of trust with his mother. Think about the unanswered question at the end of your scene. What is the answer to this question? How and when, if ever, will it be revealed?

WRAP-UP

What characters don't say is sometimes more important than what they do say. Keep exploring the secrets of your characters to learn more about who they really are, what they value, and what they fear. It is often a hidden truth that explains why characters behave the way they do, especially when their actions seem inappropriate or unusual.

Related tools in *The Dramatic Writer's Companion*. To learn more about character secrets, go to the "Developing Your Character" section and try "The Secret Lives of Characters." To explore character discoveries, go to "Causing a Scene" and try "The Aha!s of the Scene."

PHRASE BOOK

THE QUICK VERSION
Identify and define key terms important to your story

BEST TIME FOR THIS
During script revision

HOW CHARACTERS TALK
The world of a story has its own language. Certain terms are indigenous to this world and reflect the shared experiences of those who live here. These words and phrases may include nicknames, slang, cultural terms, work jargon, original terms, common terms that have acquired new meaning, and other expressions related to the time period, geography, or history of this world, whether it's a remote Aran island off the coast of Ireland, a space station in a distant galaxy, or a room at the end of time.

In my play *The Roper*, which takes place in Chicago in 1876, much of the special language of the characters is drawn from historical research. A "roper" in this world is an informant paid by authorities to keep surveillance on criminals. The term refers to the title character, who is hired by the US Secret Service to infiltrate a gang of Irish immigrants engaged in counterfeiting.

A "boodle" in this world is a bundle of counterfeit bills, and a "boodle boy" is a innocent-looking youth who holds these bills out on the street while a "dealer" goes into a store and tries to use some of the phony cash to purchase goods. That dealer might be called a "shover" or "coney man," and that phony cash might be referred to as "coney" or "queer" versus real money, which would be "rhino" or "nails and putty." The process of distributing counterfeit bills at the point of sale is a "shoving tour." If the coney is particularly good, it might be described as "next to the plate."

Even if you are writing a contemporary story that takes place on your street, your characters probably have unique ways of expressing themselves, addressing each other, and recounting the events of their lives. You can deepen your understanding of your characters by listening to how they talk: what words and phrases they choose when they have something to say.

ABOUT THE EXERCISE
Use this exercise to enrich the dialogue of your script by identifying and defining any distinctive terms that your characters use during the story.

This exercise is based on the idea that when people travel to a foreign land, they often obtain a phrase book that translates local vernacular. As you step through the exercise, you will begin to create a phrase book for the foreign land of your story.

■ WORLD OF THE STORY

First, you need to identify the world in which most of the dramatic action occurs. While *The Roper* focuses on the world of nineteenth-century counterfeiting, other writers through the ages have chosen other worlds to explore, such as those of cutthroat real-estate salesmen (*Glengarry Glen Ross*), royal families (*Macbeth*), dysfunctional families (*August: Osage County*), acting classes (*Circle Mirror Transformation*), college faculties (*Oleanna*), international espionage (*Bridge of Spies*), newspaper journalism (*Spotlight*), psychotherapy (*Beyond Therapy*), brothels (*Ruined*), and more. Think about the primary social context in which your characters operate. What is the world of your story?

■ INDIGENOUS WORDS AND PHRASES

Use the following phrase-book categories to trigger ideas about the language of your characters. For each category, identify as many terms as you can. Define each within the context of your story, and write the definition as if it were an entry in a phrase book or dictionary. The definition is as important as the term itself.

1. *Nicknames*. Some characters may use pet names when they address others whom they know well. In *Waiting for Godot* by Samuel Beckett, Estragon calls Vladimir "Didi." Vladimir calls Estragon "Gogo." Nicknames may be terms of endearment or expressions of disdain. Identify any such nicknames among your characters and who uses what for whom.

2. *Positive slang*. The values of your characters may be reflected in their informal speech. Focus first on slang terms with a positive connotation in the world of your story. In *Hurlyburly* by David Rabe, "bread" meaning money is a good thing. So is "Bolivian blow," which refers to cocaine. In *Topdog/Underdog* by Suzan-Lori Parks, "boosting" is a term for theft and also viewed as good since it yields free merchandise. Define any slang terms your characters use for something they consider positive.

3. *Negative slang*. In *Of Mice and Men* by John Steinbeck, the phrase "busted a gut" means that you worked too hard. In *Bent* by Martin Sherman, "fluff" is a derogatory term for a gay man. Define any slang terms your characters use for something they consider negative.

4. *Familiar terms with unfamiliar meaning*. For most people, "Parnassus" is a sacred mountain in ancient Greece, but for George in *Who's Afraid*

of Virginia Woolf by Edward Albee, it's the house where Martha's father lives. In *Edmond* by David Mamet, the term "health club" is code for a whorehouse. Identify any common terms that have special meaning for your characters.

5. *Original terms.* Sometimes characters use original terms to communicate with each other. For the jazz musicians in *Side Man* by Warren Leight, "Club 92" refers to the 92nd Street unemployment office, where they meet to collect their unemployment checks. In *The Piano Lesson* by August Wilson, the "Ghosts of the Yellow Dog" are the spirits of men who were killed in a railroad car over the theft of a piano and now haunt the countryside seeking revenge. Define any important terms that are unique to the world of your story.

6. *Work jargon.* Many professions have a lingo that affects how people communicate, even when they're not talking about work. In *Glengarry Glen Ross* by David Mamet, the term "leads" refers to the names and contact information of people likely to buy real estate. In *Proof* by David Auburn, the term "proof" refers to a deductive argument for a mathematical statement. Define any important work jargon among your characters.

7. *Famous people.* Characters in the world of a story may devote extra attention to certain individuals whom they find interesting. These prominent figures may be heroes or villains, and their fame may be local, global, or historical. In *Lakeboat* by David Mamet, Skippy is well known on the ship because he may have been mugged during shore leave. In *The House of Yes* by Wendy MacLeod, John F. and Jacqueline Kennedy have acquired special fame for a brother and sister who do reenactments of the Dallas assassination. Identify any individuals who are famous among your characters.

8. *Famous places.* In *Macbeth* by William Shakespeare, Lady Macbeth might be puzzled if her husband asked her to join him at the Hi Ho. But in William Inge's *Picnic*, everyone in town knows that it's a popular spot to meet for Cokes. In *Lettuce & Lovage* by Peter Shaffer, the "staircase of ennoblement" is a famous staircase where the Virgin Queen of England slipped and was rescued from falling by her host John Fustian. Identify any well-known places in the world of your story.

9. *Famous events.* In my play *The Roper*, "the war" refers to the American Civil War, "the fire" refers to the Chicago Fire of 1871, and "the blight" refers to the Great Famine in Ireland from 1845 to 1852. In *Crimes of the Heart* by Beth Henley, "the funeral" refers to the funeral for the sisters' mother, who committed suicide. Identify any special ways in which your characters refer to important events from their history.

■ HOT TOPICS

To explore the language of your story another way, review the following topics. For each one, identify any special terms related to this topic in the world of your story, and define the terms. Look for new responses that are not already in your phrase book.

Friend	Good thing	Attractive person
Enemy	Bad thing	Unattractive person
Good person	Family	Love
Bad person	Money	Peace
Sex	Success	Death
Admirable trait	Failure	God
Reviled trait	Distress	

■ TOP TERMS

You've been exploring the language of your characters and how it reflects the world they inhabit. As the dramatic journey unfolds, certain terms are more important than others. You can learn more about the world of your story by thinking about the words and phrases that command the greatest attention here or get repeated most often.

In *Doubt* by John Patrick Shanley, for example, here are twenty of the most important terms in random order: *teachers, students, vigilance, secular, religious, wrongdoing, laziness, certainty, doubt, cleverness, innocence, lying, service, self-indulgence, obedience, satisfaction, evil, wine, fingernails,* and *ballpoint pens.* Without looking back at your script, list twenty of the most important words or phrases in your story. For this round, do not include proper nouns.

■ KEY FINDINGS

Review the terms you've identified and defined during the exercise. When viewed collectively, what do these words and phrases suggest about your characters and the world they inhabit? List any new insights you've gained.

WRAP-UP

Language is a fundamental element of any dramatic script and a powerful tool to reveal character and embody action. As you develop scenes, especially during revision, keep looking for opportunities to enrich the dialogue and use it to make each of your characters distinct and engaging. As you discover new terms for the world of your story, you may find it helpful to add them to the phrase book you've started.

If your story takes place in a time period or culture different from your own, you also may find it useful to keep an etymology dictionary at hand so that you can check whether terms you wish to use are appropriate for the world you're creating. A number of online etymology sites are available to make this word check quick and easy.

Related tools in *The Dramatic Writer's Companion.* **For more about dialogue, go to the "Causing a Scene" section and try any stage 3 exercise, from "Talking and Listening" to "The Bones of the Lines."**

BETTER LEFT UNSAID

THE QUICK VERSION
Explore a character's subtext during a scene

BEST TIME FOR THIS
During scene planning, writing, or revision

THE SILENT STREAM
The art of dramatic writing often lies not in the lines of dialogue that characters speak but in the silence between the lines: the realm of subtext, where unspoken thoughts and feelings bring meaning to what the characters say and motivate what they do.

Whether positive or negative, subtext can sometimes be quite different from the words under which it lies. If a woman tells her boyfriend, "I have to leave now," she may simply mean that she needs to be elsewhere. Or, depending on the subtext, she might actually mean that she feels nervous about staying here, or that she's angry about something he did, or that she thinks he's a loser, or that she wishes he would invite her to stay longer. When it offers hidden truths that can be detected through inference and interpretation, subtext can be a powerful tool to engage the audience in a scene.

ABOUT THE EXERCISE
Use this exercise to explore how subtext—unuttered thoughts and feelings—might influence the dramatic action of a scene. Examples are from an early scene in *Seminar* by Theresa Rebeck, nominated for Best Play in 2011 by both the Drama League and the Outer Critics Circle. The story centers on four young writers in New York who hire an international celebrity teacher to mentor them in an expensive private writing seminar.

Character 1—who drives most of the action—is Kate, in her thirties. Character 2 is Martin, also in his thirties. Both are aspiring but insecure writers. Their relationship: old friends and members of a writing seminar. The main event of the scene: Kate tries to throw Martin out of her apartment for being an unsupportive friend.

To prepare for the exercise, choose a scene you wish to develop, identify the two most important characters in it—Characters 1 and 2—and define their relationship. Then sum up the main event of the scene as you see it now: what happens overall.

■ SCENIC CONTEXT

Define the context for the dramatic action.

1. *Setting.* The setting for *Seminar* is Kate's nine-room apartment on the Upper West Side of Manhattan with a river view. She pays low rent for this prestigious place because it has been in her family and under rent control for years. Define the setting for your scene.

2. *Time.* The action begins just after the first session of the writing seminar that meets in Kate's apartment. Identify the setting for your scene.

3. *Given circumstances.* Four writers have each paid $5,000 to participate in a ten-week seminar with Leonard, a pompous celebrity teacher who dislikes Kate and her writing because he assumes she is wealthy. After reading only the first half of the first sentence of her short story, he trashed her writing in front of the others and implied that she is an overeducated, sexually inadequate rich white girl with a Jane Eyre obsession. Kate had been working on the story for six years. Think about the world of your story when your scene begins. Identify any physical, psychological, social, economic, political, or spiritual circumstances that could affect the dramatic action.

■ ELEMENTS OF ACTION

Define the elements of action for a character whose subtext you wish to explore.

1. *Scenic objective.* After the tongue-lashing she received from Leonard, Kate wants Martin's reassurance her that she really is a good writer. Think about what your character wants from whoever else is present. What is the character's scenic objective?

2. *Conflict.* A number of obstacles will make it difficult for Kate to get the moral support she needs. One is her own insecurity about her writing talent. Another is Martin's tepid response to her short story. What obstacles will make it difficult for your character to achieve the scenic objective here and now?

3. *Motivation.* As she fishes for compliments from Martin, Kate's big dream of becoming a professional writer is at stake. What's at stake for your character?

■ SUBTEXT POSSIBILITIES

Use the following questions to explore possibilities for your character's subtext in the scene. These buried truths may rise to the surface later in the story and become text, but for now they are thoughts and feelings that the character wants to hide or avoid discussing. Answer each question in the character's voice, as if you were writing dialogue, and always reply beyond a simple yes or no. Feel free to repeat information. It may signal that something important is being uncovered.

To the character here and now

Is there something important that you are *not* saying about

- your physical state or condition, such as your age, ethnicity, health, physical habits, mental acuity, or use of medications or mood-altering drugs?
- something that you have discovered?
- something that you want to obtain or to achieve?
- your plans for the near or distant future?
- a recent development in your life that has you worried or afraid?
- an experience that has made you angry?
- an experience that has made you feel embarrassed or ashamed?
- your current living situation?
- events involving a family member or close friend?
- your love life?
- your financial status?
- a new development or change in your community?
- your political beliefs?
- your religious or spiritual beliefs?
- a significant success that you achieved in the recent or distant past?
- a significant failure or loss that you have suffered?
- your true feelings, positive or negative, about whoever else is here now?
- something you know about the other character that he or she doesn't realize?
- your true feelings about someone else whom you both know?
- a secret about someone else whom you both know?

■ MAIN SUBTEXT AND ITS IMPACT

You've been exploring what your character might think and feel but not say during a scene. From the possibilities you identified, focus now on what matters most and answer the following questions not as the character but as the writer.

1. *Main subtext.* In *Seminar* there are a number of things that Kate thinks and feels but does not say to Martin. Her main subtext is her fear that Leonard may be right: she's a failed writer with a lousy short story. Review your exercise findings and identify the most important thing that your character is *not* saying during your scene.

2. *Reason for silence.* Kate not only spent $5,000 on a writing seminar but also agreed to host it at her apartment. These facts would only add to her humiliation if her fears about her writing talent proved to be true.

Think about your character's main subtext. What is the reason for not discussing this with whoever else is here now?

3. *Impact on emotion.* Kate's unspoken feelings about her writing talent make her extremely anxious and upset. How does your character's main subtext affect him or her emotionally at any time during the scene?

4. *Impact on thought.* At first, Kate views Martin as a friend who can rescue her from the pain of Leonard's abusive critique. Then her fears gradually lead to the perception that Martin is not really a friend and that nobody likes her or her writing. How might your character's main subtext affect his or her thoughts and perceptions during the scene?

5. *Impact on behavior.* Kate's hidden angst leads her to eat comfort food obsessively, fish for compliments from Martin, and beg for his reassurances that she really is a good writer. When Martin fails to provide the support she needs, Kate attempts to throw him out her apartment. What are at least three examples of how your character's main subtext might affect his or her behavior during your scene?

WRAP-UP

As you write and revise your script, beware of dialogue that expresses everything a character thinks and feels. By articulating less and leaving room for interpretation, you are more likely to tap the talents of your actors and to engage the audience as they lean forward to read between the lines.

Related tools in *The Dramatic Writer's Companion*. To continue exploring subtext, try "The Secret Lives of Characters" in the "Developing Your Character" section and "Unspeakable Truths" in the "Causing a Scene" section.

ANATOMY OF SPEECH

THE QUICK VERSION
Revise and edit the dialogue of a scene

BEST TIME FOR THIS
After you have completed a draft

A TECHNICAL LOOK AT DIALOGUE
When starting a new scene, you are most likely focused on who will be in it and what will happen between them at this particular time in the story. Ideally, the dialogue you write will reveal important information about these characters, embody their intentions, and move the story forward by leading to a new event in the dramatic journey.

Once you know what happens in your story and are ready to revise and edit scenes, you can strengthen your script by reviewing the dialogue from a technical perspective. This is different from the approach you first used to develop the scene, and the shift in perspective may help you see your words in a new light.

ABOUT THE EXERCISE
This technical exercise can help you edit the dialogue of a scene. Use any or all of the following nine rounds of questions to identify lines that need to be clarified, condensed, or cut. The terms *line* and *speech* are used here interchangeably to mean what a character says at one time. This can be as short as one word or as long as several pages.

■ DRAMATIC QUALITY: ONE AT A TIME

During the revision process, it is important to remember that a dramatic story is more about what the characters do than about what they say. Unlike everyday conversation, dialogue is heightened language that usually embodies a character's efforts to affect someone else in an important way. This translates technically into objectives and the strategies and tactics that characters use to achieve them.

To review your dialogue, focus on one character at a time, and read only his or her lines from the beginning of the scene to the end. This isolation technique will highlight what each character is doing and can help you pinpoint problem areas. Keep these questions in mind as you evaluate the dramatic quality of each character's lines:

1. What does the character want?
2. What different strategies does the character use to achieve this objective?
3. What line of dialogue begins each new strategy? This is a line where a new topic is introduced or where the character's behavior has clearly changed.
4. Within each strategy, do the lines reflect what the character is doing now?
5. Does the character change strategies enough to keep the action from getting stale?
6. Does the character spend too much time on any single strategy, particularly one that is clearly not working?
7. Do any of the character's strategies feel underdeveloped?
8. Can any strategies be eliminated because they are redundant or unnecessary?
9. The importance of dialogue can be measured by how much it reveals about the characters and moves the story forward. What are the character's three most important speeches in the scene, and why?
10. Is the importance of these speeches clear, or do they need further development?

■ CLARITY

Suspense stems from knowledge more than lack of knowledge. To remain engaged in a story, the audience thus needs to know what's happening or at least have enough information to ask the right questions. Review the dialogue of your scene as if you were the audience hearing it for the first time.
1. Are there any lines that could be confusing to the audience?
2. Are there any critical terms within the lines that the audience might not know?
3. When a line includes a pronoun, is it clear to whom or what it refers?
4. How likely is it that the audience will understand any references to characters who are not present? To events that happened elsewhere or earlier in the story?
5. What clues, if any, need to be added to the dialogue to remind the audience of information they learned earlier or to communicate the meaning of a new reference?

■ EXPOSITION

An explanation of something that cannot be observed here and now is called *exposition*. It is an important part of dramatic storytelling, but it also can bring the dramatic action to a halt. For best results, keep exposition to a minimum, and don't reveal it until the story has raised questions that make the audience want to know what they're missing.

Identify any expositional speeches in your scene. These are lines that refer to offstage characters, past events, or the inner world of the speaker. They are often written in the past tense and tend to be long. Answer these questions for each expositional speech:

1. What is the character's reason for revealing this information now? If the purpose is only to explain, how can you change the character's intention so that he or she is trying to affect the other character in an important way?
2. Exposition feels talky in the absence of conflict. Look at where your expositional speeches occur. Do you need to increase the dramatic conflict here, and if so, how?
3. Think about what's at stake for whoever is revealing this information. Are the stakes high enough to justify an interruption in the here and now of the scene?
4. How much of this information does the audience really need at this time in the story? What expositional details, if any, can be eliminated?
5. Are there any important expositional details that need to be added?

■ SUBTEXT

The subtext of a scene is the unspoken flow of thoughts and feelings that underlie the dialogue and bring deeper meaning to it. A skillful dramatic writer can include enough clues in the text to enable the audience to read between the lines and infer the subtext. Dialogue can feel stilted, false, or melodramatic when characters speak "on the nose" and articulate everything they think and feel. Often the deepest truths are better left to the silent realm of subtext.

1. Look for lines that directly express a character's feelings, such as "I'm really mad at you." Would any work better as subtext so that the emotion can be shown, not explained?
2. Look for lines that state important character conclusions, such as "You don't love me anymore." Would any work better as subtext so that the audience has to infer the character's thoughts and thus become more actively engaged in the action?
3. Are there are thematic ideas or author's messages that would be more powerful if they were dramatized rather than explained?

■ UNNECESSARY DIALOGUE

Ideally, each line of dialogue is essential because it not only reveals important information about the characters but also moves the story forward. If any lines can be cut without significantly affecting the dramatic action, they probably need to go.

1. Can any lines be eliminated because they repeat what has already been said?
2. Are there filler lines—such as "What?," "What do you mean?," or "Really?"—that can be cut because they don't advance the action?
3. Are there segues—such as "Let me tell you a story" or "Then what happened?"—that can be cut because they do nothing but needlessly announce another speech?
4. Can any lines be rendered unnecessary via translation into nonverbal terms—such as an object, physical action, or visual image—that show, not tell, the story?
5. Are all of the references to offstage characters or events really necessary?
6. Do any lines exist mainly because you are impressed with their brilliance? Such "darlings" need to go if they don't advance the story.
7. Are there any filler words within the lines—such as "well," "so," or "at any rate"—that can be eliminated because they just take up space?

■ INAPPROPRIATE DIALOGUE

The dramatic voices of characters reflect who they are, where they live, and when they live there. At any given time, their speech also reflects their current needs, physical and emotional states, and relationship to whoever else is present. Review your dialogue for any lines that feel inappropriate for your characters in this particular situation.

1. Does each character's dramatic voice feel consistent with his or her voice in the rest of the story? If not, is there a dramatic reason for the difference?
2. Does the character's language fit his or her age, educational level, and upbringing?
3. Are there any technical, slang, ethnic, or other terms that these characters would not know or use or that don't fit this geographical region or period in history?
4. If there is poetic language, does it fit the character speaking it?
5. Would the dialogue benefit from more poetic language?
6. Does the dialogue match the emotional tempo of the scene? If the situation is tense, for example, does the pace of the dialogue reflect that?

■ MONOLOGUES

A monologue is a prolonged speech in which a character speaks inwardly or addresses another character, the audience, or the universe. Monologues offer the opportunity to reveal a character's inner world but can intrude on the action if they are overused or if their purpose is only to explain something for the benefit of the audience. As with most dialogue, monologues tend to work best when they are driven by objectives and rich in word imagery. If there are any monologues in the scene, consider these questions:

1. Does the character have a clear reason to speak at length now? Is this reason strong enough to carry the weight of the words?
2. How clear is the speaker's intent?
3. Is the monologue about one thing, or does it ramble on without a clear focus?
4. What is at stake during the monologue? Can the stakes be any higher?
5. Does the speaker experience anything new here and now, such as a discovery or change of emotion?
6. If the monologue is written in the past tense, can it be changed to the present tense to make it more dynamic?
7. If other characters are present, does it make sense that they would remain silent and allow the speaker to go on at length?
8. Why is this a monologue and not an exchange of dialogue between characters?
9. Are there any lines that can be cut or condensed without weakening the monologue's purpose or impact?
10. What is the most important line in the monologue, and why?
11. Do you see any opportunities to heighten the impact of the monologue through word imagery?
12. Beyond the words spoken, what new information is revealed about the speaker?
13. Why is this monologue essential to the scene?

■ OVERUSED SPEECH PATTERNS

Characters have distinct ways of expressing themselves and, in some cases, may repeat certain linguistic idiosyncrasies because of who they are. However, overused speech patterns can weaken a scene's dramatic impact and take up valuable space in the script.

1. Does your character ask too many questions, especially in a row? Multiple questions often indicate the presence of a foil, that is, a character who asks all the right questions so the other character can articulate everything the writer wants explained. Has anyone in your scene become a foil?
2. Do your characters use each other's name too often in direct address?
3. One character interrupting another can be dramatic, but too many interruptions can make a scene feel choppy. What interrupted dialogue, if any, can be replaced by robust lines that fuel the action rather than cut it short?

4. When characters speak back and forth in paragraphs, it usually means that the content of their lines is too complicated. Can any longer speeches be broken down into shorter ones that each express a single idea and intensify the characters' interaction?

■ LINE CONSTRUCTION

Dialogue in a play or film differs from that in fiction because it is heard rather than read and because the audience can't go back over it if something wasn't clear. Some dramatic writers test their dialogue by reading it aloud during script development.

1. Are any lines difficult to say because they are too long or too complex?
2. Might any words be misunderstood because of how they sound phonetically?
3. When a character speaks, there is usually a word or phrase that prompts the other character to reply. This cue typically occurs near the end of the line so the other character can respond without having to wait artificially for the rest of the speech to be completed. Do you see any cues that need to be moved closer to the end of a line?
4. Dialogue has a certain rhythm created by line length, word patterns, and sentence construction. Does the rhythm of your dialogue change enough to keep the scene from becoming monotonous (unless there is a dramatic reason for the monotony)?
5. Review your use of typographical elements, such as italics, caps, ellipses, and dashes. Are you relying too much on such elements to tell the actors how to say their lines?

WRAP-UP

Dialogue often seems like everyday speech but is actually a heightened version of it. As you edit your script, stay aware of the dramatic quality of the words your characters use. Keep looking for ways to clarify, condense, and cut lines until you can settle on those that are essential because without them the scene simply would not make sense.

Related tools in *The Dramatic Writer's Companion.* For other technical approaches to dialogue, go to the "Causing a Scene" section and try "Talking and Listening," "Universal Truths and Lies," or "The Bones of the Lines."

Building Your Story

Story is what happens when a character tries to accomplish something that is not only extremely important but also extremely difficult. The struggle to achieve this goal triggers a chain of events that challenges, reveals, and often changes the character. Use the exercises in this section to help you explore the roots of the dramatic journey, develop an effective throughline, and get a clear big-picture view of the story so that you can better understand what it's really about.

FACTS OF LIFE

THE QUICK VERSION
Define how the world of your story works

BEST TIME FOR THIS
During early story development

HOW THIS STORY WORKS
Since there is no successful formula for a dramatic story, writers need to set their own rules for each new story they want to tell. A key purpose of such rules is to define how the world of the characters operates. Once established, these facts of life become important guidelines during script development. They determine how things usually work in this world, what is possible here under unusual circumstances, and what is never possible under any circumstances.

The nature of a story's operating rules depends on the type of reality the writer wishes to create. If the story is realistic, the rules mirror the laws of nature. For example, if a crack cocaine addict wants to get sober, she will have a difficult time doing so because of the drug's physical and psychological effects (*Water by the Spoonful* by Quiara Alegría Hudes). When a realistic story includes events that are unusual or hard to grasp, the writer may need to do research to ensure that the story's operating rules have been correctly depicted. If a girl suffers from progenia, which makes her age more rapidly than normal, the writer needs to know how this genetic disorder can affect the body over time (*Kimberly Akimbo* by David Lindsay-Abaire).

If the story is nonrealistic, the writer dispenses with some laws of nature and creates special operating rules to replace them. These new facts of life may make it possible for a man to travel back through time to a different era (*Midnight in Paris* by Woody Allen), for a woman to be visited by her guardian angel (*Marisol* by Jose Rivera), or for the ghost of a tiger to haunt the soldier who killed it (*Bengal Tiger at the Baghdad Zoo* by Rajiv Joseph). When a world has nonrealistic elements, the writer needs to know exactly what these elements are and how they affect life here.

ABOUT THE EXERCISE
Whether your story is realistic or nonrealistic, this exercise can help you define the operating rules for the world your characters inhabit. For best results, focus on the rules that will have the greatest impact on story events.

In the final part of the exercise, "If Your Story Is Nonrealistic," examples are from *Birdman or (The Unexpected Virtue of Ignorance)* by Alejándro Gonzalez Iñárritu, Nicolas Giacobone, Alexander Dinelaris Jr., and Armando Bo. Recipient of the 2014 Academy Award for Best Writing, Original Screenplay, the film centers on the attempts of a former cinema superhero to stage a comeback by writing, directing, and starring in a Broadway play adapted from a short story by Raymond Carver. The film is notable for a cinematographic approach in which most of the action appears to unfold in one take and for a story that features distinct elements of magic realism.

■ REALISM VERSUS NONREALISM

A realistic story aims to create an illusion of real life in progress without acknowledging the audience. It typically features "slice-of-life" situations, emotional themes, everyday speech, and characters with whom we can empathize. *Glengarry Glen Ross* by David Mamet and *Bridge of Spies* by Matt Charman, Joel Coen, and Ethan Coen are both realistic dramas.

A nonrealistic story aims to create an artificial reality. It may feature unusual or otherworldly situations, intellectual themes, stylized speech, archetypal characters, and imaginative devices such as exaggeration, distortion, fragmentation, repetition, symbolism, or direct address to the audience. A story may be fully nonrealistic, as in *Waiting for Godot* by Samuel Beckett, which creates a desolate new world for its characters. Or a story may be mostly realistic but have nonrealistic elements, as in *After the Fall* by Arthur Miller, which presents emotional depictions of real-life events but includes a character who speaks to the audience and a set comprised of platforms without walls or furniture except for a chair.

Decide how realistic your story will be, and then move to the appropriate set of questions below.

■ IF YOUR STORY IS REALISTIC

For a realistic world, it may not be necessary to devote extra time to its operating rules since they have already been established by nature. However, if the story deals with topics that are rare, complicated, or a matter of historical record, you may need to do research to ensure that you understand what the rules are.

If any topics in your story require research, gather the information you need from the resources you have available, and focus this activity around the specific questions your story raises. Then use the following steps to integrate your findings into your script.

1. Sum up your research findings as a series of bullet points.
2. Which of these findings will most influence story events? Prioritize your bullet points by numbering them in order of importance.

3. Review your numbered bullet points, and eliminate any that have little or no relevance to your story.
4. For each important finding, how much of this information does the audience really need in order to understand story events and find them credible?
5. How will your findings affect the physical, psychological, or social traits of your characters? Which characters will be most affected, and how?
6. How will your findings affect the nature or sequence of story events?
7. What findings, if any, can be translated into visual images that eliminate the need for words of explanation?
8. What findings, if any, will need to be explained in dialogue?
9. For any findings that require explanation, who will deliver the information to whom? What will be the reason for doing so?
10. Review the findings that you wish to integrate into your script. Can you further condense any of this information without weakening its purpose for being there?

■ IF YOUR STORY IS NONREALISTIC

If you wish to create a world for your story that is artificial, whether in whole or in part, it is important to define the facts of life for this new reality. The world of *Birdman* is governed by special operating rules that reflect the increasingly nonrealistic perceptions of the main character, Riggan Thomson, as he succumbs to madness. For example:

- Riggan has the ability to levitate. When meditating in his dressing room, he can assume a lotus position two feet above the floor.
- A gravelly disembodied voice can speak to Riggan but not be heard by anyone else. This is the voice of Birdman, the superhero he once played in the movies.
- Birdman can address Riggan as "you" or "we." The "you" highlights Riggan's separation from the superhero and is meant to make him feel like a failure. The "we" highlights their unity and is meant to make him feel powerful and loved.
- Riggan has special powers that let him move objects by pointing at them. He can telekinetically turn off a TV or send a vase of roses flying across the room.
- These telekinetic powers grow as Riggan's grasp on reality weakens. At his peak, he can make a building explode or stop a giant alien from attacking the city.
- Others in the real world cannot witness Riggan's superhero powers at work. While he sees himself telekinetically destroying everything in his dressing room, his producer sees him only throwing things around.
- Birdman can evolve from a disembodied voice to a masked superhero with the ability to fly, but only Riggan can see this presence.

- A final stage of Riggan's transformation is his ability to fly like Birdman over the streets of Manhattan.

What special rules are you creating for the world of your story? Use the following questions to explore possibilities.

Nonrealistic elements

Explore the world of your story and its key nonrealistic components. For example:

1. **Human characters.** Nonrealism in a script is often the result of the characters themselves: who they are, how they appear, and what they can and cannot do. Do any of your characters have nonrealistic
   - physical traits, such as x-ray vision or hands shaped like scissors?
   - psychological traits. such as the ability to see dead people?
2. **Anthropomorphic creatures.** Do any of your characters belong to the animal, bird, fish, insect, or plant kingdom but have human traits—for example, pigs who speak and act like people?
3. **Otherworldly beings.** Some dramatic characters may be unlike anything on earth. Does your story include any
   - ethereal beings, such as ghosts or demons?
   - fantasy beings, such as vampires or werewolves?
   - mythic beings, such as dragons or unicorns?
4. **Physical realm.** The nonrealism of a story may be embodied by the physical environment and what's in it. Do any settings in your story include nonrealistic
   - physical features, such as a door that leads to the afterlife or a pond that reflects visions of the future?
   - clothing or accessories, such as shoes that can transport a girl from one land to another or a cape that can make a man invisible?
   - inventions, such as a time machine or a computer that can read minds?
   - other objects, large or small, such as a piano that can arouse the souls of the dead or a ring that can endow its wearer with extraordinary strength?
   - sensory experiences, such as unearthly sounds, smells, or physical sensations?
5. **Dramatic events.** Does your story feature any nonrealistic
   - physical phenomena, such as people turning into rhinoceroses or the water of a river turning to blood?
   - miracles, such as the unexplained cure of a physical disability?
   - supernatural events, such as demonic possession or a visit from an angel?
   - intergalactic events, such as an invasion of creatures from outer space?
6. **Backstory.** The backstory is everything that has happened in the world of the characters before the opening scene. Does your backstory include

any nonrealistic characters or events—for example, an ancestor who was born from the earth or a house that was once haunted?

The rules

Once you have identified the nonrealistic elements of your story, you need to know the rules that govern them. For each element you identified, consider these questions:

1. How does this element work? Focus on both its positive and negative features, and state the key rules that govern its existence in the world of your story. For example, Riggan has telekinetic powers: he can move a physical object by pointing his finger at it.
2. What new potential does this element create in the world of the story, even if this potential is never fully realized?
3. What specific limitations does this element impose on the characters or the world they inhabit?
4. Are all of the characters aware of this element and its effects? If not, why do some characters know about it and others don't?
5. Among characters who know about this element, how do most of them perceive it? Does anyone have mistaken ideas about it, and why?
6. Whom does this element most affect, and how? If anyone is not affected, why is that?
7. When and how is this element first introduced in the story? Is it established early enough for the audience to accept it as credible?
8. Whether the element is present from the beginning of the story or comes into existence as a result of story events, what is its primary cause?
9. Does this element change or cease to exist during the story? If so, what happens, and what causes this new development?

WRAP-UP

For any type of dramatic story, it is important to know how the world of the characters works. This is especially true when you are creating a non-realistic world with special rules. You may identify some of these new facts of life while planning the story and discover others as you write. At some point during script development, you need to settle on what the rules are, commit to your choices, and then write and revise your script with these self-imposed dictates in mind.

> **Related tools in *The Dramatic Writer's Companion*. Defining the facts of life is part of fleshing out the world of the story. To explore this world further, go to the "Building Your Story" section and try "As the World Turns."**

IN THE BEGINNING

THE QUICK VERSION
Explore ideas for how your story begins

BEST TIME FOR THIS
During early story development

FINDING THE RIGHT POINT OF ATTACK
A critical step in story development is the decision about when and how to bring the audience into the lives of the characters. This decision determines what we first see and hear in the story and thus contributes to our initial impressions of it. The moment a dramatic story begins is sometimes called the point of attack.

To find the right point of attack, you need to know how much of the story, if any, the audience should see before the inciting event: the experience that upsets the balance of the main character's life and sets a quest into motion. It is when a woman reveals to her husband that she has invited guests for cocktails in the middle of the night, or when a former drug dealer returns from prison and finds a strange man's hat in his girlfriend's bedroom.

The point of attack is often set close to the inciting event so the main character's quest can be triggered as soon as possible after the story begins. Sometimes the point of attack and inciting event are simultaneous. In *Doubt: A Parable* by John Patrick Shanley, a nun's quest to drive away a suspected pedophile priest is triggered by a sermon he delivers from the pulpit on the subject of doubt. This sermon starts the play and thus functions dramatically as both point of attack *and* inciting event.

The point of attack may occur well before the inciting event if there are things the writer wants to accomplish first. In *Hamlet* a prince's quest to avenge his father's murder is incited when his father's ghost appears to him and names the murderer. This meeting doesn't happen, however, until scene 5 so that we can first witness life in the kingdom after the king's death. Rarely does a story begin *after* the inciting event, since that would prevent the audience from witnessing a key part of the dramatic journey.

The decision about when to set the point of attack determines not only when the story begins but also when the backstory ends. The backstory is anything that happened before scene 1 that will affect the characters during the dramatic journey. In some cases, the point of attack is set early in the history of the story so there is little relevant backstory. As a result, the audience can witness all or most of the story events while they happen, as in Rajiv Joseph's *Gruesome Playground Injuries*, which starts when the characters meet in a school nurse's office at the age of eight.

In other cases, the point of attack is set late in the history of the story so that certain key events have already occurred before scene 1, as in Tracy Letts's *August: Osage County*, which begins decades after a family's web of betrayal and deceit was first spun. When events from the past play a critical role in the present, the writer must find ways to make the audience aware of them. Stories with a late point of attack often rely more on exposition—that is, explanations about what the audience cannot see for themselves.

ABOUT THE EXERCISE

Use this exercise to explore a beginning for your story. You can analyze a beginning you've already written or flesh out possibilities for a new one. Examples are from *Of Mice and Men* by John Steinbeck, recipient of the 1938 New York Drama Critics Circle Award for Best Play. The story focuses on two migrant farm workers during the Great Depression who dream of owning a farm. Originally a novella by Steinbeck, the story has been adapted twice to film—in 1938 by Eugene Solow and in 1992 by Horton Foote.

■ WHEN THE STORY BEGINS

Explore the beginning of your story in relation to the inciting event and backstory.

1. *Inciting event.* Large or small, positive or negative, the inciting event is a turning-point experience that arouses the main character's primary goal in the story.
   - Steinbeck's play focuses on the quest of George Milton, a migrant worker, to protect his mentally disabled partner, Lennie Small, from an aggressive foe. This quest is incited when they get hired at a ranch and Lennie unintentionally angers the boss's son, thus setting into motion a rivalry that will lead to murder. What is the inciting event of your story? What quest does it arouse?
   - Steinbeck begins his play the night before the inciting event, when George and Lennie are still on their way to the ranch and set up camp beside a river. When does your story begin in relation to the inciting event?
2. *Backstory.* By beginning his play the night before Lennie and George arrive at the new ranch, Steinbeck chose not to show the audience a number of earlier experiences in the history of the characters. George and Lennie have been friends since childhood and began traveling together as migrant workers after Lennie's Aunt Clara died. A key event during their travels occurred at their last job in Weed, California: they had to flee for their lives after the childlike Lennie tried to pet a

woman's dress and the locals came after him with guns. Think about when your story begins in relation to the backstory. What critical events, if any, have you chosen to keep in the past?

■ HOW THE STORY BEGINS

Flesh out the opening scene in more detail and explore why this is the best time to introduce the audience to the characters.

1. *Setting and time.* Define where and when the action takes place.
   - *Setting.* Of Mice and Men opens on a sandy bank of the Salinas River beside a stagnant stream. Surrounded by willows and blanketed with dry leaves, the area feels "sheltered and quiet." Where does your story begin?
   - *Time.* Steinbeck's play takes place during the Great Depression and begins on a Thursday night at dinnertime as the sun sets. When does your story begin?
2. *Given circumstances.* As with any scene, the opening of a story is surrounded by given circumstances that influence character behavior.
   - *Physical circumstances.* George is a small man. Lennie is a large man who doesn't know his own strength. Their campsite is a quarter mile from the ranch where they hope to get jobs in the morning. Having just walked four miles after their bus driver left them off in the wrong place, they are now tired, hungry, and thirsty. Unknown to George, Lennie has a dead mouse in his pocket. What physical circumstances are at work as your story begins?
   - *Psychological circumstances.* George is quick-minded and resourceful. Lennie is mentally disabled and has a childlike need to pet soft things, such as the dead mouse in his pocket. Both men dream of owning their own farm and raising rabbits. What psychological circumstances are at work as your story begins?
   - *Social circumstances.* Like many migrant workers of their time, George and Lennie are homeless, broke, and without families. They fight loneliness by banding together in a partnership that George rules. Because of Lennie's mental weakness and clumsy physical strength, George often has to come to his rescue. What social circumstances are at work as your story begins?
3. *Elements of action.* The first event of a story typically occurs because of certain needs, problems, and motivations that cause the characters to interact.
   - *Scenic objectives.* Knowing the trouble that Lennie can cause, George wants to convince him to keep his mouth shut when they arrive at the ranch tomorrow in search of work. Lennie wants to please George. What does each character want most in your opening scene?

- *Scenic conflict.* George wants to teach Lennie how to behave, and Lennie wants to learn, but they both have a difficult time achieving their objectives because of Lennie's impaired thinking, forgetfulness, and tendency to get distracted. What conflicts will make it hard for your characters to get what they want in scene 1?
- *Scenic motivation.* What's at stake for George is employment and thus survival. What's at stake for Lennie is George's happiness. What will motivate your characters to get what they want in scene 1? Identify what's at stake.

4. *Main event.* The main event of Steinbeck's scene is an agreement: Lennie promises to keep his mouth shut when they arrive at the ranch tomorrow and meet the boss. What is the main event of your opening scene?

5. *Grand question.* The opening scene of a dramatic story often gives the audience a sense of who and what the story will be about so that they can settle into the world of the characters and know where to put their focus. This "ticket to ride" suggests a dramatic destination ahead and often raises a grand question that the story will address. The scene between George and Lennie clearly establishes them as the characters whom we will follow and raises the question that fuels the story: how will George protect Lennie, a man who is a danger to himself? What grand question might your opening scene raise in the minds of the audience?

6. *Why now.* Of Mice and Men could have started earlier in the lives of George and Lennie—for example, when they were in Weed, where Lennie stirred up trouble by petting a woman's dress. Or the play could have started later—for example, when they first arrive at the ranch near Soledad to get new jobs. Steinbeck chose to begin his story at the riverbank between these events so that we could see how George and Lennie behave when they are alone in a safe place.

As a result, we discover character traits that will be important later, such as Lennie's simple-mindedness, his inability to control his own strength, and his fetish for petting things. We also gain the opportunity to see why these misfits have banded together. Lennie needs George for advice and protection. George needs Lennie to feel important and have a sense of purpose. In addition, the opening scene introduces their best-laid plans to own a rabbit farm, generates suspense by raising questions about how Lennie will act at the ranch tomorrow, and uses a dead mouse in Lennie's pocket to foreshadow his accidental killing of a woman whose pretty hair he will try to pet.

Think about your opening scene. Why is this the best time to bring the audience into the lives of your characters? List as many reasons as you can. Then consider these two questions:

- Does enough happen in scene 1 to engage the audience? If not, you may have started the story too soon. Is there a later point in the lives of the characters that would work better because there would be more at stake?
- Is so much happening in scene 1 that the audience may not want to get involved? If so, you may have started the story too late. Is there an earlier point in the lives of the characters that would work better because it would give the audience time to know them before their lives erupt into crisis?

■ **POINT OF ATTACK**

Once you know the first event of your story, you need to determine the moment when this event will start to unfold. In other words, you need to find the exact point of attack not only for this opening scene but also for your whole story.

1. *Opening image.* Ranch dogs bark in the distance, and a flock of startled quails flies off with the sound of beating wings as George and Lennie arrive at the secluded riverbank in single file. Both are carrying blanket rolls, which they throw down in exhaustion. Lennie then falls down and, snorting, begins to drink from the river. What is the opening image or action of your story?

2. *Opening line.* Seeing that the stream looks stagnant, George begins the play's dialogue with a scolding: "Lennie, for God's sake, don't drink so much." When Lennie fails to respond, George shakes him and adds: "Lennie, you hear me! You gonna be sick like you was last night." The first words of the story thus suggest George's role as Lennie's caretaker. The reference to Lennie's earlier illness implies that this role is a challenging one. What is the opening line of your story? What do these words reveal?

3. *Opening beat.* A beat is the smallest unit of dramatic action and usually centers on one topic, one behavior, or one emotion.

   - *Beat objectives.* In Steinbeck's opening beat, Lennie has a physical objective: to quench his thirst. George has a behavioral objective: to convince Lennie to stop drinking bad water. What do your characters each want in your opening beat?

   - *Beat conflict.* Lennie wants to drink water and George wants him to stop. The story's first conflict is thus created by their contradictory needs. Large or small, what is the first conflict of your story?

   - *Beat motivation.* George wants to stop Lennie from drinking the water because his health could be at risk. Lennie wants to keep drinking because he's thirsty. What motivates each of your characters to act in the opening beat?

4. *First impressions.* With Lennie drinking from a polluted stream and George scolding him, we see that Lennie doesn't know how to take care of himself and that George therefore must act as his guardian in spite of the fact that Lennie is much larger than him. Such traits imply an unbalanced but caring relationship. What first impressions do you wish to make on the audience as your story begins?

5. *Emotional impact.* The opening of Steinbeck's play might lead us to worry about a large man drinking from a polluted stream and a small man trying to stop him. What emotion do you wish to arouse in the audience as your story begins?

6. *Why now.* Scene 1 takes place at the riverbank where George and Lennie camp for the night. This scene could have begun after they had already set up camp, but Steinbeck chose to start when they first arrive. This point of attack creates the opportunity to show their discovery of the river, their different reactions to the water, and the parent-child relationship that underlies the dramatic journey. This point of attack also sets a mood for play, with barking dogs, fleeing quails, a polluted stream, and the onset of darkness suggesting that the world these migrants have entered is a dangerous one. Think about your point of attack. Why is this is the best moment to begin your opening scene and thus your whole story? List as many reasons as you can.

WRAP-UP

Steinbeck's play will end at the same riverbank with George once again faced with the task of protecting Lennie. The danger will have increased significantly, however, from polluted water to a mob that wants to lynch Lennie for accidentally killing someone. Knowing that the mob will be vicious if they find him, but also that he could unintentionally kill again, George will make the decision to euthanize his partner with the gunshot that ends the play.

Scene 1 sets up this ending by introducing the secluded riverbank as the place where Lennie should hide if he gets into trouble and by establishing George as the one who will come to his rescue. This opening also introduces the dream of a rabbit farm that George will recite in the end to distract Lennie from the gun behind him. The tragedy of George's final decision is heightened by its contrast to the warmth and camaraderie of the opening scene.

Once you know how your story ends, you may wish to revisit your decisions about how it begins. These two points—in their contrast or similarity—help define the main character's dramatic journey. How will your ending compare to your beginning? Will it be the right contrast for the story you want to tell?

Related tools in *The Dramatic Writer's Companion.* To explore other basic decisions in script development, go to the "Building Your Story" section and try "Whose Story Is It?" or "How Will the Tale Be Told?" To evaluate the first ten pages of your script, try "The Art of Grabbing" in the same section. For more about beats, go to the "Causing a Scene" section and try "Thinking in Beats."

CHARACTER ON A MISSION

THE QUICK VERSION
Explore your story as a character's quest to achieve a certain goal

BEST TIME FOR THIS
During early story development

A QUEST: SOMEBODY AFTER SOMETHING
Most dramatic stories center on a character who wants something important and faces obstacles that will make it difficult to get. This quest is usually triggered by an experience that somehow upsets the balance of the character's life. It may be a turn for the better—a soldier receives a prophecy from three witches that he will become a powerful leader (*Macbeth* by William Shakespeare)—or a turn for the worse: a scholar is diagnosed with ovarian cancer (*Wit* by Margaret Edson).

Whether positive or negative, this inciting event stirs something new in the character: a desire to restore the balance that has been upset. In *Macbeth*, as a result of the prophecy he receives, a solider embarks on a quest for power. In *Wit*, after her diagnosis of a terminal illness, a scholar embarks on a quest for human companionship.

Once this quest has been launched, it is usually what drives most of the dramatic action and makes the story happen. Such goals tend to work best dramatically when they have a specific measure of success: a certain outcome that would signal that the objective has been achieved. The soldier seeking power will know that he has achieved his goal if he can rule Scotland from the throne. The scholar seeking human companionship will know that she has achieved her goal if she can overcome her emotional repression enough to allow someone to call her "sweetheart." The story ends when the character's quest is finally achieved (happy ending) or when it reaches the point of utter failure (unhappy ending).

ABOUT THE EXERCISE
This exercise can help you explore your story as a quest driven by a character's need to achieve an important but difficult goal. For best results, use your main character. It you don't have a single protagonist, choose a principal character.

Exercise questions are addressed to the character near the beginning of the story. Answer each from the character's point of view and in the character's voice, as if you were writing dialogue. Keep in mind that these responses reflect what the character believes to be true but may not always be accurate in the world of the story.

■ INCITING EVENT

The event that incites a dramatic quest may be something that the character does or something that happens to the character. It may be a positive or negative experience. It may take the form of a decision, discovery, action, or external development.

To the character

1. What experience upsets the balance of your life and sets a quest into motion?
2. Where and when does this inciting event take place?
3. Why does this event occur?
4. Do you see this event primarily as a good thing or a bad thing? Why?
5. How does this experience affect you physically and emotionally?
6. What is the most important new belief that this event arouses in you?
7. How would you describe yourself *before* this event occurs? *After* it occurs?
8. Who else, if anyone, is affected by this event, and how?
9. Whether positive or negative, what part of this experience will you remember most, and why?

■ QUEST

The quest that results from the inciting event is a new course of action in the character's life. It thus reflects a need that might not have been aroused if the inciting event had not occurred. Because it will drive most of the story, this mission will not be easy to complete. The character will have to deal with many obstacles from many sources and will sometimes succeed and sometimes fail.

For best results, focus on a positive goal (something the character wants to acquire or achieve) rather than a negative one (something the character wants to avoid or eliminate). For example, the scholar diagnosed with a terminal illness will be most active dramatically if she focuses on finding companionship more than on avoiding pain.

To the character

1. Think about what you want to accomplish as a result of the inciting event. State your mission. This is the desire or need that will drive your quest.

2. Is your goal positive (toward something) or negative (away from something)? If the latter, how can you restate it as a positive goal that will keep you reaching out for what you want?

3. How will you know whether you have achieved your goal? Identify the specific measure of success.

4. You will need a compelling reason to deal with the obstacles standing in your way. Think about what will be gained if the quest succeeds or lost if it fails. What is at stake?

5. Are there any higher stakes at risk that you have overlooked?

6. As you set out on your mission, who is your greatest ally? Identify the individual, group, or organization most likely to help you succeed.

7. What do you like best about this ally?

8. What do you like least about this ally?

9. Who is your greatest adversary as the quest begins? Identify the individual, group, or organization most likely to oppose your efforts.

10. What do you fear most about this adversary?

11. What do you admire most about this adversary?

12. In days of yore, knights on a quest had to pass difficult tests—for example, to slay a dragon. What is a dragon that you will have to slay in order to succeed?

13. A truly difficult quest will require you to use all resources at your disposal. Some will be personal assets, such as intelligence, imagination, or charm. Others will be external, such as the key to a locked room, a rich uncle, or an in at city hall. What key resources do you expect to have available as you pursue your goal?

14. A difficult quest will expose your weaknesses. Without repeating a previous response, what shortcomings will add to the challenge of achieving your goal?

15. What will this quest require you to do that you have never done before?

16. What is the worst thing that could happen if your quest fails?

17. Think about your decision to pursue this goal. What does it reveal about your values and beliefs?

18. As you face the quest ahead, what is your biggest fear?

19. Large or small, what is the first step you will take to pursue your goal?

WRAP-UP

You've been exploring your story as a character's mission to achieve an important but difficult goal. By looking at the start of the mission from your character's perspective, you have taken an important step toward setting the story in motion and understanding the character at a deeper level. It is through this character's desire to succeed that the dramatic journey will take shape and ultimately reach its final destination.

Related tools in *The Dramatic Writer's Companion*. To explore more about your character's quest and what sets it into motion, go to the "Building Your Story" section and try "Inciting Event."

DECISION POINTS

THE QUICK VERSION
Flesh out two related character decisions

BEST TIME FOR THIS
After you are well into the story

MOMENTS OF TRUTH
A dramatic story is a series of decision points: forks in the road where characters have to choose which direction to head next. These decision points vary in significance. Some are routine matters, such as deciding what to have for lunch. Others are critical choices that affect lives—for example, deciding whom to marry. Most decisions fall somewhere between the routine and the critical.

When a character has to make a difficult decision under pressure and has high stakes hanging in the balance, superficialities tend to get stripped away and glimpses of the character's true nature come into view. Whether such choices are thoughtful or impulsive, wise or unwise, each is thus an opportunity to reveal something important about the decision maker. Each is a moment of truth.

ABOUT THE EXERCISE
This exercise can help you find new ideas for your script by exploring two important decision points in the story. You can focus on the same character for both decisions or a different character for each. Either way, look for decisions that are in some way related. Examples are from Edward Albee's play *The Goat, or Who Is Sylvia? (Notes toward a Definition of Tragedy)*. Winner of the 2002 Tony Award for Best Play and a nominee for the 2003 Pulitzer Prize for Drama, *The Goat* presents the story of a successful married architect whose life crumbles when he falls in love with a goat.

■ BIG DECISION

Characters have to make a number of big decisions in the course of a dramatic journey. If these decisions truly matter, they have an impact not only on the decision maker but also on others and the rest of the story. The main character of *The Goat* is Martin, a man in love with a goat. One of his most difficult decisions occurs in scene 1 when he must decide whether to trust his best friend, Ross, with his unusual secret.

Identify an important decision that one of your principal characters must make at any time during the story. For best results, choose a difficult decision that you wish to understand better and that could significantly affect your story's chain of events.

1. *Paths A and B*. When viewed as a fork in the road, a decision point presents the character with at least two possible courses of action. For Martin, Path A is to confess to Ross that he is in love with a goat. Path B is to continue hiding this fact. Restate your character's decision point as a fork in the road. What is Path A? What is Path B? There may be more than two forks ahead, but for now, focus on the two that matter most.

2. *Why Path A*. From Martin's perspective, Path A—to confess his love for a goat—could be a viable alternative. It might help him escape the isolation and confusion he has felt from keeping this secret for half a year. Regardless of what actually happens in your story, imagine that your character has a compelling reason to choose Path A. Why might he or she see this as a viable option?

3. *Why Path B*. From Martin's perspective, Path B—to keep his love of Sylvia secret—also could be viable. He has a wife and son whom he still loves. Revealing his secret love life could hurt them both and ruin the family. Imagine that your character also has a compelling reason to choose Path B. Why might he or she see this as viable?

4. *What's at stake*. As he struggles with his decision, Martin feels forgetful and confused. Ross describes him this way: "You act like you don't know whether you're coming or going, like you don't know where you are." What's most at stake for Martin is his sanity. What is at stake for your character at the decision point you are exploring?

5. *Path C*. Difficult decisions often present more than two options. Martin, for example, could consider Path C: to confess the affair but stop short of revealing that the "other woman" is a goat. The upside of Path C is that it would let him vent his guilt about his infidelity without looking like a freak. The downside is that he would not be dealing with the problem fully. If there were a Path C for your character's decision, what would it be? What would be its upside? Its downside?

6. *Which path*. After much beating around the bush, Martin chooses Path A: to confess his love for a goat. Which path will your character actually choose?

7. *Why now*. Since Martin has been hiding his love of Sylvia for six months, the question arises: *why now* is he suddenly wrestling with the decision to tell or not tell? The answer lies in Ross's introduction of him for a TV interview: "Three things happened to you this week, Martin. You became the youngest person ever to win the Pritzker Prize, architecture's version of the Nobel. Also this week, you were chosen to design the World City, the two hundred billion dollar dream city of the future. . . . Also, this week, you celebrated your fiftieth birthday."

It has thus been a high-pressure week for Martin, with the eyes of the world upon him and the milestone of his fiftieth birthday prompting him to reevaluate his life. Yet he finds himself in an isolated state, unable to discuss his true feelings. He is now at a breaking point. Being alone with his best friend is an opportunity to relieve the pressure that has left him dazed. Think about your character's decision point. Why now? Why can't this decision be avoided or put off until later?

8. **Action**. Big decisions in a dramatic story usually lead to action. Martin's decision to reveal Sylvia's identity leads him to show Ross her photo. What important action results, now or later, from your character's decision?

9. *Expected response*. Characters make decisions based on how they expect the world to respond. In choosing to air the truth about Sylvia, Martin hopes that Ross will understand his plight and lend needed support. What does your character expect, or hope for, as a result of the path chosen?

10. *Actual response*. The world doesn't always respond in expected ways. Ross reacts to Martin's news not with understanding and support but with bewilderment and concern. What actually happens as a result of your character's decision?

11. **Who's affected**. The importance of a decision can be measured in part by whom it affects. Over time, Martin's decision will negatively affect not only himself but also his wife, son, and best friend as well as Sylvia herself. Who is affected by your character's decision, and how?

12. **Truth shown**. Martin's choice of Path A—to confess his love for a goat—is a moment of truth. It shows how desperate he has become in his isolation from other humans. It also shows how much he trusts Ross and sees him as a friend. What does your character's decision reveal about him or her?

13. *Discovery*. When Martin reveals his love for Sylvia, he does not realize how devastating the consequences will be. By the story's end, he will have lost everything—all because he told the truth. This leads him to conclude that what matters in life is not what we do but what others find out about what we do. Think about the impact of your character's decision. What will the character learn or conclude from this?

■ **RELATED DECISION**

In a dramatic story, one big decision often leads to another that must be made either by the same character or by someone else. This new decision produces consequences that, in turn, lead to another big decision, and so on, so that the key decision points in the story are linked through cause and effect and a throughline is formed. Because Martin decides to tell Ross about

Sylvia, for example, Ross must now decide whether to share this news with Martin's wife, Stevie. Think again about the consequences of your character's decision. What is another difficult decision that it will trigger for your character or for another character later in the story?

1. *Paths A and B.* Thanks to Martin's honesty, Ross finds himself facing a critical fork in the road. Path A is to honor Martin's request for secrecy and say nothing about the strange affair. Path B is to tell Stevie the truth if Martin won't. Restate your new decision as a fork in the road. What is Path A? What is Path B?

2. *Why Path A.* From Ross's perspective, Path A—to honor Martin's request for secrecy—could be a viable choice. It would further cement his relationship with Martin, who is not only a longtime friend but also an important man in the news. Regardless of what actually happens in your story, imagine that your character has a compelling reason to choose Path A. Why might he or she see this as viable?

3. *Why Path B.* From Ross's point of view, Path B—to tell Stevie what's going on—could also be a viable choice. Stevie is a close friend, too, and it would be a betrayal *not* to tell her. In addition, she might be the only one who can stop Martin from ruining his life. Imagine that your character has a compelling reason to choose Path B. Why might he or she see this as viable?

4. *What's at stake.* Ross has been a close friend of both Martin and Stevie for years. The issue of Sylvia is a threat to their marriage and the well-being of their teenage son. What is at stake for your character at this particular decision point?

5. *Path C.* Ross could consider more than two possible courses of action. Path C might be to keep Martin's secret if he agrees to end the affair now and see a psychiatrist. The upside is that it would force Martin to get professional help. The downside is that Ross would still be betraying Stevie. If there were a Path C for your character's decision, what would it be? What would be its upside? Its downside?

6. *Which path.* Ross chooses Path B: to tell Stevie what's going on because Martin won't do it himself. Which path will your character actually choose?

7. *Why now.* As the host of a TV show called *People Who Matter*, Ross values social status and public image. He knows that Martin is now in the public eye and that he would be ruined if anyone else found out about Sylvia. Think about your character's decision point. Why now? Why can't this decision be avoided or put off until later?

8. *Action.* Ross's decision leads him to write a tell-all letter to Martin's wife that begins: "Dearest Stevie, this is the hardest letter I've ever had to write . . ." These words are written offstage after scene 1 and then read aloud by Stevie to Martin during scene 2. What action results from your character's decision? When does this occur?

9. *Expected response*. In choosing to tell Stevie about Martin's strange affair, Ross hopes that she will be able to help him. Ross also expects her gratitude for being such a good friend. As he states in his letter: "I felt it my obligation to be the one to bear these tidings, as I'm sure you'd rather hear it from a dear friend." What does your character expect, or hope for, as a result of the path chosen?

10. *Actual response*. Stevie responds to Ross's letter not by getting Martin to change his ways and thanking Ross for his support, but by finding Sylvia, killing her, and dragging the carcass back to the house. What actually happens as a result of your character's decision?

11. *Who's affected*. Over time, Ross's decision will contribute to the ruin of everyone else in the story. Who is affected by your character's decision, and how?

12. *Truth shown*. Ross's choice of Path B—to tell Stevie what's going on—is a moment of truth. It shows that Ross has switched his loyalty from Martin to Stevie. It also shows that Ross has mostly washed his hands of the matter. Think about your character's decision as a moment of truth. What does it reveal about him or her?

13. *Discovery*. The impact of Ross's decision leads to his realization near the end of the story that those he once saw as friends are actually strangers capable of unthinkable acts, such as bestiality and slaughter. This prompts him to ask the haunting question "Is there anything you people don't get off on?" Think about the consequences of your character's decision. What will the character learn or conclude as a result of this?

WRAP-UP

Dramatic characters are decision makers who cause stories to happen. From the writer's perspective, each decision is an opportunity not only to move the story forward in a certain direction but also to reveal character information. Whether a decision is good or bad, for example, the choice of one alternative over another suggests what the character believes, values, and expects at this particular time. Such moments of truth become essential to the throughline when they are the result of previous story events and have consequences that affect future events. No decision of importance occurs in a vacuum.

Related tools in *The Dramatic Writer's Companion*. To flesh out the most difficult choice your main character must make, go to the "Building Your Story" section and try "Crisis Decision."

LIVING IMAGES

THE QUICK VERSION
Translate an important story development into dynamic imagery

BEST TIME FOR THIS
After you are well into the story

IMAGES THAT CAN BE WATCHED AND HEARD

Visual images on stage or on screen are different from those in a book or on canvas. They include elements, such as movement and sound, that make them dynamic. These living images can heighten dramatic action and leave lasting impressions on the audience because of the physical and emotional power they bring to the story. Such images in a production are created by a director and actors as well as the artists and technicians responsible for sets, props, costumes, makeup, lighting, sound effects, music, and other elements. All of this is set into motion by the choices the dramatic writer makes during script development.

Sometimes the writer combines stage directions and dialogue to create a memorable living image. In the opening of *Dead Man's Cell Phone*, Sarah Ruhl uses stage directions to describe the nearly empty café where her play begins. A dead man sits alone at one table with his back to the audience and his cell phone lying in front of him. A woman sits alone at another table with an empty soup bowl in front of her as she drinks coffee and writes a letter. After a moment, the man's cell phone begins to ring and ring. Not realizing he is dead, the woman becomes increasingly concerned about the phone. She finally asks, "Excuse me, are you going to get that?" The dead man doesn't respond, and the scene goes on. In the meantime, through a living image, we have been drawn into the world of a story that has just begun.

While stage directions do most of the work in the blueprint for Ruhl's image, the line of dialogue is also important because it requires the man to *not* answer his phone. The dialogue thus reinforces what the stage directions describe. Sometimes, however, dialogue does all of the work in creating a living image.

In David Mamet's *Lakeboat*, two men on a ship—an old-timer and a college student hired for the summer—are in the galley getting to know each other. The old-timer says, "I'm going to get some pie." Then he says, "You can see the bridge. You can just make it out. Like a landmark out there. You know, that is one pretty bridge. We been going under that bridge for once or twice a week since I was your age off and on, but that sure is a pretty bridge." The kid replies, "Yeah, I like it."

With no stage directions, the playwright has created the living image of an older man in a ship's galley heading toward a pie, then stopping to look out a porthole in awe, and finally drawing the younger man to gaze out as well. This dynamic, or a variation of it, must occur in order for the dialogue to make sense.

Whether a living image arises from stage directions, from dialogue, or from both, its usual purpose is to reveal something important about the characters and story, to do so in an interesting way, and to stir the audience's feelings and thoughts.

ABOUT THE EXERCISE

This exercise can help you explore possibilities for a living image that can heighten the impact of your script. For best results, focus on a critical time in the story, such as the opening scene, inciting event, end of an act, crisis, climax, other major turning point, or final scene. Look for a story development that you wish to understand better.

■ BRINGING A VISUAL IMAGE TO LIFE

Use the following steps to translate your story development into a living image. As you do this, try to work from an instinctive and emotional point of view.

1. *Color.* When you think about what's happening at this point in your story, what color speaks to you the loudest for any reason?
2. *Emotion.* Whether positive or negative, what emotion do you associate with the color you just named?
3. *Character(s).* Identify who's here now. It may be one character alone or two or more characters interacting.
4. *Setting.* Consider where you are at this point in the story, and identify the setting. Whether indoors or outdoors, familiar or unfamiliar, this place will provide a visual context for your image.
5. *Visual description.* Imagine the setting you identified. With a focus on what matters most, describe what you see.
6. *Mood.* Describe the mood, or emotional atmosphere, of this place at this time.
7. *Object.* Look for an object or physical element in this setting that could be an important part of your image. Describe what you find.
8. *Emotion.* Think about whoever is here now in relation to the setting and what's in it. What emotion do you associate with these choices? This may be the same emotion you named before or a new one.
9. *Lighting.* Whether it is day or night, your setting has a certain quality of

light that affects what it looks like and perhaps how it feels. Describe the light here now.

10. *Sounds.* If you listen carefully to your setting at this particular time in the story, you may hear sounds coming from something in the setting, from the setting itself, or from somewhere else. These sounds may be loud or quiet, pleasant or unpleasant, familiar or unfamiliar. Listen carefully and describe what you hear.

11. *Smells.* Continue to use your senses to explore the setting and describe what you smell. This smell may be strong or slight, pleasant or unpleasant, familiar or unfamiliar.

12. *Sensation.* The setting has a certain temperature, air quality, and texture. Describe how it feels here—not emotionally but physically.

13. *Music.* As an exercise that might lead to discovery, imagine that your image is accompanied by music. What do you hear? You might identify a musical genre, such as rock or jazz, or name a specific song, such as "Jingle Bells" or "Happy Birthday."

14. *Color.* You began this instinctual exploration with a color. Think about what you've learned since then. Does that color still feel like a dominant color for this image? If not, what color does?

15. *Color placement.* Keep thinking about the dominant color here. Where in the image does it reside?

16. *Apparel.* Think about who's here now, and describe what each character is wearing. This may include clothing, headwear, footwear, jewelry, or anything else that is visible on the character's body and that you find interesting enough to mention.

17. *Physical description.* Keep looking at the characters, and for each one, identify any distinguishing physical traits—for example, tall or tattooed.

18. *Action.* Describe what you see your character(s) doing. This activity may be routine or unusual, pleasant or unpleasant, relaxing or strenuous. If two or more characters are present, they may be interacting or in separate worlds.

19. *Dialogue.* Find some dialogue to bring your image to life. Identify who is speaking to whom, and write at least three lines of dialogue not in your script now.

20. *Title.* As a focusing exercise, give your living image a title that reflects what matters most.

■ **IMAGE ANALYSIS**

You've been working instinctually to find a living image that can add dramatic weight and staying power to an important moment in your story. Begin to work more analytically now as you review your findings.

1. *Summary.* Think about what you've learned so far about your living image and the details it might include. Sum up what you imagine seeing and hearing at this particular time in the story. Your image may or may not include dialogue, and for now it does not need to be written as it will appear in your script.

2. *Insights.* If your script gets produced, the audience—a group of strangers—will come to see it. Imagine them experiencing the living image you described. Right or wrong, what impressions might they gain from this image about your characters and your story? List whatever insights might come to mind.

3. *Cause.* This living image is the consequence of some action or event earlier in the world of the story. What was the primary cause of this image?

4. *Change.* What is the most important change that this image depicts?

5. *Impact.* If your image truly matters, it will have consequences. Identify the most important thing that will happen later in the story as a result of what is happening now.

■ SCRIPTWRITING

How will you actually enter your living image into your script? Use the best of what you found during the exercise to write first-draft stage directions and/or dialogue that will begin to make this image an integral part of your story .

WRAP-UP

Your script is a blueprint for what the audience will see and hear. This blueprint can suggest a living image through stage directions that spell out what should happen in production, dialogue that implies what should happen, or a combination of directions and dialogue. As you write, keep finding opportunities for the audience to experience your story so they don't they have listen to explanations about what they missed.

> **Related tools in *The Dramatic Writer's Companion*. To use visual imagery to map out a scene, go to the "Causing a Scene" section and try "Seeing the Scene." To use visual imagery to map out a story, go to the "Building Your Story" section and try "Picturing the Arc of Action."**

WHAT JUST HAPPENED?

THE QUICK VERSION
Examine different types of events in your story and explore one in more depth

BEST TIME FOR THIS
After you are well into story development

STEPS OF THE JOURNEY
Story is the series of events that occur when a character pursues an important but difficult goal. Each event is something that happens at a certain time and place in the world of this story. It may be a discovery or disclosure that someone makes. Or it may be primarily a beginning, ending, or change of some kind. Whether positive or negative, intentional or accidental, each event has two dramatic functions: to reveal new information about the characters and to move the dramatic journey forward.

ABOUT THE EXERCISE
This exercise can help you learn more about your story by identifying different types of events in the dramatic journey and then examining in more depth the one you understand least. You need to have a principal character in mind during this process. Which character will it be?

■ DIFFERENT TYPES OF DRAMATIC EVENTS
Use the following categories to identify different types of events in your character's dramatic journey. Since many can be viewed from more than one angle, you need to focus on what matters most about each event so that you can find a new response for each category. For best results, do not repeat a response you've already given.
  1. *Discovery*. Some events center on an important discovery that someone makes. These *aha!* moments may be positive or negative, accurate or inaccurate. They may be self-realizations or insights about someone else. They may relate to specific events in the world of the story or to broader aspects of humanity, nature, the universe, or beyond. For example, she realizes that she is going mad. Or he finds out that his best friend has betrayed him. Or she concludes that people are incapable of changing who they are. Identify your character's most important discovery during the story.

2. *Disclosure.* Some events center on a disclosure that someone makes to someone else or to the public. Whether positive or negative, true or false, something important is confessed or shared. This revelation might be about oneself, someone else, or something related to the world of the story. For example, she reveals that she loves him. Or he admits that he robbed the office. Or she announces that the father of her child is God. Identify a big disclosure that your character makes in the course of the story.

3. *Beginning*, Some events matter primarily because they are beginnings. The character, or someone close to the character, initiates a new course of action or adopts a new way of thinking or being. Whether positive or negative, intentional or accidental, such starting points suggest movement toward something new. For example, he enrolls in an acting class. Or she lands a job in another city. Or he and his brother get arrested for reasons they don't understand. Identify an event in your story that is important primarily because it starts something new.

4. *Ending.* Beginnings and endings often go hand in hand, but in some cases the fact that something has ended is more important than the fact that something new will begin. Such endings may be positive or negative, intentional or accidental. They suggest a movement *away from* something. For example, he is deposed from the throne. Or she stops smoking crack. Or her son gets kidnapped. Identify an event in your story that is important primarily because it ends something that once mattered.

5. *Change for the better.* Some events center on a positive change in the life of the character or someone close to the character. This change for the better might be the result of deliberate action. Or it might happen by accident or chance. Such upturns may have negative consequences later, but they are perceived as good when they first occur. For example, she wins the lottery. Or they fall in love at first sight. Or she finally agrees to accept her sister's help. Identify an event that is important because of the positive change it brings to your character's dramatic journey. Remember not to repeat a response you've already given.

6. *Change for the worse.* Some events center on a negative change in the world of the story. This change for the worse might be caused by the character or someone else. Or it might occur by accident or chance. Such downturns may have positive consequences later, but they are perceived as bad when they first occur. For example, she is diagnosed with a terminal illness. Or his pretentious sister-in-law tries to ruin his marriage. Or the city streets are invaded by foreign tanks. Identify an event that is important because of the negative change it brings to your character's journey.

■ THE EVENT YOU UNDERSTAND LEAST

Review the events you highlighted from your story. Identify the one you understand least, and then use the following steps to learn more about it.

1. *Title.* As a focusing exercise, write a title for the event that reflects what matters most—for example, "A Prophecy from Three Witches."

2. *Nature of event.* In the first round, you categorized this event primarily as a discovery, disclosure, beginning, ending, change for the better, or change for the worse. You may learn more about this event now by looking at it from other angles as well. For example, a certain "beginning" might also involve a certain "ending" and a "change for the better" and a "change for the worse" as well. Which of the other exercise categories, if any, could also apply to this event, and how? What new insights do you gain by looking at the event from one than one angle?

3. *Obvious causes.* In many cases, the causes of a dramatic event are obvious. For example, she died because she accidentally drank poison. Identify at least one obvious cause of the event you are exploring.

4. *Underlying causes.* Some events have underlying causes that may not be immediately apparent. For example, she died because her husband would not acknowledge that he had poisoned a drink that was intended for her son. Identify at least one underlying cause of your event. See if you can discover something new.

5. *Positive impact on character.* Your character may view this event initially as a good or bad experience. Either way, it can have positive consequences. What is an example of how this event affects your character in a good way now or later?

6. *Negative impact on character.* What is an example of how this event affects your character in a negative way now or later?

7. *Positive impact on someone else.* What is an example of how this event affects someone else in a good way?

8. *Negative impact on someone else.* What is an example of how this event affects someone else in a bad way?

9. *Impact on the world of the story.* The importance of a dramatic event can be measured by how much it affects the world of the story, with the most important events having the greatest and most far-reaching consequences. Whether positive or negative, what is an example of how this event could affect the world of your story? Look for an impact that encompasses more than one or two characters—for example, a family, business, neighborhood, organization, society, or even the whole world.

10. *Character strengths.* Dramatic events often expose important information about those involved. Identify any physical, psychological, or social strengths that are revealed in your character as a result of what happens.

11. *Character weaknesses*. Identify any physical, psychological, or social vulnerabilities that are revealed in your character as a result of what happens.

12. *Key consequence*. Think about how this event moves the story forward. What is the most important consequence of this event? For this final step, you may repeat a previous response or find a new one. Focus on what matters most.

WRAP-UP

A dramatic event may be something that a character does—for example, he decides to become a ballet dancer against his father's wishes. Or it might be something that happens to a character—for example, her house is destroyed in a fire. Either way, the character crosses a river of no return and ends up in uncharted territory where new resources must be tapped and new skills learned.

To understand the impact of an event and how it affects the rest of the dramatic journey, you need to know what the event entails, how it arose, why it matters, and how it differs from other events. By fleshing out each event fully, you can build a story that keeps moving forward as your characters continue to be challenged and revealed.

> **Related tools in *The Dramatic Writer's Companion*.** To learn more about a dramatic event, go to the "Building Your Story" section and try "Turning Points" or "Twelve Word Solution." To explore how story events connect, try "Step by Step," "What Happens Next," or "Picturing the Arc of Action" in the same section.

THE DRAMATIC CONTINUUM

THE QUICK VERSION
Explore how an event arises from a certain past and leads to a certain future

BEST TIME FOR THIS
After you are well into the story

THROUGHLINE: ONE THING LEADING TO ANOTHER
The lives of most dramatic characters often begin long before the opening scene and continue long after the final one. The only characters without a backstory are those who, like Frankenstein's monster, are born or created during the story. The only characters without an afterstory are those who, like Hamlet, die before the story ends.

To understand any story event is to know how the past brought each of the characters to this particular place and time. It is also to know how their actions here and now are paving the way for a certain kind of future. The events of the story thus occur not in isolation but in relation to one another. Each is part of a dramatic continuum, or throughline, that holds the story together and enables it to unfold.

ABOUT THE EXERCISE
This exercise can help you strengthen your story's throughline by exploring how the dramatic event of a scene connects to both past and future events. Examples are from a scene in act 2 of *Our Town* by Thornton Wilder. Recipient of the 1938 Pulitzer Prize for Drama, the play introduced the world to the fictional town of Grover's Corners, New Hampshire. Character 1—who drives most of the action—is George Gibbs, age seventeen, a popular small-town boy. Character 2 is Emily Webb, also age seventeen, a popular small-town girl. Their relationship: classmates who grew apart after a flirtation last year. The main event of the scene: George and Emily rekindle their romance.

Choose a scene from your script that you can use as a focal point for this story exercise. Identify the two most important characters in the scene—Characters 1 and 2—and their relationship. Then sum up the main event of the scene as you see it now.

■ THE PRESENT

Define the here and now of the scene through which you will enter the throughline of your story.

1. *Setting*. The scene between George and Emily takes place on Main Street in Grover's Corners, New Hampshire. Define where your scene takes place.
2. *Time.* It is springtime, 1904, near the end of the school year. Classes have just let out for the day, and everyone is heading home. Identify when your scene takes place.

■ THE RECENT PAST

In any story, the past includes events that happened both recently and long ago. Some of these experiences were positive, some negative. Some were things that characters did. Some were things that happened to the characters. Begin to focus on the *recent* past of your characters and how it might influence them in your scene. You can define "recent" any way you wish, from moments to days to weeks ago.
1. *Fact from the recent past*. George has just been elected president of the junior class, and Emily has just been elected secretary and treasurer. This fact from the recent past is important because it will influence their interaction on Main Street here and now. Identify a fact from the recent past that will affect your scene. This fact may pertain to any or all of those present.
2. *Character most affected*. George is the one most affected by the election victory. Which of your characters has been most affected by the experience you identified from the recent past? Focus on this character for the next few steps:
   - *Impact on self-perception.* George's election victory has boosted his self-esteem. How will your character's self-perception be affected during your scene by the fact you identified from the recent past?
   - *Perception of other character.* While harboring a secret crush on Emily for the past year, George has viewed her as unfriendly and unattainable. She still seems unfriendly, but, as a result of their election victories, they have a new common ground, which could make her more available. In your scene, how will the fact from the recent past affect your character's perception of whoever else is here.
   - *Impact on feeling.* George's success at school has made him feel more confident and less shy. In your scene, how will the fact from the recent past affect your character physically or emotionally?
   - *Impact on behavior.* Buoyed by his election victory, George will speak to Emily for the first time in a year and attempt to walk her home. He will approach this daring task by offering to carry her schoolbooks. Identify at least one thing your character will do in your scene as a result of what happened in the recent past.

■ THE DISTANT PAST

The past of the characters stretches back to the start of their lives and may thus include events that happened long ago. Whether the characters know it or not, some of these experiences may still be influencing them. Begin to focus on the *distant* past of your characters and how it might affect them during your scene. You can define "distant" any way you wish, from months to years to decades ago.

1. *Fact from the distant past.* Last year George became the star of the school baseball team. That success was a turning point in his life: he became a big fish in a small pond. At the same time, however, his friendship with Emily mysteriously ended. That falling-out from a year ago will influence their interaction now as he walks her home from school. Identify a fact from the distant past that will influence your scene, whether the characters are aware of it or not. This fact may involve any or all of those present.

2. *Character most affected.* George's baseball success had an impact on both Emily and him—it ended their friendship—but it was George who was most changed. Which of your characters has been most affected by the experience you identified from the distant past? Focus on this character for the next few steps:

   • *Positive impact.* George's baseball success boosted his popularity and set him on a path that led to his election more recently as president of the junior class. For your scene, think about who is most affected by the fact from the distant past. How has that experience affected your character in a positive way?

   • *Negative impact.* George's new popularity as star of the baseball team made him feel self-conscious and awkward in social situations—traits that others, especially the girls at school, interpreted as "conceited and stuck up." This misperception was the reason Emily stopped being friendly to him. How has the experience from the distant past affected your character in a negative way?

   • *Impact on behavior.* George's loss of Emily's friendship last year affects much of what he does in the scene on Main Street. It is what triggers his scenic objective—to win her back—and makes him emotionally vulnerable when she reveals her true feelings. Identify at least one thing your character will do in your scene as a result of what happened long ago.

■ THE NEAR FUTURE

Dramatic writers have the gift of knowing the future of their characters. This future includes events that will happen soon and events that will happen later—even after the story ends. Begin to think about the near future of your characters, how it will be shaped by the present, and how it might help you understand what needs to happen now so that the near future will make sense. The term *near future* here refers to anytime soon after the scene you are developing—for example, the next scene.

1. *Fact from the near future.* George and Emily are on Main Street trying to patch things up after a year of unhappily misunderstanding each other. This present-tense action concludes with her accepting his invitation to have an ice-cream soda at Morgan's Drugstore. But what will happen in the near future as a result of this? After spending more time together, George and Emily could discover that they no longer have much in common. Or they could instead form a deeper bond. Perhaps they will go steady. Whether positive or negative, many near futures are possible as a result of their reunion now.

   In the actual near future—the next scene in the story—George and Emily will share that ice-cream soda through two straws while awkwardly expressing their love for each other. Their connection will be so strong that George will make the decision not to go to the State Agricultural College so that he can stay here with Emily and never be apart from her again. Think about how the main event of your scene might affect the lives of any or all present. Identify an important event in the near future that will occur as a result of what happens now.

2. *Impact on the present.* The renewal of George and Emily's relationship will lead to a proclamation of love so strong that George will change the direction of his life. This near-future event dictates that in the present, as her carries her schoolbooks down Main Street, we must see that they really do care for each other in spite of their differences and that they are both trying to repair their friendship. All of this paves the way for his big decision in the next scene. Think about your near-future event and how it will reflect back on the scene you are developing now. What needs to happen in this scene so that the later event will feel truthful and logical in the world of your story?

■ THE DISTANT FUTURE

The future of your characters stretches forward to include the rest of the story and, in most cases, the afterstory, where the characters continue their lives without the audience. Any given scene may thus have important long-term effects. Unless the story ends with a *deus ex machina*—a purely coincidental event—its conclusion will be the result of everything that happened along the way. Begin to think about what lies further ahead for your characters and how the scene you are developing now might help pave for the way for that distant future.

1. *Fact from the distant future.* In the present scene, George and Emily are on Main Street trying to revive their friendship, and in the next scene

he will cement their reunion by deciding to give up college in order to stay with her. But what will happen in the distant future as a result of this? They could end up getting married and having children. Or they might discover that they can't have children. Or they might never marry for one reason or another. Many distant futures are possible as a result of their reunion now.

In the actual future, George and Emily will get married and live happily together for four years. During the delivery of their second child, however, Emily will die. She will then join the other dead citizens of Grover's Corners to watch the world of the living from a distant hilltop and to see her grieving young husband lying prostrate on her grave. Think about what happens in your scene. Identify an important event in the distant future that will occur as a result of what is happening now.

2. *Impact on the present.* In *Our Town* an innocent young love will end in tragedy while the rest of the world continues its everyday activities. This future outcome dictates that in the present, as we watch George carrying Emily's schoolbooks down Main Street, we must see that what is beginning to blossom is not only love but great love. It is the nature of this love that will make the loss of Emily so tragic that George will have no words to express his grief. The story will end with the Stage Manager drawing the curtain as George lies on his wife's grave. Think about your future event and how it will reflect back on the scene you are developing. What needs to happen in this scene so that the later outcome will feel truthful and logical in the world of your story?

WRAP-UP

The dramatic continuum is a chain of events. It is referred to as a chain because each event in it is connected to at least one other event—either as its cause or as its effect. At the same time, each event differs from the others so that something new keeps happening as the story unfolds. To build a strong throughline, keep looking at your story events in relation to one another. Know how each is not only a product of the past but also a gateway to the future.

Related tools in *The Dramatic Writer's Companion.* To use visual imagery to map out key points in your story's throughline, go to the "Building Your Story" section and try "Picturing the Arc of Action."

AN END IN SIGHT

THE QUICK VERSION
Use the end of the story to flesh out the beginning and middle

BEST TIME FOR THIS
Anytime during story development

WHEN THE ENDING IS THE BEGINNING
At some point during script development, the writer must figure out how the story will end. Some writers don't make this discovery until they reach the final pages of the script. Others like to know the ending well in advance so that they can have a specific destination in mind as they make writing choices. Their knowledge of the ending helps them figure out the sequence of events that will be necessary in order to make that final outcome understandable and credible.

Regardless of when it is crafted, the ending of the story is one of its most critical parts. The final moments often define what the dramatic journey has been about and contribute significantly to its impact on the audience. A weak ending can deflate the power of an otherwise great story, just as a strong ending can sometimes make up for flaws earlier in the script.

ABOUT THE EXERCISE
Use this exercise to flesh out your story by exploring possibilities for the ending. You may or may not already know what this conclusion will be. Either way, the exercise may lead to discoveries that can help you develop your script further.

Examples are from my play *The Roper*, which was nominated for a 2014 Joseph Jefferson Award for Best New Work. Set in Chicago in 1876 and based on actual events, the story explores what happens when a convicted horse thief is hired as an informer by the US Secret Service and assigned to infiltrate a gang of Irish counterfeiters. What he uncovers is more than he bargained for: a plot to steal the body of Abraham Lincoln and hold it for ransom from the state of Illinois.

■ KEY STORY ELEMENTS

Define the basic elements of your story.
 1. *Main character.* The main character of *The Roper* is Lewis Swegles, a
    horse thief living in nineteenth-century Chicago after being released

from prison. Describe your main character. If you have more than one protagonist, focus for now on one of them.

2. *Quest.* Every story is a quest: the pursuit of an important but difficult goal. The quest of Lewis Swegles is to do something important in his life that will be remembered after he is gone. More specifically, he wants to get his name in the newspaper for something other than stealing horses. Identify your main character's overall goal. Ideally, this is the need that drives most of the action and makes the story happen.

3. *Inciting event.* The quest is usually set into motion by an event that occurs early in the story and upsets the balance of the character's life. Whether positive or negative, this turning point is often known as the inciting event. For Swegles, it occurs in scene 1 when he is hired by the US Secret Service to be an informer, or "roper," who will work undercover in pursuit of criminals. What event sets your character's quest into motion?

4. *Reversal.* Dramatic stories usually lead to unexpected developments—some good, some bad—that turn the quest in new directions. Big changes of this nature are often known as reversals. In a two-act story, for example, the event that ends act 1 is typically a reversal that brings the characters into the new territory of act 2. A key reversal for Swegles is a discovery he makes in act 1: he learns that the gang he infiltrated is planning to kidnap Lincoln's body from the tomb in Springfield. Identify a reversal that occurs at any time during the first half of your script.

5. *Ending.* The quest will ultimately succeed, fail, or end up in a mix of success and failure. Try a few "what ifs" to explore different possibilities for your story's ending, Stay open to new possibilities—even if you already know what the ending will be.

   - *Happy ending.* If *The Roper* had a happy ending, Swegles would do something important and receive public recognition for his success. More specifically, he would help the Secret Service arrest grave robbers in the act of stealing Lincoln's body and would be hailed in the press as a hero who will be remembered for years to come. If your story had a happy ending, what would it be?

   - *Unhappy ending.* If *The Roper* had an unhappy ending, Swegles would fail to become a hero. Perhaps he would begin to identify more with the criminals than with the government agents and would secretly help the grave robbers escape. He would then lose his job as a roper and be sent back into obscurity without the legacy he had sought. If your story had an unhappy ending, what would it be?

   - *Mixed ending.* If *The Roper* had a mixed ending, Swegles would manage to do something important, such as protect Lincoln's body from harm, but, instead of being hailed as a hero, would lose his job after being unjustly accused of allowing the grave robbers to escape.

If your story had a mixed ending—a blend of success and failure—
what would it be?

■ WHAT THE ENDING REVEALS

Review the three endings you imagined for your story and choose one to
explore further, such as Swegles's mixed ending. Then answer the following
questions.

1. *Impact on character.* The ending of a story, in its contrast to the
   beginning, usually shows that the main character has undergone a
   big change—either for better or for worse. Swegles starts out with
   the hope that he can rise above his criminal past and accomplish
   something important. He ends up a failure in the eyes of the law and
   loses hope of becoming a better person. As a result, he will return to
   a life of crime and spend most of his remaining years in prison. Think
   about the ending of your story in relation to the beginning. How will
   the character change as a result of what happens?

2. *Impact on a key relationship.* The changes that a character experiences
   often affect his or her relationships over the course of the story.
   Swegles's primary relationship is with Jack Hughes, one of the gang
   members whom he was assigned to watch but whom he comes to
   understand and like. In the end, Swegles must betray this friendship
   in the name of good. This ending shows that his quest for legacy is
   more important than the well-being of his closest ally. Identify your
   character's primary relationship. What new information will the
   ending of your story reveal about this relationship?

3. *Enduring truths.* Regardless of the changes that occur during a story,
   there are usually important aspects of the character that remain the
   same. These traits lie at the unshakable core of the character's true
   nature. The ending of *The Roper* shows that in spite of his efforts to
   reform himself, Swegles has a lawless bent that he cannot overcome.
   This is why he retreats to criminal activity when the world fails to
   respond the way he expected. Think again about the ending of your
   story in relation to the beginning. In what important ways will your
   character stay the same?

4. *Broader impact.* A character's dramatic journey often changes the world
   of the story or uncovers its hidden truths. Swegles tries to use the
   system to reform himself and create a legacy, but the system proves
   to be more powerful than he had imagined. Those on top, such the
   Secret Service, stay on top. Those on the bottom, such as Swegles and
   the grave robbers, stay on the bottom. In the end, the system does not
   allow him to rise above the criminal underclass. How will the world
   of your story be changed or revealed by the time the dramatic journey
   ends?

5. *Contributing character facts.* For a story's conclusion to be credible, certain character traits, qualities, and experiences need to be introduced during the dramatic journey. These facts will contribute to our understanding of how and why the story ends the way it does. A look back from the ending of *The Roper* suggests that certain facts about Swegles need to be established along the way—for example, that he has

- lived a hard life as a horse thief, one of the most hated types of criminals,
- developed a true desire to change who he is,
- felt inspired by Lincoln to want a legacy of his own,
- developed a need to win the respect of his boss, Captain Tyrell,
- maintained a strong love of money, and
- developed an increasing affinity for others who live outside of the traditional laws of society.

Think about the ending you chose to explore. Then look back through your story to see what facts about your character need to be revealed along the way. List at least six character facts that must be introduced earlier for your ending to make sense.

6. *Contributing story events.* For a story's ending to be credible, certain events need to occur during the dramatic journey. Some of these events will contribute directly to the final outcome, some indirectly. A look back from the ending of *The Roper* suggests that events like these must occur along the way:

- Swegles's boss, Tyrrell, must have a reason to suspect that Swegles has a certain affinity for the grave robbers. On the morning of the tomb break-in, for example, when Tyrrell refers to them as swine, Swegles defends their humanity, blaming poverty and social oppression for their desperation.
- Swegles must actually accomplish something good. For example, he protects Lincoln's body from harm by preventing Mullen, one of the grave robbers, from using an ax to smash open the sarcophagus and coffin.
- The grave robbers must be able to escape from the tomb due to circumstances that do not involve Swegles. It is the accidental firing of a distant Pinkerton's gun that alerts them to the hidden presence of the law.

Think again about the ending you chose to explore. Then look back through your story to see what events need to occur during the dramatic journey. List at least three events that the story must include for your ending to make sense.

7. *Theme.* A story's ending often demonstrates the themes being dramatized. In the end, Swegles has a life-changing reaction to not getting the credit he deserves for protecting Lincoln's body. This

reaction shows how much he values his reputation and demonstrates the main idea that the desire for legacy is a common human need. Think again about the ending you chose to explore. What theme does it illustrate?

WRAP-UP

Your story's ending can teach you many things about your characters and plot. Once you know the ending, you may better understand what needs to be added, clarified, or removed during the dramatic journey that leads to it. From a technical perspective, a key purpose of this journey is to pave the way for the ending so that when it finally occurs, it is a believable outcome in the world of this story.

> **Related tools in *The Dramatic Writer's Companion*. To continue exploring how story events connect, go to the "Building Your Story" section and try "Pointing and Planting." To clarify your story's subject and theme, try "What's the Big Idea?" in the same section.**

TWO CHARACTERS IN SEARCH OF A STORY

THE QUICK VERSION
Explore the arcs of action for your two most important characters

BEST TIME FOR THIS
After you are well into the story

CHARACTERS IN TRANSITION
Most dramatic characters undergo a fundamental change as a result of what happens in the story. Sometimes this is a change for the better. When we first meet Lane in *The Clean House* by Sarah Ruhl, her obsessive need for perfection has alienated her from her husband, sister, and maid. Lane thus begins her dramatic journey in isolation. By the time the story ends, she has learned to accept life's messes and, in doing so, to develop meaningful connections with those around her.

In other cases the character's transition may be a change for the worse. In *Topdog/Underdog* by Suzan-Lori Parks, Booth begins his dramatic journey in hope. He believes that he can get rich quick by playing three-card monte, win back his beautiful ex-girlfriend, and outshine his older brother. Booth's journey ends, however, in hopelessness. He has abandoned his dream of wealth, murdered both his girlfriend and his brother, and ended up alone in a seedy furnished room.

In a story driven by a single protagonist, such as Nora in *A Doll's House* by Henrik Ibsen, it is the main character's transition—or arc of action—that provides a framework for all that happens. The transitions of the other characters typically influence this journey. It is thus important for the writer to know how these various arcs of action inform and affect one another.

In a story with two or more protagonists, such as the Ranevskaya family in *The Cherry Orchard* by Anton Chekhov, it is even more important for the writer to know how the arcs of the central characters relate to one another. It is the intersections of these dramatic journeys that hold the story together as one main event.

ABOUT THE EXERCISE
Use this exercise to explore the dramatic journeys of your two most important characters: where these journeys begin and end, how they unfold, and how they affect each other. This is a focusing exercise that asks you to simplify, set priorities, and decide what matters most in each character's arc of action.

Examples are from *Hamlet* by William Shakespeare. Written over four hundred years ago, the play focuses on a young man's attempt to avenge the death of his father who, he believes, was murdered by his uncle. This quest is complicated by the fact that the uncle has since married the young man's mother and is now therefore also his stepfather. The quest is further complicated by the fact that the young man is the prince of Denmark, the murdered father was the king of Denmark, and the evil uncle/stepfather is now the reigning monarch.

To begin, identify the two characters in your story who matter most. Write down their names in order of importance—for example, Character 1 is Hamlet, prince of Denmark; Character 2 is Claudius, his uncle, stepfather, and king.

■ CHARACTER ARCS

Ideally, each of the characters you named will experience an overall transition, or arc of action, as a result of story events. You can understand each arc by identifying the starting and end points of the character's dramatic journey and then seeing how they compare. These points are not physical locations but rather states of being. For example, a character might travel from hatred to forgiveness (Nancy in *Frozen* by Bryony Lavery) or from facade to exposure (Amir in *Disgraced* by Ayad Akhtar).

Character 1. As a result of what he experiences in the story, Hamlet travels dramatically from injustice to revenge: he starts out as the son of a murdered man and ends up as the avenger of his father's death. What are the starting and end points of your Character 1's dramatic journey? Identify each point in a word of phrase.

Character 2. As Hamlet moves from injustice to revenge, Claudius also undergoes a dramatic journey, moving simultaneously from success to ruin: he starts out as a powerful king and ends up as a dead traitor. How would you define the starting and end points of your Character 2's dramatic journey?

■ STARTING POINTS

The start of each character's dramatic journey often ties to the backstory: what happened in the lives of the characters before the story begins.

Character 1. When we first meet Hamlet, something is rotten in Denmark. This state of injustice is due to such backstory facts as these:

- Hamlet's father, the king, was murdered in his sleep.
- The murderer has not been found.
- A ghost resembling the dead king has been seen wandering the castle at night.

Think about how your Character 1's dramatic journey begins. Identify at least three facts from the backstory that contribute to this starting point.

Character 2. When we first meet Claudius, he is in a position of success due to such backstory facts as these:

- He had two burning desires: to be king and to marry his brother's wife.
- He fulfilled both desires by poisoning his brother in his sleep.
- He has been perceived in the Kingdom of Denmark as a capable monarch.

Think about how your Character 2's dramatic journey begins. Identify at least three facts from the backstory that contribute to this starting point.

■ OPENING IMAGES

The beginning of a character's dramatic journey can be translated into a visual image that occurs early in the story and shows, not tells, important information about this point of departure. Early images matter because they create a first impression that can influence our perception of the character as the story unfolds.

Character 1. Hamlet's dramatic journey begins in injustice. This starting point might be depicted by an image of him in the moonlit courtyard of the castle at night, staring in horror at the ghost of the king, who addresses him while pointing to the castle tower. Translate the beginning of your Character 1's dramatic journey into a visual image that depicts something important about it. Describe what you see.

Character 2. The dramatic journey of Claudius begins in success. This starting point might be depicted by the image of Claudius in a grand room of the castle, sitting on the throne with his wife, Gertrude, beside him. He holds a letter in his hand and speaks to his courtiers, who listen with rapt attention. Translate the beginning of your Character 2's dramatic journey into an image that depicts something important about it.

■ END POINTS

The conclusion of each character's dramatic journey is the result of what has happened in its course. Whether positive or negative, the events of the story have worked together to bring the character to this final destination.

Character 1. Hamlet travels dramatically from injustice to revenge. His final destination is the result of certain major story events, such as these:

- His father's ghost appears and claims that Claudius murdered him.
- Hamlet exposes Claudius by presenting a play about murder and watching his reaction.
- Hamlet, though wounded in a duel by Laërtes, kills Claudius.

Identify at least three major story events—successes, failures, or discoveries—that contribute to your Character 1's final destination.

Character 2. Claudius moves from success to ruin. Here are three of the most important story events that lead to his final destination:

- His guilt is exposed by his victim's son, Hamlet.
- His attempt to have Hamlet killed in exile fails.
- He is slain by Hamlet and thus loses both the throne and his life.

Identify at least three major story events that contribute to your Character 2's final destination.

■ CLOSING IMAGES

The end point of a character's dramatic journey can also be translated into a visual image that shows, not tells, important information. Final images matter because they can leave an impression that stays with us after we leave the theater.

Character 1. Hamlet's dramatic journey ends in revenge. This final destination might be depicted by an image of him, wounded and bleeding, forcing the dying Claudius to drink from a poisoned cup as he lies on the floor. Translate the end of your Character 1's dramatic journey into a visual image. Look for contrast between this and the image you found for Character 1 at the start of the journey.

Character 2. Claudius's dramatic journey ends in ruin, a final destination that intersects with Hamlet's revenge and can be depicted by the same final image. As Claudius lies on the floor bleeding from the wound of a poisoned sword and being forced to drink from a poisoned cup, he could not be further from the royal stance with which he began the play. Add more dead bodies, such as those of his wife, Gertrude, and the fallen Laërtes, and the picture of ruin is complete.

Your Character 2's final destination may or may not intersect with that of Character 1. If these end points do intersect, you may already have found a final image that includes Character 2. If they do not intersect, find a telling image that depicts Character 2's final destination. Again, look for contrast between this and the image you found for Character 2 at the beginning of the journey.

■ MOST DIFFICULT DECISION

Dramatic stories show us characters at crucial decision points. These decisions tend to get more difficult and more risky as the story goes on.

Character 1. One of Hamlet's most difficult decisions occurs near the end of the play, when he must decide whether to remain in Claudius's presence and risk death or flee to safety and let his father's murder go unavenged. What is the most difficult decision your Character 1 must make? Identify at least two options the character faces.

Character 2. One of Claudius's most difficult decisions is whether to allow his wife to accidentally drink poison rather than acknowledge his wrongdoing. Think about your Character 2's most difficult decision. Identify at least two options the character faces.

■ HOW THE DRAMATIC JOURNEYS INTERSECT

The dramatic journeys of your characters most likely intersect in different ways at different times. What your Character 1 does probably affects what happens to each of the other characters in the story. At the same time, the other characters affect what happens to Character 1.

How Character 1 affects Character 2. As Hamlet moves from injustice to revenge, Claudius moves from success to ruin. Many steps of Hamlet's journey intersect with, and affect, Claudius's journey. When Hamlet exposes Claudius's guilt through the play within the play, for example, Claudius's confidence is so shaken that his kingship is put into jeopardy. This a significant development in his road to ruin. Identify a few key examples of how your Character 1's journey directly affects your Character 2.

How Character 2 affects Character 1. After he realizes that Hamlet knows the truth about the murder, Claudius uses Hamlet's accidental killing of Polonius to send him to England. This is a major obstacle in Hamlet's quest for revenge. Identify a few key examples of how your Character 2's journey directly affects your Character 1.

WRAP-UP

Your two most important characters are the ones you need to know best. Once you figure out how they begin and end the dramatic journey, you can clarify the step-by-step transition that each must experience in order for these opposite points in the story to connect in understandable ways. Keep these arcs of action in mind as you continue to develop your script, and know how each affects the other and the story overall.

Related tools in *The Dramatic Writer's Companion.* For more about character arcs, go to the "Building Your Story" section and try "Before and After." For help with outlining the steps of these transitions, try "Step by Step" in the same section.

FOUND IN TRANSLATION

THE QUICK VERSION
Learn more about your story by translating key topics into dramatic elements

BEST TIME FOR THIS
After you have completed or nearly completed a draft

DRAMATIC WRITER AS TRANSLATOR
A dramatic story addresses a number of topics as the characters interact and cause certain events to take place. The writer's challenge is to figure out how to translate this intellectual content into dramatic elements, such as character traits, behavior, and visual imagery so that the story can be shown to the audience more than explained. During this process, some topics matter more than others. One topic can be so important that it determines who the characters will be and how the dramatic journey will unfold.

ABOUT THE EXERCISE
This exercise can help you explore your story from new angles by translating some of your key topics into different types of dramatic elements. Examples are from *The Cripple of Inishmaan* by Martin McDonagh. Set in 1934 on a remote Aran island off the coast of Ireland, the story is incited by news that a famous Hollywood director is filming a documentary on a neighboring island. Among those who wish to be in the film is Billy Craven, a crippled teenager who yearns for an escape from the loneliness and boredom of his life.

This exercise asks you to associate topics and dramatic elements with characters from your story. As you do this, you may use some characters repeatedly and others not at all. To prepare, list your characters so you can see them all at a glance—for example, Billy, the village cripple; Kate and Eileen, the aunts who raised him; Helen and Bartley, other teenagers in the village; Babbybobby, a fisherman; Johnnypateenmike, the town crier; Mammy O'Dougal, Johnny's mother; and Dr. McSharry, the village doctor.

■ STORY TOPICS
McDonagh's story tackles such topics as life in the Aran Islands, being crippled, Hollywood, tuberculosis, England versus Ireland, truth, isolation, gossip, drowning, matricide, worry, and death at an early age. In random

order, list twelve topics your story addresses at any time during the dramatic journey. This will be your master list.

■ FIRST SET OF TOPICS

Of the topics listed from *The Cripple of Inishmaan*, the four that spark my interest most are life in the Aran Islands, being crippled, Hollywood, and tuberculosis. Review your master list of topics, and choose the four that seem most interesting to you now for any reason. Let this be an instinctive process, without concern for how the topics relate or compare in importance. Then copy your choices in a new short list.

1. *Objective.* My first topic is life in the Aran Islands. From Billy's perspective: "Life in the Aran islands is so fecking boring and so fecking awful that I want to go to America and become a movie star if they take cripple fellas." Match the first topic on your short list to one of your characters. Then translate the topic into something important that this character wants at any time in the story.

2. *Three actions.* My second topic is being crippled. Billy has been viewed as the village cripple all his life and has been taunted by nearly everyone around him. At various times in the story, his disability prompts him to retreat from the world of people into the realm of cows and books; to demand that others call him "Billy" instead of "Cripple Billy"; and to convince his neighbor Bobby to take him by boat to the film shoot on the next island. Translate your second topic into three important actions that one of your characters might take at any time during the story.

3. *Misinformation.* My third topic is Hollywood. Billy believes that Hollywood is a paradise where all of his problems will be solved. When he actually gets to Hollywood, however, he ends up in a squalid one-dollar rooming house with no one to care for him as he lies in bed gasping for air. Remember that characters are not always right: they can be misinformed, delusional, or deceptive. Translate your third topic into a falsehood that involves any of your characters.

4. *Stakes.* My fourth topic is tuberculosis. For Billy, this is an extremely important topic for different reasons. At first, it is a fake TB diagnosis that enables him to convince his neighbor Bobby to take him by boat to Inishmore. Later, it is a real TB diagnosis that explains why Billy is coughing up blood. Explain why any of your characters might view your fourth topic as extremely important.

■ SECOND SET OF TOPICS

Of the remaining topics listed from McDonagh's play, the next four that attract my attention are isolation, truth, drowning, and death at an early age. Review the remaining eight topics on your master list, and choose the next four that seem most interesting to you now for any reason. Then copy these into a new short list.

1. *Three character traits.* My first topic in this set is isolation. Because of his lonely life as a cripple on a remote island, Billy has become resourceful: whether he's staring at cows or reading books, he knows how to amuse himself. Isolation has also made him restless: he yearns for a new life elsewhere. In addition, isolation has made him desperate: he will do anything—tell lies, forge a doctor's letter, take advantage of others—to escape his loneliness. Match your first topic in this set to one of your characters. Then translate the topic into three of his or her defining traits.

2. *Conflict.* My second topic is truth. After his dreams of Hollywood fail and Billy ends up back on Inishmaan, he feels the need to confess his worst sin: that he faked a TB diagnosis to get Bobby's sympathy and a boat ride to the next island. Billy's confession is difficult, however, because Bobby's wife died of TB. Billy will thus have to expose himself as a heartless manipulator who preyed on Bobby's deepest vulnerability. Translate your second topic into a conflict that any of your characters must face.

3. *Double-sided fact.* My third topic is drowning. Billy's parents were thugs who tried to kill him because he was crippled but ended up drowning themselves instead. The upside of this tragedy is that it enabled Billy to be raised by two loving aunts. The downside is that many unanswered questions surround his parents' deaths. This uncertainty has left Billy feeling confused and alone in the world. Translate your third topic into a double-sided fact, past or present, about one of your characters.

4. *Visual image.* My fourth topic is death at an early age. Like his parents, Billy is likely to die before the age of twenty. His death will be due to either TB or suicide. The latter possibility leads to this visual image: Billy alone in his aunts' store, tying a burlap sack to his wrist and filling the sack with cans of peas so that he can drown himself in the sea. Translate your fourth topic into a visual image that reveals something important about any of your characters.

■ **THIRD SET OF TOPICS**

The remaining topics on the sample list are gossip, worry, England versus Ireland, and matricide. Review the last topics on your master list, and copy them in a new short list.

1. *Advice or warning.* My first topic in this set is gossip. From Johnnypateenmike, the town crier who goes from door to door announcing the news of the day, here is a piece of advice: "When you're telling your news to people, always save the best news for last

and make sure they know you are doing this so they will have to wait and listen to the other less interesting news first." Translate your first topic in this set into a bit of advice or warning that one of your characters might offer.

2. *Unusual fact.* My second topic is worry. When Billy's auntie Kate worries, she talks to stones and believes they talk back to her. This is why she keeps a large stone handy after Billy disappears from the island for two months. Translate your second topic into an unusual fact about one of your characters.

3. *Emotion.* My third topic is England versus Ireland. Helen is angry about the oppression that the Irish have suffered historically at the hands of the English. She vents her anger by giving her brother, Bartley, an "Irish history lesson" in which she represents England and he represents Ireland. She then breaks raw eggs over his head. Identify a strong emotion, positive or negative, that one of your characters associates with your third topic, and give an example of this emotion in action.

4. *Question.* My fourth topic is matricide. Johnnypateenmike has been plying his elderly mother with liquor against her doctor's orders. After she falls down a flight of stairs, he leaves her lying on the floor with a pint of porter. Such facts might lead one to wonder why Mammy O'Dougal doesn't seem to care that her son has been trying to kill her for the past sixty years. Translate your fourth topic into a question your story might raise about any of your characters.

■ MAIN TOPIC AND THEME

You've identified twelve topics your story tackles, grouped them instinctively, and translated them into character and story specifics. Review your findings now from a more analytical perspective.

1. *Three most important topics.* Of the topics listed from McDonagh's story, the three that feel most important to me are isolation, being crippled, and truth. Return to your master list of topics, and identify the three that feel most important.

2. *Main topic.* Of the three highlighted topics from McDonagh's play, the one that feels most important is truth. All of the characters are struggling with truth in some way, whether they're trying to hide it, figure out what it is, or recover from the pain it causes. What is the main topic of your story?

3. *Main theme.* Many dramatic stories center on the theme that the truth shall set you free. McDonagh's story does this as well, but with a dark side. Near the end of the story, Billy confesses that he used a fake TB diagnosis to trick Bobby into taking him to the film shoot. This confession lifts Billy from his guilt and shame but results in a beating from Bobby with a lead pipe. The implied message appears to

be that the truth shall set you free, but you'll be a bruised, bloody mess because of it. State your story's main theme. Then translate it into the story event that illustrates it best.

WRAP-UP

Drama is primarily an emotional experience but also tends to be rich in intellectual content, such as facts, ideas, opinions, insights, realizations, and other information. Know what topics you want to dramatize in your story, which matter more than others, and which matters most of all. Then keep looking for ways to translate this information into character and story specifics that the audience can experience.

> **Related tools in** *The Dramatic Writer's Companion.* **For more about the main topic and theme of your story, go to the "Building Your Story" section and try "What's the Big Idea?" or "The Forest of the Story."**

LIST IT

THE QUICK VERSION
Gain new insights about your story by listing key elements

BEST TIME FOR THIS
After you have completed or nearly completed a draft

SETTING PRIORITIES
At various times during script development, and especially after you have completed a first draft, you need to step back from the details of your story to get a clear vision of what it's all about. Knowing the big picture can help you make more informed decisions about what needs to happen in each scene. It also can be a critical guide during revisions, when you are evaluating your story and figuring out what works best, what should be developed more, and what needs to be trimmed or cut.

ABOUT THE EXERCISE
A list is a series of related items that are recorded in random order one after another. This exercise can help you use lists to explore the big picture of your story. In the end, each list will have ten items. The first half of each list will probably come more easily than the latter half, which may require you to stretch creatively in order to reach a total of ten. It is during this creative stretch that you may make the most interesting discoveries. Work instinctively to complete each list without concern for how the items on it relate or compare. If appropriate, feel free to repeat items from other lists.

Examples are from *Glengarry Glen Ross* by David Mamet. Recipient of the 1984 Pulitzer Prize for Drama, the play focuses on four ruthless real-estate salesmen in Chicago who will do anything to unload worthless land on unwitting buyers. Mamet later adapted the play to film for a 1992 release.

■ YOUR STORY AS A SERIES OF LISTS

Develop twelve numbered lists with ten items in each.

Character 1
Mamet's story centers on a group of real estate salesmen. The most important is Shelley "The Machine" Levine. Identify your Character 1.
  1. **Traits.** In random order, list ten words or phrases that describe your Character 1 at any time during the story—for example: real

estate salesman, aging, in a slump, desperate, frightened, deceitful. Remember this is a list, not a paragraph.

2. *Desires.* List ten things that your Character 1 wants at any time during the story—for example, decent customer leads, money, moral support, recognition, respect, help for his sick daughter.

3. *Deeds.* List ten things that your Character 1 does at any time during the story. Use verbs or verb phrases—for example, begs, lies, bribes, threatens, complains, robs.

Character 2

Mamet's second most important character is Roma. Identify your Character 2.

4. *Traits.* List ten words or phrases that describe your Character 2 at any time during the story—for example, top salesman, smooth-talking, ruthless, greedy, duplicitous, methodical.

5. *Desires.* List ten things that your Character 2 wants at any time during the story—for example, the Glengarry leads, sales, his name at the top of the contest board, money, respect, kickbacks.

6. *Deeds.* List ten things that your Character 2 does at any time during the story. Use verbs or verb phrases—for example, charms, persuades, manipulates, plots, deceives, sells.

Character 3

Mamet's third most important character is Williamson. Identify your Character 3.

7. *Traits.* List ten words or phrases that describe your Character 3 at any time during the story—for example, unfriendly, greedy, smart, stoical, spiteful, mistrustful.

World of story

The world of *Glengarry Glen Ross* is the Chicago real estate business in the 1980s. Define the world of your story.

8. *Physical characteristics.* A story's physical landscape includes the settings in which observable action occurs, the unseen settings in which other action occurs, the physical elements that make up these settings, and the objects that can be found there. List ten important features of your story's physical landscape—for example, real estate office, paper files containing customer leads, a contest board on the wall that shows who sold what this month, a Cadillac, Chinese restaurant, a check signed by a customer named James Lingk.

9. *Psychological characteristics.* The psychological landscape includes the collective inner world of the characters, such as their ideas, beliefs, emotions, memories, values, and ambitions. List ten important

features of your story's psychological landscape—for example, greed, anger, jealousy, success, fear of extinction, self-loathing.

10. **Social characteristics.** The social landscape includes the relationships and communities in which your characters operate as well as the rules, expectations, and power structures that govern these groups. List ten important elements of your story's social landscape—for example, real estate industry, office politics, sales contests, private lunch meetings, brotherhood of the oppressed, honor among thieves.

Big picture

A dramatic story addresses different topics as it unfolds in a series of events.

11. **Topics.** Topics in a dramatic story are dramatized through such elements as character, plot, imagery, sound, dialogue, and action. List ten topics that your story addresses—for example, capitalism, greed, success, failure, manhood, revenge.

12. **Events.** Some dramatic events are caused by the characters. Some happen by chance or by accident. List ten events that occur in your story—for example, bribing the boss, closing a sale, failing to close a sale, plotting revenge, robbing the office, getting caught in a lie.

■ LIST ANALYSIS

You have now randomly identified 120 elements of your story. Some of these elements matter more than others. Use the following steps to evaluate your findings.

- **Lists 1, 2, and 3** describe the most important character in your story. Mark the three items in each list that feel most important. Then record whatever insights occur to you now about your Character 1.
- **Lists 4, 5, and 6** describe your second most important character. Mark the three items in each list that feel most important. Then record your insights about Character 2.
- **List 7** describes your third most important character. Mark the three items in this list that feel most important. Then record your insights about Character 3.
- **Lists 8, 9, and 10** describe the world of your story. Mark the three items in each list that feel most important. Then record your insights about the world your characters inhabit.
- **Lists 11 and 12** focus on the big picture. Mark the three items in each list that feel most important. Then record your insights about the story overall.

■ MASTER LIST

Create a master list that highlights what matters most in your script.

- *Top ten elements.* Of the thirty-six items you marked in your lists, which ten are most important? In random order, copy them into a master list. These final choices will be distributed unevenly among the original lists.
- *Observations.* What are you really writing about? Review your master list, and record whatever insights occur to you now.

WRAP-UP

You have created three levels of information about your script: the dozen lists that you developed first; the entries that you marked in these lists; and, the master list. During this process, you have sorted through the many details of your script to find the ten elements that most clearly reflect the big picture of your story.

To see this big picture is to know its subject, theme, and plot and to be able to express these elements in simple terms. It is also to know how these elements work together to form one story. If the subject is love, for example, the main character may be, or may wish to be, a great lover. If the theme is that love conquers all, the character's pursuit of love will be empowering. If the plot centers on a miser who becomes generous through love, the character will embody a set of traits, experiences, and actions that work together to cause this transition.

What is the subject, theme, and plot of your story as you see it now?

> Related tools in *The Dramatic Writer's Companion.* For other approaches to the big picture of your story, go to the "Building Your Story" section and try any stage 3 exercise, such as "The Incredible Shrinking Story," "The Forest of Your Story," or "Ready, Aim, Focus."

DIFFERENT SIDES OF THE STORY

THE QUICK VERSION
Explore your story from different perspectives

BEST TIME FOR THIS
After you have completed a draft

YOU AND YOUR CHARACTERS
As a dramatic writer, you know more about the world of your story than any single character does and have the most objective view of the dramatic journey. Since your characters see story events from their individual perspectives, they may not agree with each other—or with you—about what really happens. Knowing these differences may help you gain new insights about your material.

ABOUT THE EXERCISE
Use this exercise to explore your story from different perspectives: the objective view of the writer and the subjective views of different characters. The goal is to learn more about your script by letting your characters challenge some of your conclusions about them and the dramatic journey.

Examples are from the one-act farce *A Marriage Proposal* by Anton Chekhov. First performed in St. Petersburg and Moscow in 1890 and set in the Russian countryside of the nineteenth century, the play shows what happens when a nervous landowner decides to propose marriage to his feisty neighbor. Character 1—who drives most of the story—is Ivan Vassilevitch Lomov. Character 2—the second most important character in the story—is Natalia Stepanovna.

To begin, identify the two most important characters in your story. In each round you will need to identify a third character, who may change from one round to the next and, if appropriate, may be selected from your story's offstage population.

■ SUBJECT: CHARACTER 1

Focus first on the most important character in your story.
1. *Objective view.* Lomov, age thirty-five, is an unmarried Russian landowner who is in good health but tends to be a hypochondriac. How would you objectively describe your Character 1?
2. *Character 1's view.* Lomov would describe himself as a lonely man who

is approaching middle age with several serious medical conditions that even the best of doctors have been unable to diagnose. Right or wrong, how would your Character 1 describe himself or herself?

3. *Character 2's view.* Natalia would describe Lomov as an irritating but not-bad-looking man who lives alone with a mangy, half-dead dog on the land adjacent to hers. Lomov comes from a long line of scandalmongers but is one of the few men she knows who are still single. Right or wrong, how would your Character 2 describe Character 1?

4. *Another view.* Natalia's father, Stepan Stepanovitch Chubukov. would describe Lomov as a strange, annoying scarecrow of a man who is not to be trusted. Like every member of the Lomov family, he is probably mad. Identify a third character from the world of your story. Right or wrong, how would this character describe Character 1?

■ SUBJECT: CHARACTER 2

Focus next on the second most important character in your story.

1. *Objective view.* Natalia, age twenty-five, is the lonely daughter of a Russian landowner and the only one of his children who has not yet married. She tends to be competitive and has a quick temper. How would you objectively describe your Character 2?

2. *Character 1's view.* Lomov would describe Natalia as an educated, hardworking, and not-bad-looking woman who is certainly not an ideal mate but has begun to look better as he gets older and lonelier. She does, however, have a temper that often makes her insufferable. Right or wrong, how would your Character 1 describe Character 2?

3. *Character 2's view.* Natalia would describe herself as a dutiful daughter and hardworking member of the Chubukov estate who is not afraid to get her hands dirty. She is self-conscious of the fact that, unlike her siblings, she is not married. She attributes her solitary existence to the belief that she lives in a countryside full of idiots. Right or wrong, how would your Character 2 describe himself or herself?

4. *Another view.* Chubukov would describe his daughter as a fickle young woman who should have gotten married ages ago but still lives in his house and mooches off him at a time in his life when he would rather be alone. Though he loves Natalia, he wishes she would move out and get a life. Identify a third character from the world of your story. This may or may not be the same third party you used before. Right or wrong, how would this character describe your Character 2?

■ SUBJECT: THE MAIN EVENT

Think about the most important thing that happens in your story.

1. *Objective view.* As the title suggests, the main event of Chekhov's play is a marriage proposal: Lomov and Natalia get engaged. How would you objectively describe the main event of your story?

2. *Character 1's view.* As Lomov sees it, the main event is that his heart palpitations and other medical conditions lead to such a state of confusion that he accidentally finds himself engaged to a woman who annoys him. Right or wrong, what is your Character 1's version of what really happens in the story?

3. *Character 2's view.* As Natalia sees it, the main event is that while she is distraught in the mistaken belief that Lomov has died, her father tricks her into getting engaged and has her celebrating with champagne before she can realize what's happened. Right or wrong, what is Character 2's version of what really happens?

4. *Another view.* As Chubukov sees it, the main event is that he finally unloads his last daughter and will soon have the house to himself. Identify a third character from the world of your story. Right or wrong, what is this character's version of what really happens?

■ SUBJECT: THE BACKSTORY

The backstory is what happened in the lives of the characters before the story begins.

1. *Objective view.* The Lomov and Chubukov families have lived for decades on adjacent estates that are separated by the beautiful Volovyi meadows. Through the years the families have feuded viciously over who owns the meadows. This history will trigger one of the battles between Lomov and Natalia as they try to woo each other but keep getting distracted by their own need to be right. Objectively speaking, what fact from the past will most influence what happens in the present of your story?

2. *Character 1's view.* For Lomov, the most important backstory event was his recent thirty-fifth birthday, a milestone that sparked fears of ending up alone in his old age. That birthday was what motivated him to visit the Chubukov estate today and consider marriage to a woman who does not meet his impossibly high standards. From your Character 1's perspective, right or wrong, what past experience matters most?

3. *Character 2's view.* One of the most significant events in Natalia's past was her youngest sister's marriage. As a result of it, Natalia became the only daughter still living in her father's house and developed the belief that she might be doomed to solitude. It is because of this belief that she will entertain the possibility of marrying a scoundrel and fool like Lomov. From your Character 2's perspective, right or wrong, what past experience matters most?

4. *Another view.* While the death of Chubukov's wife was a tragedy, it

made him a free man who could do whatever he pleased, were it not for the daughters who still occupied his house. Now that only one daughter remains, he will do whatever is necessary to marry her off and satisfy the desire for independence that his wife's departure aroused. From a third character's perspective, right or wrong, what past event matters most in the world of your story?

■ SUBJECT: THE AFTERSTORY

The afterstory is what happens in the lives of the characters after the story ends.

1. *Objective view.* The marriage of Lomov and Natalia will end the long-standing feud between the Lomov and Chubukov families over who owns the Volovyi meadows. Now the ownership will be legally shared by husband and wife, who will devote their time to arguing about other things. Think about the main event of your story and how it changes the world of your characters. Objectively speaking, what is the greatest consequence of this event after the story ends?

2. *Character 1's view.* As Lomov sees it, he will have a partner by his side to nurse him through the many mysterious illnesses from which he suffers. Right or wrong, what is your Character 1's vision of what will happen in the future?

3. *Character 2's view.* As Natalia sees it, she will be able to set up her own household and run an estate without her domineering father constantly telling her what to do. Right or wrong, what is your Character 2's vision of what will happen in the future?

4. *Another view.* As Chubukov sees it, he will finally have the house to himself. All of his problems will end, and he will live happily ever after. Right or wrong, what vision of the future might a third character offer for the world of your story?

WRAP-UP

This big-picture exercise is designed to help you learn more about your story's main event by looking at it from different perspectives. Knowing this outcome can help you build a more cohesive plot as you juggle details at the scenic level and try to figure out what needs to be included, step by step, in order for the main event to occur.

> Related tools in *The Dramatic Writer's Companion.* To continue exploring the big picture of your story, go to the "Building Your Story" section and try any stage 3 exercise, such as "Main Event," "Your Story as a Dog," or "Six Steps of Revision."

COMING SOON TO A THEATER NEAR YOU!

THE QUICK VERSION
Learn more about your story by imagining a marketing poster for it

BEST TIME FOR THIS
After you have completed a draft

SEEING YOUR STORY THROUGH NEW EYES
When a dramatic script goes into production, a number of other people will step in and begin to look at the story from different angles. These newcomers include the director and actors who will bring the script to life and the various other artists who will contribute their talents to the production, such as the set designer, light and sound designers, property master, and costume designer.

During writing and revision, you can learn a lot about your work by looking at it occasionally from some of these other perspectives. To see your script through the eyes of a set designer, for example, is to translate it into a physical place that reflects the lives of its inhabitants. To see your script through the eyes of a property master is to translate it into the objects that will be needed to support the dramatic action. Such translations can lead to important new insights about your characters and story.

ABOUT THE EXERCISE
In the spirit of exploring your work from a new perspective, this exercise asks you to look at your script as if you were a marketer developing specs for a theatrical poster. This is an exercise not in advertising but in dramaturgy, since you need to know your script thoroughly in order to figure out how best to promote it. Examples are from actual posters that have been created for successful plays and films.

■ CONTENT

Use the following steps to sum up the content of your script.
1. *Title.* Identify your title. If you don't have a title yet, make one up for now.
2. *Length and genre.* Define the length and genre of your script—for example, a one-act drama (*The Zoo Story*), two-act comedy (*Vanya and Sonja and Masha and Spike*), or three-act thriller (*Cape Fear*).

3. *Audience.* Your script may be geared to a general audience. Or it may appeal to a particular interest group defined by such factors as age, ethnicity, geography, history, politics, religion, sports, or lifestyle. Define the audience for your play.
4. *Sentence synopsis.* In *The Crucible* by Arthur Miller, the seventeenth-century town of Salem is terrorized by teenage girls who claim the power to expose witches. Write a one-sentence summary of your story.
5. *Paragraph synopsis. The Crucible* takes place in seventeenth-century Salem, Massachusetts, where teenage girls get caught performing a satanic ritual in the woods. Accusations of evildoing spread through the town and lead to public trials, in which the girls claim the power to identify witches among the local residents. John and Elizabeth Proctor become prey to the hysteria that has gripped the community and soon find themselves facing not only the ruin of their marriage but also the threat of being sent to the gallows. Write a paragraph summary of your story.
6. *Emotional impact.* What is the main emotion you wish to stir in the audience, such as love, laughter, anger, or fear?
7. *Point of interest.* What is the most compelling aspect of your story? This may relate to the characters, plot, social or historical significance of the material, your reason for writing the script, or your storytelling style if there is something unusual about it.
8. *Casting.* If you could cast anyone in your script, living or dead, famous or otherwise, who would star in the principal roles? Think big. Your responses may help you discover something new about your characters.
9. *Color.* Think instinctively about the power of color and your emotional associations with it. What is the dominant color of your story, and why?
10. *Poster medium.* In addition to graphics, theatrical posters use photography, art, or collage to deliver their message. Photography is often used for realism. Art and collage suggest nonrealism. Which medium feels best for your story, and why?

■ TAGLINES

A tagline is a marketing slogan, or teaser, designed to attract an audience by revealing something interesting about the characters or story.
1. *Sentence fragment(s).* Since teasers are designed to grab the audience's attention, they tend to be short. Write a tagline that sells your story in less than a sentence. For example:
   - "The true story of a real fake." (*Catch Me If You Can*)
   - "The untold story of the witches of Oz." (*Wicked*)
   - "Five criminals. One lineup. No coincidences." (*The Usual Suspects*)

2. **Sentence.** Some teasers make a statement. Write a tagline that uses a complete sentence to sell your story. For example:
   - "A lot can happen in the middle of nowhere." (*Fargo*)
   - "You don't get to 500 million friends without making a few enemies." (*The Social Network*)
   - "Some memories are best forgotten." (*Memento*)
3. **Question.** Some taglines appeal directly to the audience's curiosity. Write a tagline in the form of a question that your story will address. For example:
   - "Think politics today is as bad as it gets?" (*Julius Caesar*)
   - "How much does life weigh?" (*21 Grams*)
   - "It's 4am. Do you know where your car is?" (*Repo Man*)

■ IMAGES

While some marketing posters are simply typographical, most are dominated by an attention-getting visual image.
1. *Portrait of a character.* Describe a poster image that highlights the physical appearance or action of a principal character in your story. For example:
   - A woman in an elaborate multilayered Victorian dress, including shoulder pads and a bustle, leans against a closed door of a room, as if eavesdropping. The intense look on her face suggests both shock and interest. (*In the Next Room*)
   - Dressed in hat and coat, a man walks away with his shoulders slumped and head bowed in defeat. He carries suitcases that appear to be extremely heavy. (*Death of a Salesman*)
   - In a room darkened by venetian blinds, a woman lies on her stomach on a bed, propped up by her elbows, with her legs crossed in the air behind her as she smokes a cigarette. A gun, paperback novel, and pack of cigarettes lie on the bed in front of her. (*Pulp Fiction*)
2. *Portrait of more than one character.* Describe a poster image that reveals something interesting about two or more characters in your story. For example:
   - The rear-view mirror of a car reflects the face of a black chauffeur in the driver's seat and the face of an older white woman in the back seat. They look at each other in the mirror. (*Driving Miss Daisy*)
   - Thirteen characters, mostly family members, all face us, with the mother dominating the mix. She wears a black dress with pearls and holds a cigarette as she points at us and smiles. A white frame house rises in the background. (*August: Osage County*)
   - Two men in colorful Elizabethan attire stand side by side— one looking off and the other facing us while scratching his head. Strings rise up from both figures to a large pair of hands

manipulating them from above as if they were puppets. (*Rosencrantz and Guildenstern Are Dead*)

3. **Setting.** Describe a poster image that focuses on the setting for your story. Look for something unusual or evocative about it. For example:
   - A lonely wooden farmhouse stands in the distance under a cloudy sky surrounded by a field of tall dried grasses. The foreground reveals what lies underground: tangled roots stretching down to darkness. (*Buried Child*)
   - A Southern California ranch house faces a swimming pool at night with silhouettes of palm trees in the background. The adjacent rooms of the house are brightly lit and reflected in the water of the pool. All of this is seen through shards of broken glass. (*Other Desert Cities*)
   - The silhouette of a rain forest rises against the sky at sunset, with the edge of the sun barely visible behind the lush treetops. Darkness envelops the foreground. (*The Night of the Iguana*)

4. **Still life.** Think about the physical life of your story. Describe a poster image that focuses not on characters but on things. For example:
   - An ornate armchair with lines of Arabic writing in the print of the back and seat. Blood is splattered over the image. (*Homebody/Kabul*)
   - A close-up of a grinning skull wearing a red clown nose. (*Hamlet*)
   - An army helmet with "Born to Kill" written on it beside a peace sign and a row of bullets tucked inside the helmet's outer band. (*Full Metal Jacket*)

5. **Event.** Think about what happens in your story. Describe a poster image that depicts an important story event. For example:
   - A giant underwater shark with prominent teeth swims up from the dark ocean depths as it eyes a woman swimming alone on the sunny surface above. From this angle, the swimmer looks small and vulnerable. (*Jaws*)
   - A hand from above reaches down to grasp a smaller hand from below, as if helping to pull someone up. A list of names is faintly superimposed over the joined hands. (*Schindler's List*)
   - A soldier in heavy protective gear stands alone on barren ground. He is surrounded by improvised explosive devices (IEDs) that have been unearthed and is attempting to disarm them. (*The Hurt Locker*)

6. **Dreamscape.** Describe a poster image of something not normally seen in the everyday world. If your story is realistic, the image might serve as a metaphor for a character or story event. If your story is nonrealistic, the image might depict an important story development. For example:
   - A woman with pale white skin and dark eyes looks at us while a butterfly, wings spread, rests on her mouth, as if keeping her from speaking. The butterfly's head is a tiny skull. (*The Silence of the Lambs*)

- In the night sky, a boy in silhouette rides a bicycle past a giant full moon with a figure sitting on his front handlebars. (*E.T. the Extra-Terrestrial*)
- A woman in profile looks up at the night sky. It is filled not with stars but with isolated letters of the alphabet. (*Wit*)

■ THE POSTER

Which tagline and image would work best together to interest an audience in your story? Describe your hypothetical marketing poster now. Then answer the following questions.
- Imagine how someone unfamiliar with your script might react to this poster. What thoughts and feelings might it trigger?
- How well does this poster suit your script, and why?
- Think about what you have learned from reviewing the content of your script and exploring possible taglines and poster images. What new insights have you gained about your characters and story?

WRAP-UP

While theatrical posters for plays and films are designed to sell tickets, they also display what is most important or interesting about the work. Knowing these selling points can be a useful guide not only when you are revising your script but also when you are promoting it later to potential producers.

Related tools in *The Dramatic Writer's Companion*. Even if you are happy with your current script title, you can use the naming process to learn more about your story. Go to the "Building Your Story" section and try "What's in a Name?"

Fixing That Problem Scene

However easily your writing flows, it is inevitable that you will encounter stubborn scenes that demand extra attention. This section offers twelve sets of questions to help you tackle such scenes. These sets can be used in any order. Each concludes with examples of tools from this guide that can help you explore the topic further.

As you answer questions, trust your first instinct, keep it simple, and guess at what you don't know. Don't worry if you find yourself responding to different questions the same way. Some overlap is likely as you look at the scene from different angles. If you have trouble answering a question, skip it. This exercise is about getting unstuck—not stuck. Keep moving forward until you find a solution.

You can return to this section anytime you need extra help with a scene. Once you're familiar with the different sets of questions, you can streamline your analysis and focus only on the sets that feel relevant to the problem at hand.

■ CHARACTERS

Each scene of your story is populated by a certain combination of characters who interact and cause a dramatic event to occur. Your decision about which characters to include—and which to exclude—is a fundamental step in storytelling.

Character 1

1. Who's here now? Identify the characters in the scene.
2. Which character drives most of the action and makes the scene happen? This is Character 1 for this particular scene.
3. Is the right character driving the scene? If not, who should be Character 1 instead?
4. Character 1 in this scene may or may not also be the main character of the story. If the main character is present but not driving the scene, is there a reason for that, or should the main character be more active?

Other character(s)

5. How do the other characters rank in order of importance for this particular scene? This will be your Character 2 and, if appropriate, Character 3, Character 4, et cetera.
6. What is the relationship between Characters 1 and 2? If more than two characters are present, what relationships exist among them, and what is their relationship overall?
7. Is there any character present who does not really need to be here now? How would the scene change if this character were removed?
8. Is anyone important missing, and if so, is there a good reason for that?
9. If an important character were added to the scene, who would it be, and how would his or her presence affect the dramatic action?
10. Offstage characters can be important if they influence what happens in a scene. Who, if anyone, is the most important offstage character now, and why?
11. Are there any references to offstage characters that can be eliminated because they're not relevant to this scene? Any references that need to be added?

Related tools in this guide. To learn more about your characters, try any exercise in the "Developing Your Character" section, including "The Emotional Character," "Character Fact Sheet," or "Nothing but the Truth." To find out what characters are hiding, go to the "Causing a Scene" section and try "Classified Information."

■ TIMEFRAME AND SETTING

The dramatic action of a scene is also affected by when and where it occurs. The timeframe and setting can contribute to how the characters feel, what they want, and what they can accomplish here and now. Most scenes unfold in real time in one setting.

Timeframe
1. When does the scene take place in the lives of the characters?
2. Whether it's an ordinary day or a special occasion, why is this the best timeframe for this scene?
3. How would the dramatic action be affected if the scene happened at a different time in the lives of the characters?

Setting
4. Where does the scene take place in the world of the story?
5. Why is this the best setting for this scene?
6. How would the dramatic action be affected if the scene happened elsewhere in the world of the story?
7. Large or small, what is the most important object in this place at this time?
8. What role, if any, does this object play in the dramatic action? Could it play a more important role, and if so, how?
9. Have you overlooked opportunities to use the physical life of the scene—the setting and what's in it—to show, not tell, the story?

Related tools in this guide. To learn more about a certain setting at a certain time, go to the "Causing a Scene" section and try "The Real World" or "The Color of Drama."

■ HOW THE PAST AFFECTS THE PRESENT

Characters enter a scene with knowledge, needs, and problems that are consequences of what they have experienced in their lives up to now. Some of these experiences may have occurred earlier in the story. Others may have happened before the story begins. Knowing this past can help you gain new insights about your characters and why they behave the way they do.
1. What previous event in your story ties most directly to this scene, and how? If this is scene 1, look for the previous event in the backstory.
2. Are there any other events earlier in the story that also contribute to the main event of this scene, and if so, how?
3. Have you overlooked opportunities to use the physical, psychological, or social consequences of a past event to influence the characters in the present?
4. Experiences from long ago may still be affecting the characters now,

even if they are unaware of this influence. Do you need to dig deeper into the backstory to uncover facts from the distant past that could influence character behavior during the scene?

Related tools in this guide. To dig deeper into the backstory, go to the "Developing Your Character" section and try "Meet the Parents" or "What Is the Character Doing Now?" Or go to the "Causing a Scene" section and try "The Past Barges In."

■ GIVEN CIRCUMSTANCES AND POINT OF ATTACK

The moment a scene begins is sometimes called the point of attack. Ideally, it is a moment when something important is in progress but there is still room for conflict to build. Setting the point of attack is a key decision because it determines who is doing what as the scene begins and sets the emotional tone for the dramatic action.

Given circumstances
1. Think about the world of your story as the scene begins. Identify any physical, psychological, social, economic, political, or spiritual circumstances that could affect the dramatic action here and now.
2. Should any of these circumstances have more of an impact on the dramatic action of the scene, and if so, how?
3. How would the scene be affected if any given circumstances were changed or eliminated? If any new circumstances were added?

Point of attack
4. How does each character feel physically and emotionally when the scene begins? Are these feelings appropriate for this character in this situation, and why?
5. What is on each character's mind as the scene begins? These thoughts may be trivial or profound and may or may not relate to the dramatic action at hand.
6. What is each character doing as the scene begins?
7. Who has the first line of dialogue in the scene, and what is the line?
8. Have you found the right point of attack for this scene? How would the scene change if it began earlier in the lives of the characters? If it began later?
9. Think about what we see as the scene begins. Have you overlooked opportunities to create a compelling visual image that will engage us immediately in the action?

Related tools in this guide. To learn more about what's happening in the world of the story as the scene begins, go to the "Causing a Scene" section and try "What's New? What's Still True?," "The Emotional Onion," or "Why This? Why Now?"

■ OBJECTIVES, CONFLICT, AND MOTIVATION

Story is what happens when a character wants something important (objective), faces obstacles that will make it difficult to get (conflict), and has a compelling reason to deal with those obstacles here and now (motivation).

At the scenic level, Character 1's embodiment of these elements is what makes the scene happen. The other characters present also have certain needs, problems, and reasons to act. These dynamics often create the conflict of the scene. For example, if Character 1 wants something contrary to what Character 2 wants, and if they are equally determined to succeed, they will find themselves on a collision course that will force a dramatic event to occur.

Character 1

1. In most cases, Character 1's scenic objective is behavioral: to affect whoever else is here now. For example, Character 1 may want to make Character 2 feel good or feel bad. Or Character 1 may want to convince Character 2 of something important or to find out something important. Character 1 may occasionally have a physical objective—for example, to acquire a certain object or to complete a physical task. Using the specific terms of your story, what does your Character 1 want most in this scene?

2. Why does this scenic objective make sense for this character in this situation?

3. Suppose Character 1 wanted something else. What would the new objective be, and how would that change the scene and the story?

4. A character may enter a scene with an objective in mind or may develop this desire during the scene as a result of something that happens early on. Either way, there is a specific stimulus for the objective, such as an idea, memory, discovery, action, or event. What triggers your Character 1's scenic objective? When does this occur?

5. A character objective generates the most focused action when there is a measure of success: a certain statement, action, event, or other outcome that would let the character know that the objective has been achieved. What is the measure of success for your character in this scene?

6. What problems make it difficult for Character 1 to achieve this objective here and now? These conflicts may arise from the character's own physical or psychological limitations, from other characters with opposing needs, or from the current situation in the world of the story.

7. Have you overlooked opportunities to increase the conflict of the scene? Can you add any new problems or strengthen existing ones?

8. Remember that conflict means obstacle—anything that stands in the way of an objective—and that argument is only one form of this. Is conflict present to some degree from the beginning of the scene to its end?
9. Think about what's at stake for Character 1. Why is it important and urgent to achieve the scenic objective now? In other words, why might the character consider compromise or surrender impossible? If the character doesn't have that level of urgency, you may need to rethink the terms of the scene.

Other character(s)

10. For whoever else is present—Character 2 and, if appropriate, Character 3, Character 4, et cetera—what does he or she want most in the scene?
11. Why does this character's objective make sense at this time in the story?
12. How would the scene be different if the character's objective were changed?
13. What triggers the character's objective? When does this occur?
14. How will the character know whether or not the objective has been achieved? Define the specific measure of success.
15. What obstacles make it difficult for the characters to achieve this objective? Identify at least one significant conflict.
16. Why is it important and urgent for the character to achieve the objective here and now? Identify what's at stake.

Related tools in this guide. Any tool in the "Causing a Scene" section can help you flesh out the dramatic action of the scene. Try "Levels of Desire" to explore objectives, "Mother Conflict" to identify obstacles that make objectives hard to achieve, or "Why Did the Character Cross the Road?" to examine motivations.

■ STRATEGIES

When characters want something badly and have obstacles standing in the way, they usually have to employ a number of different strategies. Whether these efforts succeed or fail, each begins a new beat, or unit of dramatic action, that can reveal a different dimension of the character and bring variety to the action.

Like scenic objectives, strategies are usually behavioral. If a real estate agent wants to convince a coworker to rob their office, for example, he might try to put the coworker in a good mood to make him more receptive to the idea, get him angry enough about the company to want revenge, and convince him that the endeavor will be lucrative. Or the plotting agent might try all of these strategies at different times in the same scene.

Character 1

1. Think about what your Character 1 wants. What are at least three different strategies that he or she could try here and now in pursuit of this goal?
2. Using verbs to sum up your character's strategies can help you sharpen your focus on these actions so that you can see how they compare. Such verbs might identify the character's behavior literally—for example, *cheers up, angers, convinces*. Or they might reflect a more figurative approach—for example, *tickles, inflames, dazzles*. What verbs or verb phrases best sum up your Character 1's strategies in this scene?
3. Are these strategies truly distinct, or does the character keep repeating the same action? If the latter, how can you bring more variety to the scene?
4. Does Character 1 keep using a strategy after it becomes clear that it doesn't work? If so, when should the character change strategies? What should the new strategy be?

Other character(s)

5. Think about what the character wants. What are at least two different strategies that he or she might try to achieve this objective?
6. What verbs or verb phrases best sum up these strategies? As before, you can identify your character's actions literally or figuratively.
7. Have you overlooked opportunities to make these strategies more distinct or to add new strategies that make sense for this character in this situation?

Strategies in sequence

8. When pursuing an objective, characters typically begin with the strategy that feels easiest, most logical, or most timely. If this doesn't work, they may have to try increasingly difficult and risky steps. Look at each character's action plan. Does this sequence of strategies feel logical and truthful for this character in this situation?

Related tools in this guide. To explore different actions that characters might take to get what they want, go to the "Causing a Scene" section and try "The Strategics of the Scene."

■ FRENCH SCENES

A French scene is a unit of action demarcated by the entrance or exit of a character. Each time someone comes or goes, a new combination of characters occurs, and something new happens. Ideally, each French scene contributes in an essential way to the main event of the scene. Address the following questions if your scene consists of more than one French scene—that is, if someone enters after the scene has started or exits before it ends.

Entrances and exits

1. Characters may enter a scene for reasons that range from ordinary to extraordinary. What is each character's reason for being here now?
2. How would the dramatic action be affected if at least one character had a different reason for being here now?
3. For any character who exits before the scene ends, what is the reason for doing so?
4. Exits tend to work best dramatically when they are emotional. Instead of leaving to get a cup of coffee, for example, he is too angry to remain here. Or instead of leaving to go to the bathroom, she is worried about someone elsewhere. For any character who exits before the scene ends, does he or she need a stronger motivation for leaving?

Scene structure

5. How many French scenes does this scene include? What combination of characters occurs in each one?
6. Ideally, something important happens in each French scene. For example, something is accomplished or fails to be accomplished. Large or small, what event occurs in each of your French scenes? If there is no distinct event, what changes do you need to make?
7. How is each French scene essential to the main event of the scene?
8. Too many entrances and exits can make the action feel choppy. Are there any French scenes that can be combined or cut? If so, how would that change the scene?

Related tools in this guide. To explore how and why a scene divides into French scenes, go to the "Causing a Scene" section and try "The Scenes within the Scene."

■ EXPOSITION

Exposition is anything that cannot be observed by the audience and thus needs to be explained so they know what's going on. Frequent subjects for exposition include past events in the world of the story, events that are currently taking place elsewhere, characters who are not here now, and inner life, such as ideas, feelings, and memories.

Exposition is an essential part of any story but is often viewed negatively because it can bring the action to a halt. When handled well, however, exposition can be a powerful storytelling tool. It tends to work best when someone is forced to reveal the information in order to achieve an objective, when it is suggested in bits and pieces rather than articulated in long narratives, or when it answers a question that the audience has been wanting to know.

1. Flag any significant expositional passages in your scene. Common signs of exposition include long speeches that have stopped the characters from interacting; a sudden absence of conflict; several lines written in the past tense; and revelations that are offered for no purpose other than to inform or to display the character's brilliance.

2. For each expositional passage, how important is it for the characters and the audience to know this information at this time in the story, and why? Which passages are not necessary and can thus be eliminated?

3. For any critical exposition, what is the character's reason for revealing this information now? If the character is not doing it to affect someone else, you may need to rethink how and why this information is being imparted.

4. For any critical exposition, how much detail is really necessary to communicate what matters most?

5. Subtext is what the characters don't say and is often more important than what they do say. Can any exposition in this scene be converted to subtext that is inferred by how the characters appear, the emotions they display, or the actions they take?

6. Think about what the characters and audience must know at this time in the story. Do you need to add any exposition about a past experience, an offstage person or event, or a character's inner world? If so, what is the purpose of this revelation?

Related tools in this guide. To analyze dialogue, including exposition, go to the "Causing a Scene" section and try "Phrase Book" or "Anatomy of Speech." To explore subtext, try "Better Left Unsaid" in the same section.

■ VISUAL IMAGERY

What the audience sees during a dramatic story is often more telling and more lasting than what they hear. A visual image can speak a thousand words about the characters, the world they inhabit, and the events that occur during the dramatic journey. This imagery draws its power from the physical life of the character's world, such as the setting and what's in it, and the physicality of the characters themselves, such as how they appear and what they are doing. You can create such images by describing them in stage directions and/or by implying them through dialogue.

1. What are the three most interesting visual images in the scene?

2. Which of these images matters most? What does it reveal about your characters? About what's happening in the world of the story?

3. Think about how your visual images work together in sequence. What story do they tell without words? Is this the right story for this scene?
4. If any of your key visual images seem similar, is there a reason for the repetition? If not, how can you add more visual variety to the scene?
5. Have you overlooked opportunities to add visual imagery that would heighten the dramatic impact of an important moment or reduce the need for words of explanation?

Related tools in this guide. For help with translating character and story information into visual imagery, go to the "Building Your Story" section and try "Living Images."

■ SCENIC EVENT

Ideally, scenes are the essential steps of a dramatic story. Whether positive or negative, each centers on an experience that reveals something new about the characters, changes their lives in some way, and moves the dramatic journey forward. A scenic event may take the form of a discovery, revelation, beginning, ending, or other development.

What happens overall
1. What is the main event of this scene? Sum it up in a sentence or so.
2. Think about how the end of the scene differs from the beginning. What has changed in the lives of the characters as a result of what happened here and now?
3. The change that occurs often has an impact on the main character, even if he or she is not present. This impact may be positive or negative, direct or indirect. How does the main event of this scene advance or hinder your main character's dramatic journey?
4. What is the most important moment in the scene? The most important line? How clearly have you established this importance?
5. In what significant ways have the characters *not* changed when the scene ends?
6. Should the scene have a different outcome? If so, what would it be, and how would that affect the rest of the story?

How scene relates to rest of story
7. Why is this scene essential to the whole story?
8. Is this scene similar to any other scene in the story? If so, can the scenes be combined, or can one be eliminated?
9. Complicated or unusual events may need to be foreshadowed earlier in the story so they are understandable and credible when they occur. If a wife decides to leave her husband of many years, for example, earlier scenes may need to depict signs of trouble in the marriage so that we

are prepared to accept this outcome as believable. Would the main event of your scene benefit from foreshadowing? If so, how and when can you pave the way for it earlier in the script?

Related tools in this guide. To map out a scenic event through the filter of a character relationship, go to the "Causing a Scene" section and try "Relationship Storyboard." For more about events, go to the "Building Your Story" section and try "What Just Happened?" For more about foreshadowing, try "An End in Sight" in the same section.

■ HOW THE PRESENT AFFECTS THE FUTURE

If this is not the final scene, it will have repercussions later in the story. Because of what happens now, the characters will enter the next scene or a later scene with new experience that will affect how they behave. Knowing what happens later can help you make decisions about what needs to happen now so that the future will feel truthful and logical for these characters in this story.

1. What future scene will be most directly affected by this scene, and how?
2. Have you overlooked opportunities to strengthen the connection between this scene and the rest of the story? Be sure to consider any character beliefs, feelings, needs, or problems that arise during this scene and could affect what happens later.
3. Think about how the present paves the way for the future. Is there an important event later in the story that needs foreshadowing now so that it will be understandable and believable when it occurs? If so, what clues can you plant in this scene?
4. If this is not the final scene, you can generate suspense by raising at least one new question during the scene and leaving it unanswered for now. This creates the need for future scenes by implying that something important remains unresolved. What is the unanswered question at the end of this scene?
5. What specific elements in the scene might trigger this question?
6. What is the answer to this question? How and when will this answer be revealed, if at all, during the story?

Related tools in this guide. To explore how scenes connect, go to the "Building Your Story" section and try "The Dramatic Continuum."

■ SHAKING THINGS UP

If you have not already uncovered the source of the scene's problem, this final set of questions can help you shake up your material and explore new possibilities. As you address each question, stay open to new discoveries. You may find a solution where you least expect it.

1. Think about when the scene occurs in the chain of events that make up the story. What if this scene happened earlier or later in the script? How would moving this scene affect the dramatic action? The rest of the story?

2. Do you really know your characters well enough, or can you surprise yourself by learning something new about them? For example, does any character have a secret that you were not aware of?

3. Are you trying to force your characters to do something they don't want to do? If so, what would they rather do instead? How would that change the story?

4. Think about the setting for the scene and what's in it. Suppose there were an object here that you have overlooked and that could play an important role in the scene. What is this object, why does it matter, and how would it affect the dramatic action?

5. Each character enters the scene feeling a certain way. What if at least one character were in a different physical or emotional state when the scene begins? Instead of being sober, for example, he's drunk. Or instead of being angry, she's amused. Who might start the scene feeling differently? How would this affect the scene?

6. Characters also enter the scene with certain beliefs, right or wrong, that influence their behavior. What if someone in the scene were misinformed about something important or operating under a delusion? Who might not know the truth, what would the error be, and how might this affect what happens in the scene?

7. Think about who has the most power here and now. This control might be physical, psychological, or social. What if this character had the least power? What would cause this shift, and how would that affect the character interaction?

8. Suppose Character 1's scenic objective were the *opposite* of what you originally imagined? Instead of trying to save his marriage, for example, he is trying to destroy it. How would flipping the character's objective affect the scene and the story?

9. Characters pursue their objectives because something important is at stake. What if the stakes were higher? What if, for example, a greater number of people could be affected by what happens here and now? Who else's well-being could be at risk, and how would that change the dynamics of the scene?

10. Conflict can grow stale if the characters are unable to affect each other—that is, if the punches never land. What if a character were more vulnerable than you realized? How would this vulnerability affect the dramatic action?

11. What if the conclusion of the scene were the *opposite* of what you

originally imagined? Instead of getting fired from her job, for example, she ends up getting a promotion. How would flipping the scene's outcome affect the action leading up to it? The action that occurs later as a result of it?

12. Have you truly created different and compelling images in the scene to help you show, not tell, the story? Or is this primarily a visual sequence of talking heads? If the latter, what new visual imagery can you build into the script?

13. Are you revealing the story as a sequence of different steps, or do you keep repeating the same story over and over?

14. Am I emotionally moved in some way by this scene? If not, what can you do to change that?

Related tools in this guide. You can use any exercise in any section of this guide to shake up your material and make new discoveries about your story. Scenic problems often can be traced back to characters who need more development. To address this issue, go to the "Developing Your Character" section and try "Character Interview," "Beyond Belief," "The Imperfect Character," or "Objects of Interest."

WRAP-UP

This has been an in-depth analysis of one scene. Not every scene requires this level of scrutiny. Much story development will happen instinctively as you live in the moment with your characters. However, these questions may be helpful when you reach a stumbling block or don't know which way to head next.

Writing a story is a process that involves both creativity and analysis. If you are only creative, you may construct some great dramatic moments but end up with a script that doesn't hold the audience from beginning to end. If you are only analytical, you may create a logical sequence of events but end up with a script that has no emotional impact or life. Find the right balance between creativity and analysis, and you will be on the way toward writing a great story.

Related tools in *The Dramatic Writer's Companion*. To continue exploring script issues, go to "Fixing Common Script Problems" at the end of the guide.

GLOSSARY

Following are definitions of key terms used in Will Dunne's books for dramatic writers. While you may already be familiar with many of these terms, they are included here because their definitions highlight many of the dramatic principles underlying guide exercises.

act. A major unit of dramatic action that is typically composed of scenes and ends with a significant change, or reversal, in the dramatic journey. Most full-length plays today are structured in two acts; most full-length screenplays are structured in three acts.

adjustment. The attitude or emotion that a character manifests at any given time. The adjustment may be true (this is how the character really feels) or affected (this is how the character wishes to appear). At the scenic level, adjustments often change from beat to beat as characters make discoveries that shift them closer to, or further from, their scenic objective.

afterstory. Anything that will happen in the world of the characters after the story ends. Knowing this future can deepen the writer's understanding of what needs to occur or be revealed during the dramatic journey.

antagonist. One who opposes a main character's efforts to pursue a goal.

arc of action. The behavioral and emotional transition of a character during a specific period of time. A character typically has an arc within each scene as well as an arc that spans the course of the whole story.

backstory. Anything that happened among the characters in the past and will somehow influence them in the present. In the first scene, the backstory includes any relevant event that occurred before the story begins; in later scenes, the backstory expands to include whatever has previously occurred onstage or offstage.

beat. 1. The smallest unit of dramatic action. A scene is made up of beats; each centers on one topic, one behavior, or one emotion. Beats bring variety to the dramatic action of a scene and determine its structure and rhythm. 2. A pause in dialogue for dramatic effect. *This guide uses only definition 1.*

beat action or objective. The character need that drives one beat of a scene. Beat actions often are strategies or tactics that a character tries in order to achieve a scenic objective.

beat change. A shift in the dramatic action caused by a change of topic, behavior, or emotion, or by the entrance or exit of an important character.

behavioral objective. A character's need to get a certain response from another character. Operating at the beat, scene, and story levels, behavioral objectives boil down to four basic categories: to make another character feel good, to make another character feel bad, to find out something important, or to convince another character of something important.

character. A metaphor for a human being composed of a unique mix of physical, psychological, and social traits that are revealed and changed through dramatic action. This guide builds on the principle that character is the root of scene and story: it is usually character, not plot, that drives a dramatic journey.

Character 1. The main character of a scene: the one who drives most of the dramatic action and causes the scene to happen. Different characters may play this role from scene to scene. Character 1 is also often, but not always, the main character of the story.

Character 2. The second most important character in a scene. Different characters may play this role from scene to scene.

climax. The peak of action within a beat, scene, or story. At the beat level, the climax is usually a single line of dialogue or physical action; at the scene level, the climax may include one or more beats of action; at the story level, the climax may include one or more scenes.

conflict. Anything that makes a character objective difficult to achieve. Such obstacles may arise from the character's inner world, from other characters with incompatible needs, or from the current situation in the world of the story. The term *conflict* is often equated incorrectly with *argument*; however, argument is only one form of conflict. Also referred to as *obstacle* or *problem*.

crisis decision. The most difficult decision in the story. Traditionally, the crisis decision is made by the main character, reflects a choice between incompatible goods or the lesser of two evils, and triggers the story's climax and resolution.

deus ex machina. A solution to a problem which arises from coincidence or other external forces rather than from the character actions and story events that led up to it. The term refers to a device in ancient Greek theater where gods would arrive conveniently in chariots at the end of a play to solve everyone's problems.

dialogue. The words that characters speak as they talk and listen to each other in order to satisfy needs, address problems, or express ideas and emotions. In realism, dialogue has the feel of everyday conversation but is actually a heightened version of it. In nonrealism, dialogue may be stylized. Either way, the usual function of dialogue is to reveal character and advance the story.

dramatic action. Character interaction or other activity shaped and driven at its most fundamental level by three elements: objective, obstacle, and motivation.

dramatic journey. The main character's pursuit of an important but difficult goal and the effects of this pursuit on the character and the world of the story. Also known as the *quest*.

emotional life. The feelings of the character at any given time. Emotional life is both a cause and effect of dramatic action, and often minimizes the need for dialogue.

event. An important happening, positive or negative, in the world of the story—for example, something is achieved or not achieved, discovered or not discovered. Dramatic events often center on a beginning, end, or change of some kind.

exposition. Explanation or description of that which cannot be observed here and now, such as past or offstage events in the world of the story, or the inner life of a character. Though often viewed as negative, exposition can be a vital and powerful part of dramatic storytelling when used judiciously to expose specific character traits, ideas, and facts.

feather duster. An expositional scene in which characters explain things to each other, often at length, only for the sake of the audience. The term refers to old-fashioned dramas that would begin with servants dusting the room and gossiping about their employers so that the author could set up the story.

foil. A character who exists in a scene only to ask just the right questions and lend an eager ear so that another character can ramble on about all of the things that the author wants him or her to say for the sake of the audience.

foreshadowing. Preparation for a future story revelation or development. In the case of a "plant," this preparation may be transparent so that its real purpose is not known until later. In the case of a "pointer," this preparation calls attention to itself in order to generate anticipation of what might happen later.

fourth wall. The imaginary wall that separates the audience from the events on stage or on screen. In some cases, such as stories that feature a narrator, characters "break the fourth wall" to address the audience directly.

French scene. A unit of action demarcated by the entrance or exit of a principal character. Each time a new configuration of characters occurs, a new French scene begins. Ideally something important happens in each French scene.

genre. A category or type of dramatic story characterized by a certain style, form, or subject matter. Through the ages, a variety of genres and subgenres have evolved as blends or subsets of the two basic theatrical genres: comedy and tragedy.

given circumstances. The current situation in the world of the story, including any fact, event, state, or condition that will affect how a scene begins or unfolds. Each scene occurs within a unique set of given circumstances.

inciting event *or* incident. The phenomenon, large or small, positive or negative, that sets the dramatic journey into motion by upsetting the balance of the character's life and arousing the story goal or superobjective. The inciting event is often the first important event in the story.

interior dramatization. Imagery, sound, or dramatic action that suggests or depicts what is going on in a character's mind, such as a memory, idea, or perception.

interior monologue. Words spoken by a character that can be heard by the audience but no one in the story. Interior monologues typically reflect what a character is thinking and feeling. Also known as *soliloquy*.

measure of success. A specific statement, action, event, or other outcome that would indicate that a character's objective has been achieved.

melodrama. A story dictated more by plot demands than by character motivations so that exaggerated conflicts and emotions can be presented to the audience for "dramatic effect."

monologue. A long speech in which a character speaks to the self, or to someone else who is present or not present, or to the world at large.

motivation. Why a character says or does something. Motivation is a basic element of dramatic action and reflects something at stake for the character.

nonrealism. A storytelling style that creates an artificial reality. It may feature unusual or otherworldly situations, intellectual themes, stylized speech, archetypal characters, and imaginative devices such as exaggeration, distortion, fragmentation, repetition, symbolism, or direct address to the audience.

objective. What a character wants. A basic element of dramatic action, an objective may be behavioral or physical and, depending on its size and importance, may drive a beat (*beat action*), scene (*scenic objective*), or whole story (*story goal*).

obstacle. Anything that makes a character's objective difficult to achieve. Obstacle is a basic element of dramatic action. Also referred to as *conflict* or *problem*.

physical life. The specific setting for a scene as well as the objects in it and the physical elements that compose it.

physical objective. The desire or need to complete a physical task.

pivotal object. A thing that has special positive or negative meaning for the characters and significantly affects their interaction in a scene. The pivotal object often embodies what the character most values or fears here and now.

plant. A speech, action, image, or object that will make a future story development understandable and credible to the audience by discreetly paving the way for it. Ideally, a plant's true purpose is not known until its payoff occurs later on.

pointer. A speech, action, image, or object that paves the way for a future story development by overtly suggesting that it might happen. Unlike a plant, a pointer draws attention to itself in order to make the audience anticipate an outcome.

point of attack. The precise moment when a story or scene begins.

point of view. The vantage point from which the story will be revealed to the audience. This vantage point may be unlimited or limited.

protagonist. A classical term for the main character of a dramatic story. The role of protagonist may be played by more than one character.

quest. What the main character is after in the story. Also known as the *story goal* or *superobjective*.

realism. A storytelling style that creates the illusion of real life without acknowledging the audience. It typically features "slice of life" situations, emotional themes, everyday speech, and characters with whom we can empathize.

resolution. How things end up for the characters; the final outcome of the story. Also referred to as the *denouement*.

reversal. A turning-point experience, positive or negative, that sets the dramatic journey into a radically different, often opposite, direction. Each act of a dramatic story typically ends with a reversal.

rule of three. The storytelling principle that something which is said or done three times is funnier, more important, or more dramatic than something which is said or done any other number of times. This "rule" suggests that thrice provides the best emphasis for an important fact or action, since once is not enough to stress something, twice seems like a mistake, and four times feels repetitious.

scene. A unit of dramatic action that is driven by a character's need to accomplish something important and unfolds in one setting in real time. Most scenes add up to one main event that changes the world of the story in a good or a bad way.

scenic objective. The character need that drives most of a scene. Once aroused, either prior to the scene or during it, the scenic objective does not change until it is achieved or reaches a point of failure.

sense memory. A technique in which actors relive a past experience emotionally by recalling a physical detail from it. Writers can adapt this technique to explore their characters at a visceral level.

speech. What a character says at one time. A speech may be as short as one word or as long as several pages, depending on the complexity and importance of the content. Also referred to as a *line*.

spine of the character. The root action from which all of the character's other actions flow.

step outline. A writing or revision tool that gives the writer an at-a-glance view of the story structure by listing the key events in the order in which they happen.

story. The series of events that occurs when a character pursues an important goal that is difficult to achieve.

story goal. The character desire or need that is aroused by the inciting event, drives most of the story, and does not reach its conclusion—whether successful or unsuccessful—until the story ends. Also known as the *quest* or *superobjective*.

story structure. The selection and sequence of events used to depict a story. Classically referred to as *plot*.

strategy. How a character attempts to achieve an objective. Different strategies create the different beats of a scene. Also known as *tactics*.

style. The manner in which characters and story events are depicted. The style of a dramatic work may be realistic or nonrealistic.

subtext. Character thoughts and feelings that influence character behavior but are not stated in the dialogue. Subtext is that which remains "between the lines."

superobjective. See *story goal*.

suspense. A state in which the audience is in two places at the same time: the present (what is happening here and now in the story) and the future (what might happen later in the story as a result of what is happening now).

theme. A universal idea that the writer believes to be true and attempts to demonstrate through the characters and story. The theme is usually not stated in the dialogue but is often reflected most clearly in the crisis, climax, and resolution of the story. Also known as *controlling idea* or *premise*.

throughline. The spine of the story: the key events and how they connect so that the dramatic journey maintains a forward movement from beginning to end and enables a transition to occur.

turning point. A dramatic event, large or small, positive or negative, that creates an observable change in the world of the story. A major turning point is sometimes referred to as a *reversal*.

voice. How a character expresses thoughts and feelings through language. This voice is a core component of character identity and speech.

ACKNOWLEDGMENTS

Thank you to the dramatic writers in my workshops who helped me select the exercises that appear in this guide, particularly Susan Bazargan, Janet Burroway, Jan Chatler, Amy Crider, Patricia Curtis, Anita Delaria, Cathy Earnest, Joshua Fardon, David Finney, Dennis Fisher, Hope Hommersand, Christine Hodak, Corinne Kawecki, Charles O'Connor, Nancy Schaefer, Anthony Seed, and Diane Watry.

Thank you as well to the University of Chicago Press and the staff who encouraged and supported the development of this guide, particularly Paul Schellinger, who was the first to champion the project; Christie Henry, who helped steer it in the right direction; my editor Mary Laur, who helped move it to publication, and my manuscript editor Ruth Goring, who helped refine the words. Special thanks also to the theater experts who, through the Press, were generous enough to review my materials and offer invaluable insights, especially Alvaro Saar Rios.

Chicago Guides
to *Writing*, Editing,
and Publishing

Permissions, A Survival Guide
Susan M. Bielstein

The Craft of Research
Wayne C. Booth, Gregory G. Colomb,
Joseph M. Williams, Joseph Bizup,
and William T. FitzGerald

Immersion
Ted Conover

The Architecture of Story
Will Dunne

The Dramatic Writer's Companion
Will Dunne

*The Chicago Guide to Grammar,
Usage, and Punctuation*
Bryan A. Garner

The Art of Creative Research
Philip Gerard

Getting It Published
William Germano

Storycraft
Jack Hart

A Poet's Guide to Poetry
Mary Kinzie

The Subversive Copy Editor
Carol Fisher Saller

The Writer's Diet
Helen Sword

Write Your Way In
Rachel Toor

*A Manual for Writers of Research
Papers, Theses, and Dissertations*
Kate L. Turabian